Backwater Blues

Backwater Blues

The Mississippi Flood of 1927 in the African American Imagination

RICHARD M. MIZELLE JR.

UNIVERSITY OF MINNESOTA PRESS
MINNEAPOLIS · LONDON

Portions of chapter 5 previously appeared in "Black Levee Camp Workers, the NAACP, and the Mississippi Flood Control Project, 1927–1933," *Journal of African American History* 98, no. 4 (Fall 2013): 511–30.

Published by the University of Minnesota Press
111 Third Avenue South, Suite 290
Minneapolis, MN 55401–2520
http://www.upress.umn.edu

Library of Congress Cataloging-in-Publication Data

Mizelle, Richard M., Jr.
Backwater blues : the Mississippi Flood of 1927 in the African American imagination
Includes bibliographical references and index.
ISBN 978-0-8166-7925-6 (hc : alk. paper)
ISBN 978-0-8166-7926-3 (pb : alk. paper)
1. African Americans—Social conditions—20th century. 2. African Americans—Migrations—History—20th century. 3. Floods—Mississippi River—History—20th century. 4. Disaster victims—Southern states—Social conditions—20th century. 5. United States—Race relations—History—20th century. I. Title.
E185.6.M76 2014
305.896′0730750904—dc23

2014001434

Printed in the United States of America on acid-free paper

20 19 18 17 16 15 14 10 9 8 7 6 5 4 3 2 1

For my parents

Richard *and* Julye Mizelle

CONTENTS

ACKNOWLEDGMENTS

Writing a book is an exercise in patience and stamina. I am fortunate to have benefited along this path from the support of family, friends, colleagues, mentors, and institutions. I thank the Rutgers Center for Race and Ethnicity and the McKnight Foundation for fellowships that provided valuable research and writing time. I am also grateful to the Council for Research and Creativity at Florida State University for a first-year assistant professor award, a research planning grant, and a summer writing grant that gave the space necessary for me to complete this book.

This book has taken me to countless archives in search of "nuggets of truth." I am particularly thankful for the help offered by librarians and archivists at the Mississippi Department of Archives and History, the Louisiana State Archives, the Louisiana State Museum Historical Division (Old U.S. Mint), the New Orleans Public Library, the Amistad Research Center, the Southern Historical Collection at the University of North Carolina at Chapel Hill, the Newberry Library, the Carter G. Woodson Library, the Herbert Hoover Presidential Library, the Hill Memorial Library at Louisiana State University, the McCain Library at the University of Southern Mississippi, the Arthur Capps Library at Delta State University, the National Archives and Records Administration, and the Library of Congress. I am especially indebted to archivists at the Hogan Blues Archive at Tulane University. They reached deep into their stacks for obscure recordings by well-known and virtually anonymous singers. These recordings provide the backbone of this book. Even songs whose lyrics were too muffled to make out from the old-school LPs and could not otherwise be tracked down contributed to my argument that the blues archive represents a crucial theoretical and material framework for the 1927 Mississippi River Flood. The existence of these songs shows how much of a watershed event the disaster was in the imagination of blues singers.

This book has benefited significantly from opportunities for me to present at conferences and works-in-progress sessions over the past decade. Valuable feedback from audiences and co-panelists at the Association for the Study of African American Life and History in Milwaukee and the Society for the History of Technology in Amsterdam helped me think through ideas around race and technology. I am especially indebted to organizers of the first Workshop for the History of Environment, Agriculture, Technology, and Science (WHEATS) held at MIT. I am also grateful for the opportunity to present parts of the book and engage scholars at the Medical History Society of New Jersey, the Robert Wood Johnson Health and Society Scholars Working Group in African American History and the Health and Social Sciences at Columbia University, the Symposium on Civil Rights and the Body in the American South at the University of North Carolina at Chapel Hill, the University of Georgia (WHEATS) workshop, the History of Science Department at the University of Oklahoma, the Workshop on Energy, Urban History, and Environment at the University of Houston, and the Department of History at the University of South Carolina.

I am extremely thankful to have had the opportunity to work with Jason Weidemann and the editorial staff at the University of Minnesota Press. Jason supported the many intricacies and oddities of my project from the very beginning and provided valuable and critical feedback. I thank Danielle Kasprzak for quickly and enthusiastically answering every question I had about the publishing process.

At Rutgers University I benefited from the training and mentorship of Keith Wailoo, who pushed me to always "cast a wide net" in my formulation of history. Wailoo fostered and promoted my intellectual curiosity into other disciplines and fields and helped me to see the strategic importance of different kinds of texts and "ways of knowing" when writing about what is not easily accessible. I marvel at his unique ability to weave complicated ideas and arguments together in histories that are both necessarily broad and intricately detailed, and I am thankful for his continued professional and scholarly advice. Mia Bay and Julie Livingston read multiple drafts of chapters and have been constant advocates for me over the years, while Neil Maher helped me think through what were, at the time, foreign ideas of environmental history.

Many others at Rutgers were supportive of my research and provided outstanding mentorship. I thank Deborah Gray White, Christopher Leslie Brown, Herman Bennett, David Levering Lewis, Jennifer Morgan, Stephen Lawson, Nancy Hewitt, Allison Isenberg, Paul Clemons, Carolyn Brown, Kim Butler, Ann Fabian, Roland Anglin, and Paul Israel. I also benefited from a very tight-knit circle of friends at Rutgers from various departments, especially Monique Porow, Unique Fraser, Danielle Maguire, Joe Gabriel, Stephen Pemberton, Khalil Gibran Muhammad, Kristen Block, Marsha Barrett, Curt Cardwell, Franklin D. Turner, John Johnson, and Rebecca Scales. I would particularly like to thank Soyica Colbert, Kelly Josephs, and Krystal D. Frazier—members of my Rutgers writing group—for pushing each other to the finish line.

It has been my good fortune to come across many great scholars, mentors, and friends who in their own way helped me through this process. Some read parts of or the entire book while others gave timely words of encouragement over the years. Thank you to Samuel K. Roberts, William P. Jones, Sherwin K. Bryant, Minkah Makalani, Donna Murch, Clarence Lang, Kathleen Brosnan, Freddie Parker, Dwight Watson, Richard Gragg III, Jenny Leigh Smith, Martin Melosi, Nell Irvin Painter, Dineo Brinson, James L. Williams, Deborah Fitzgerald, Sharita Jacobs, Rayvon Fouche, Joy L. Anderson, Nancy Beck Young, Paul Sutter, Carlton Wilson, Sian Hunter, Akil Mensah, Joseph Pratt, Sowande Mustakeem, Jimmy Schafer, Foloshade Alao, Sylvia Hood Washington, Kennetta Perry, Daina Ramey Berry, and Alan Kraut.

Many colleagues and friends at Florida State University made it a congenial and supportive place to work. I am grateful to Robinson Herrera, Darrin McMahon, Andrew Frank, James Jones, Peter Garretson, Ronald Doel, Jennifer Koslow, Charles Upchurch, Elna Green, Sally Hadden, Maxine Jones, Jonathan Grant, Will Hanley, Neil Jumonville, Kris Harper, David Ikard,

Martell Teasley, Eyitayo Enifade, Patricia Hightower, Eric Stewart, Jeffrey Lowe, Daniel Tope, Alicia Gaines, Rhea Estelle, Verna Keith, Robert Patterson, and Ramona Pittman. I particularly want to thank Fritz Davis and Michael Creswell for their mentorship and friendship. Their advice on the matrix of publishing, critical commentaries on drafts, gentle nudging to stay on time with the writing process, and brainstorming over coffee breaks or lunch were invaluable.

I thank Mr. Frank Broussard, lifelong resident of Frenchtown and head of the Frenchtown Community Association, for opening his home and personal archive to me. His willingness to accept calls and visits from a stranger was absolutely necessary for me to understand the interesting and largely unknown story of Frenchtown.

My family deserves the greatest and deepest debt of appreciation. My parents, Richard and Julye Mizelle, both educators and freedom fighters, were my first mentors, putting the tools of success in my hands at an early age through their love of reading, attention to social justice, and commitment to education. They inculcated their tremendous love of reading and information into my sisters and me, sometimes in spite of much resistance from us. As kids I can still vividly recall their response to our statement of being bored: “Well, why don’t you read a book!” They continue to be the foundation of love and inspiration for everything this family does. My sisters, Nathalie Mizelle-Johnson and Dezmona Mizelle-Howard, and my brothers-in-law, Keith Johnson and John Howard, all supported me and helped keep me grounded. I must especially thank John and Dezmona for the free board and meals on countless archival trips to the Library of Congress and the National Archives over the years. My grandparents Clifford (deceased) and Mary Roberts also gave unconditional support and love during this process. We have had three wonderful additions to the family over the past decade, my nephews, John Cameron and David McKinley Howard, and my niece, Julye Simone Howard. They each have provided tremendous spirit and love to the entire family, not to mention much-needed breaks for me during the writing process. This book is dedicated to my family.

INTRODUCTION

John Lee Hooker's Blues

What I know of the Mississippi are facts, and facts are the uncut jewels which grind false theories to powder.

—James Eads, Engineer

It Rained and It Rained

The sheer breadth of the Mississippi River Flood of 1927 continues to present an interesting challenge to scholars. While other disasters such as the 1900 Galveston Hurricane, the 1906 San Francisco Earthquake, and Hurricane Katrina might have resulted in more physical damage and loss of life, the 1927 flood stands alone in the ways in which it influenced both environmental policy and culture. No other single environmental catastrophe affected so many states and encompassed such a wide area of devastation. Hurricane Katrina, now universally considered the worst environmental disaster in American history, destroyed property and claimed lives in the Gulf Coast states of Louisiana, Mississippi, and Alabama. The 1927 flood affected seven states, resulting in a logistical nightmare for the federal government and the American people in terms of how best to respond to citizens in need. Scholarship on the 1927 flood is similarly uneven, with a heavy focus on Mississippi, Louisiana, and to a lesser degree, Arkansas. We know very little about how the 1927 flood played out locally in Illinois, Kentucky, Missouri, or Tennessee, and just a bit more about how it played out in Arkansas. It would be extremely difficult to write a monograph on the 1927 flood that provided equal attention to all seven states. Historians Robyn Spencer, Pete Daniel, and John Barry have made clear the importance of the

1927 flood's aftermath for understanding local Yazoo Mississippi Delta politics and how the disaster set the stage for the ascendency of an Iowan with Quaker roots by the name of Herbert Hoover to the White House.[1] For these scholars and others the focus on Mississippi, Louisiana, and Arkansas was the result of thinking through race and politics in places where segregation and violence toward African Americans was the most egregious, and where the backwaters overflowed cotton-producing areas considered by the country to be at the heart of the region and America's future prosperity. *Backwater Blues* also focuses mostly on the Yazoo Mississippi Delta, Louisiana, and through migration patterns, Texas. I focus on these areas because it was not until areas of the lower Mississippi Valley were inundated with backwaters that the federal government and nation began to take notice and mobilize resources around the disaster, and because the cultural commentators who bore witness to the flood were most familiar with the Yazoo Delta. At times in the following pages, however, the narrative is necessarily rootless in terms of place. By framing parts of the disaster through a historical blues and literary archive, I am not so much talking about particular places as describing universal experiences of blackness and citizenship in America.

The Mississippi River has meant different things to different people across space and time, and not everyone feels like Mark Twain when confronted with one of nature's most powerful wonders. Proverbially known as the Father of Rivers, the Mississippi River stretches close to 2,500 miles from its origin in northern Minnesota's Lake Itasca to the Gulf of Mexico and has a drainage basin encompassing 1.2 million square miles; only South America's Amazon River and the Congo River in West Central Africa surpass it.[2] The Mississippi River and tributaries move like a pulsating bloodline through thirty-one U.S. states and two Canadian provinces; by the turn of the twentieth century it provided not only life-sustaining water and rich alluvial soil but also a transportation network of goods and commerce vital to the entire country's prosperity.[3] This vast network of tributaries and distributaries (tributaries are smaller water systems that flow into a larger body of water, while distributaries are smaller bodies of water that break away from a water system and form their own channel), which includes the Missouri River, Illinois River, Ohio River, Tennessee River, St. Frances and White Rivers in Arkansas, Arkansas River, Yazoo River in Mississippi, and Ouachita, Red, Atchafalaya, Old,

Morganza, and Bonnet Carre Rivers in Louisiana, connects the main stem Mississippi River to roughly 40 percent of the coterminous United States.[4]

A series of floodplains, drainage basins, runoffs, tributaries, distributaries, swamps, marshes, headwaters, and backwaters in the upper and lower halves of the Mississippi River have come to define its complicated hydraulic makeup. The area most well known in culture and memory is the Yazoo-Mississippi floodplain, approximately two hundred miles long and eighty miles wide, making up the dynamic environmental and cultural region known as the Yazoo Mississippi Delta. This region forms the backdrop of this book as both the birthplace of blues and the site where the 1927 Mississippi Flood is remembered most in cultural memory. Writer David Cohn provided an apt definition of the Mississippi Delta when he suggested that "the Mississippi Delta begins in the lobby of the Peabody Hotel in Memphis and ends on Catfish row in Vicksburg."[5] Cohn's description is truer as a cultural representation of the Yazoo Mississippi Delta than as a physical description of environmental hydraulics developed over centuries. Memphis, for example, once part of the alluvial plain of the Mississippi Delta, is now only part of the Mississippi Delta in culture and memory.[6] The physical landscape of the Yazoo Mississippi Delta includes ten counties—Bolivar, Coahoma, Humphreys, Issaquena, Leflore, Quitman, Sharkey, Sunflower, Tunica, and Washington—as well as parts of other border counties, including Carroll, DeSoto, Grenada, Holmes, Panola, Tallahatchie, Tate, Warren, and Yazoo. Together these Delta counties encompass more than seven thousand square miles of physical landscape.[7] Prominent towns located in the Yazoo Mississippi Delta floodplain include Mound Bayou, Cleveland, Greenville, Rosedale, Clarksdale, and Friars Point.[8] The Yazoo Mississippi Delta makes up a regionally distinctive political, social, and cultural landscape resting within the southern half of the United States.[9] As historian James Cobb argues, the Mississippi Delta is distinctively more southern than any other part of the South, including the North Carolina Piedmont, Appalachia, the Gulf Coast, the Florida Panhandle, Chesapeake, and the South Carolina Lowcountry. Eight years after the 1927 flood, sociologist Rupert Vance described the relations between blacks and whites and the region's political and economic culture as still reminiscent of slavery. "Nowhere but in the Mississippi Delta," he wrote in 1935, "are antebellum conditions so nearly preserved."[10]

Recorded history of the Yazoo Mississippi Delta is fraught with interactions between human beings and the Mississippi River during periods of "high water." What riparian landscapes provided to the region from the richness of soil and alluvial content was easily taken away by seasonal flooding in the nineteenth and twentieth centuries, making survival alongside the Mississippi River a precarious give and take with nature. By the mid-nineteenth century the Mississippi Delta was already on the verge of becoming a vast cotton kingdom, but landowners and politicians knew the region's profitability was predicated on their ability to bridle seasonal flooding. Controlling nature was necessary to inhabit the landscape and extract resources from the land to build an alluvial empire. In the century preceding the 1927 Mississippi River Flood, the Yazoo Mississippi Delta experienced spring floods in 1828, 1844, 1850, 1851, 1858, 1862, 1865, 1867, 1882, 1883, 1884, 1890, 1897, 1903, 1912, 1913, and 1922.[11] The control of nature was essential for the region's growth, but it also set the stage for an epic battle between humans and the Mississippi River that led to the 1927 flood.

At the center of this battle was the construction of artificial levees. For centuries before human habitation, the Mississippi River hydraulic ecology created its own naturally forming barriers called "high ridges," which were the result of soil deposited by seasonal flooding on the border where land meets water. Artificial levees (from the French *lever* meaning "to lift") entered the social environmental landscape in the early nineteenth century as an attempt to channel the Mississippi River. The responsibility of building levees fell primarily on individual landowners, who often used black slave labor or Irish workers to build and maintain the structures.[12] Compared to their twentieth-century counterparts, antebellum levees were simple embankments, normally no more than three to six feet high, built of a combination of sod, clay, and cypress slabs.[13] But levees also reflected wealth and power: while noticeably uneven and poorly designed levees and gaps in coverage existed in poorer areas, there was better protection for the property of wealthier residents. With no centralized standard or federal intervention for how levees should be built, the size and scope of early nineteenth-century artificial levees reflected the wealth and power of individual landowners and communities.[14] Throughout most of the nineteenth century, New Orleans built its levees closer to six to eight feet high, while hinterland parishes shadowed by the growing commercial and international port city could maintain levees of only three to six feet.[15] The higher levees of New Orleans not only showed the city's wealth and power, but as historian Ted Steinberg reminds us in *Acts of God: The Unnatural History of Natural Disaster in America,* those with resources and wealth are better situated to survive environmental disasters.

By the 1840s federal agencies faced considerable pressure to take action against seasonal floods that were hampering the development of a powerful plantation economy in Mississippi, Arkansas, and Louisiana. This pressure set the stage for passage of the 1849 and 1850 Swamp Land Acts, which allowed Congress to donate federally owned swamp and overflow lands to applicable states. Individual states throughout the Mississippi Valley in which flooding from the Mississippi River and its tributaries proved costly and burdensome were given opportunities to raise money from federally donated lands to build or shore up levees within their own borders; the goal was to stimulate construction of a contiguous levee system. Ultimately it was the lack of coordination and cooperation between mostly southern states that marred this early effort of a standardized levee system. Although the Swamp Land Acts of 1849 and 1850 were considered a failure, they nevertheless marked the beginning of a federal presence in levee construction that, for better or worse (and through the Civil War), was fortified in the ensuing decades.[16] The brief momentum of federalism initiated by the Swamp Land Acts suddenly ground to a halt in the early 1860s as valuable resources were shifted away from the improvement of levees by the war. The sectional conflict also had a more immediate impact on levees in what Civil War historian Charles Royster describes as the "destructive war." Union and Confederate armies destroyed levees as part of tactical maneuvering and sabotage, and the entire system suffered neglect during the war years.[17]

A more complete standardization of levees was realized with the Mississippi River Commission (MRC), created by Congress in 1879 to develop and maintain a unified federal system of levee construction and management. In addition to improving navigation of the world's third-longest river, the MRC also marked a more concrete presence for the United States Army Corps of Engineers in levee construction. Centralized authority and standardization in construction, as opposed to community or individual responsibility, was the Mississippi River Commission's primary goal. Emergence of the MRC did not necessarily mean an end to localism in levee construction—local levee boards and private citizens continued to bear the costs and responsibilities of levee construction well into the twentieth century. Nonetheless, the MRC served an important function in moving the nation toward a single policy of flood control, effectively summed up in two words: "levees only." As a consequence, flood control politics at the turn of the twentieth century became fraught with debates regarding the most appropriate measures of protection, and the question of whether levees alone, or a combination of levees along with spillways, reservoirs, and dams, should make up flood-control dynamics emerged as a serious issue.[18] The levee question came of age during Progressive Era politics, where everything, from the proper use of nature's resources to eugenicists' and settlement workers' racialized codification of a pure Anglo Saxon "race" through federally and state-sanctioned segregation and sterilization of African Americans, poor whites, and immigrants deemed unfit to marry and reproduce, was brought under the gaze of reform.[19] For the construction of levees, the question hanging in the balance during this era was exactly who had the authority to make decisions about levee building.

In many ways, Progressive Era debates about levees were just as much about what to do with water (or an overabundance of water) in the Yazoo Mississippi Delta region, compared to the arid west.[20] How to effectively make water and land productive for human use and consumption was a fundamental tenet of early twentieth-century conservation theory. In his epic work, *Conservation and the Gospel of Efficiency,* Samuel P. Hays describes the movement: "Conservation, above all, was a scientific movement, and its role in history arises from the implications of science and technology in modern society.... Its essence was rational planning to promote efficient development and use of all natural resources."[21] Conservation leaders believed not only that science and new forms of technology made the rational planning of landscapes a realm of endless possibility but also that decisions over proper use of the land should be in the hands of individuals most qualified to make those decisions. In other words, the rational and efficient use of landscapes was a scientific and technical enterprise best performed by those trained to make technical assessments of resources. Hays puts it this way: "Foresters should determine the desirable annual timber cut; hydraulic engineers should establish the feasible extent of multiple-purpose river development and the specific location of reservoirs; agronomists should decide which forage areas could remain open for grazing without undue damage to water supplies."[22] In terms of flood control and the "levees only" policy, the United States Army Corps of Engineers was pushing for its voice to supersede all others in terms of river design and levee construction during the conservation period. Importantly, the "levees only" policy was never absolute, and the corps' authority over the matter was tenuous at best during the early 1900s. Civilian engineers suggested the corps plan was untenable because it unnecessarily confined the Mississippi River, keeping it from spreading over its natural watershed and taxing the system's artificial levees to an unsustainable degree. Corps engineers refuted those claims, relying on a conservationist and progressive faith in science, making the case that confining the Mississippi River within its natural floodplain with artificial levees would only cause the river to deepen its river bed naturally over time without major environmental damage. In the process, this shift in hydraulic makeup would lessen the pressure placed on artificial levees. For his part, Teddy Roosevelt came out in favor of a "multipurpose" flood-control system that would employ levees alongside additional river and flood-control mechanisms.[23]

Nonetheless, by the second decade of the twentieth century, the "levees only" policy had firmly taken shape and was increasingly blamed for record-breaking floods in the Yazoo Mississippi Delta. One chief officer of the corps, writing internally after the disastrous 1912 and 1913 Mississippi and Ohio River floods, reaffirmed the case: "There is only one way to protect the Mississippi Valley from floods, and that is by an adequate system of well-designed levees."[24] It would take a disaster the caliber of the 1927 flood to shake the stubborn "levees only" policy and dissuade engineers from their conviction that levees alone could protect the region.

The 1927 flood was the result of unusually heavy and frequent rainfall throughout the entire country. Above-average rain totals began accumulating in states with tributary access to the Mississippi River during the late months of 1926 and did not cease until the spring of 1927.[25] By late February, Yazoo Delta residents, fearing they would become the unfortunate recipients of heavy rainfall from other states via Mississippi River tributaries, were already voicing strong concerns about the ability of levees to hold.

Rainfall was consistently high in Nebraska, Kansas, and Iowa, while South Dakota, Oklahoma, Illinois, Arkansas, and Tennessee experienced torrential downpours. Runoff from melting snowfall in Montana and Minnesota saturated vulnerable Upper Mississippi River watersheds already struggling with excess water, and Mississippi and Louisiana added their own share of the burden to the Lower Mississippi watershed thanks to downpours that occurred every day for a month during the spring. One Yazoo Mississippi Delta resident recounted in diary entries the overwhelming feeling of being constantly surrounded by water: "rainy"; "pouring rain almost constantly for 24 hours"; "rain almost all night"; "steady unrelenting flood came down for four hours"; "I don't believe I ever saw so much rain"; "a tremendous storm of rain"; "still raining hard tonight"; "still cold and showery"; "too dark and rainy to do anything"; and "rain last night of course."[26]

A storm on Good Friday proved to be the tipping point in Mississippi and Louisiana, pouring an additional five to fifteen inches of rain across the two states on watery grounds that could take no more.[27] While the Yazoo Mississippi Delta's floodplain is notoriously flat, it does slope ever so slightly downward going south in the range of one-quarter to one-half foot per mile.[28] As floodwaters rushed southward to the Gulf of Mexico, the "levees only" policy was put to the ultimate test. The river wanted to spread over its natural floodplain and reclaim what was once its own, but was too confined between mountains of artificial levees and dirt. Finding no other way, the Mississippi River ultimately had to make its own outlets, bursting and conquering humans' feeble attempt at levee control throughout the Mississippi Valley basin.[29] By late spring, flood waters had crushed more than 120 levees and created 42 major crevasses on the Mississippi River and tributaries, flooding land from Cairo, Illinois, to the Gulf of Mexico, approximately 1,100 square miles in area. The breadth of the disaster was equally astonishing as flooding created over a billion dollars (calculated in 1927 figures) of damage in the states of Arkansas, Kentucky, Missouri, Tennessee, Mississippi, Illinois, and Louisiana. Millions of people in the flooded states were temporarily or permanently displaced and untold numbers perished.[30] The roughly two hundred deaths quoted by the American Red Cross is, without question, a vast underrepresentation that reflected sensibilities of race. African American dead bodies were not considered important, so most were not included in the official toll. When a levee broke near Greenville, Mississippi, in the spring of 1927, black men were forced to work at gunpoint to secure the levee. Eyewitness accounts corroborated stories that countless black and white workers perished, though the official Red Cross's narrative was that not a single life was lost during the break. Even Red Cross officials hinted at the unreliability of drowning figures and acknowledged the countless unconfirmed reports of drowning victims.[31] Drowning was, however, not the only concern for black flood survivors—they also faced the threat of murder from lawless whites. Black murder at the "hands of persons un-known" was part of the racialized experiences of black people "down by the riverside."

The flood also tied directly into the idea of backwater flooding. In a strictly environmental sense, backwaters can be defined as the thousands of square miles located away from the main stem of the Mississippi River along smaller tributaries and streams inadequately protected from flooding either by the absence of levees or by levees that were poorly constructed. Flooding along the hundreds of streams and tributaries connecting into the Mississippi River drainage basin and backflow from the Mississippi River created these vulnerable landscapes. The idea of a backwatered community cannot be understood simply in environmental terms, however. It also implies the marginalization and vulnerability of certain groups and communities within the broader society and the disciplining of poor people and African Americans into neglected spaces that, later in the century, would become defined as environmental racism. In his work on early twentieth-century scientific discourses linking criminality with race, historian Khalil Muhammad describes how the North House Association, a social work agency in Philadelphia during the Progressive Era, described the mostly poor white and Eastern European immigrant residents of one particular community as the "stagnant backwater of humanity."[32] In varying contexts the intellectual idea of backwater suggests an operation on the fringes of society, less than American and less than human. Where one lives and the protection afforded shapes historical relationships with the Mississippi River and the backwater identity. In *Caste and Class in a Southern Town,* a 1937 sociological study of class and power in a typical southern town, John Dollard highlights the connection between historical vulnerability and environmental landscapes. In what is best described as ethnographic and historical participant-observation research, Dollard did not disclose the town he researched, but most scholars suggest it was the Yazoo Mississippi Delta town of Indianola, Mississippi, in Sunflower County. He described this typical southern locale by writing, "It is a small town, just about large enough to qualify under the census as an urban area. It is flat as a tennis court but with a bit of a tilt, the white people living on the upper half. Should floods come, the Negro quarter would be first under water. Southerntown is bisected by a railroad, and its tracks divide people according to color, the whites living on one side and the Negroes on the other."[33] The vulnerability associated with certain environmental spaces is imbued with important ideas of race and class. For African Americans living under the yoke of Jim Crow in the deepest South, the 1927 flood was not only an environmental event but also a racial one. While class and immigrant distinctions are often put aside under the umbrella of whiteness during moments of extreme crisis such as the 1919 Chicago Race Riot or the 1927 flood, these moments have always provided a particular type of window into the meaning of blackness. For black survivors of the 1927 flood, they had to deal with the dangers of both the environmental world and their second-class status as citizens where skin color alone was all the justification needed to be murdered.

Backwater Blues represents this historical mixture between an environmental backwater and a social, political, and cultural backwater, reciprocal in the ways in which they influence each other in history and culture. The story I tell is about more than the failing levees and "levees only" policies. *Backwater Blues* represents an intellectual engagement with race and place through nature and the ways in which African Americans in the Yazoo Delta and other parts of the country made sense of this disaster. As a result, the story is not so much a traditional history of the 1927 flood; rather it serves as a brief window into what the flood tells us about race and citizenship during a period between 1927 and 1934.

Mapping the Blues (Voice)

Contrary to what your parents told you as a kid, there was such a thing as the boogie man. His name was John Lee Hooker. Considered the last of the great Delta singers with ties to the classic and country era, his unique sound was born from the Yazoo Mississippi Delta's rich soil. Hooker was born around

August 22, 1917, in Clarksdale, Mississippi, into a family of sharecroppers. Like many of his predecessors, he left Mississippi to record and perform his music, settling at various times in Memphis, Knoxville, Cincinatti, and Detroit. In 1948 during his stretch in the Motor City, he worked at a local auto factory by day and played gigs on the legendary Hastings Street at night. His first recorded song, "Boogie Chillen," which debuted in 1948, along with other hits like "Boom Boom," "Crawling Kingsnake," "I'm in the Mood," and "The Healer," catapulted Hooker to legendary stature. My first recollection of Hooker comes from a scene in the 1980 movie *The Blues Brothers,* with Cab Calloway, John Belushi, and Dan Aykroyd. Immaculately dressed, matching down to his socks and shoes, he looked like a hip dude while singing his "Boom Boom" in a street scene right before the Blues Brothers (Belushi and Aykroyd) attempt to persuade Matt Guitar Murphy to rejoin the band.[34] While this cameo appearance largely encompassed the extent of John Lee Hooker's movie career, his superstardom in music lasted five decades, until his death in 2001.

In 1959 Hooker recorded a song called "Tupelo" on his *Country Blues of John Lee Hooker* album, paying homage to a record-setting 1936 tornado and flood in Tupelo, Mississippi. This was perhaps the first song I ever listened to with an eye toward explaining environmental disasters of the past, and I made the decision that indigenous black music would be an important part of this project on one of the greatest environmental disasters in American history. I realized that in the absence of official accounts of historical narratives, songs like "Tupelo" are especially important in chronicling the experiences of poor black people. Like griots of the past, black blues musicians kept the experiences of those displaced and marginalized folks alive in the music. Among the second wave of great country blues singers, Hooker vocalized the thoughts and desires of historically nameless and faceless people through words and instrumentation. The song opens with Hooker's signature deep and rich tonal humming over guitar. "Tupelo" is a haunting song and situates the listener squarely in the middle of a disaster. "Did you read about the flood, a long time ago? In a country town, way back in the east, Tupelo, Mississippi. One Friday evening, the dark clouds rolling. It rained and it rained, both night and day."[35] The song is driven by a constant dripping sound that resembles rain. Ominous and powerful, the instrumentation demands the ear perhaps even more than the words do. The pounding beat and sound of rain becomes psychological, even maddening. What must it have been like for the black survivors of this flood to hear this song? As Ralph Ellison reminds us, "The blues is an impulse to keep the painful details and episodes of brutal experience alive in one's aching consciousness, to finger its jagged grain, and to transcend it, not by consolation of philosophy, but by squeezing from it a near-tragic, near-comic lyricism."[36] The blues paradox bespeaks the plight of African America, particularly as it concerns representing those experiences in master narratives. The blues, then, is much more than an art form—it can, and does at times, operate to both bear witness to and help folks cope emotionally with such tragic black experiences. The rub is that these experiences are often conspicuously omitted or discounted in the master narratives of history, making such cultural modes all the more crucial to representing black historical realities. "It rained and it rained, it rained and it rained." Those who survived the 1927 flood would have found solace in Hooker's interpretation.

Backwater Blues is a study of what I call the racial *flood diaspora* of black protest, charity, environmental displacement, structures of labor, and cultural critique that informed the most significant environmental disaster of the twentieth century. The 1927 flood represents a polysemy of both an engineered environmental ecology of vulnerability and a blues ideology of group expression, drawing attention to the multiple narratives that created a backwater flood. In particular, I build on Earl Lewis's contention that scholars of African American history consider "overlapping diasporas" and the necessity of stretching temporal boundaries to fully understand identity formation between "dispersed" African American communities rooted in the commonality of race, gender, religion, and class. The disaster represents a distinct type of cultural diaspora where various expressions of race are connected to this specific historical event. It was the most significant event in America following the end of World War I, as postwar limitations of black citizenship became fodder for protest against racial discrimination. In the process, black people used what was at their disposal to create a rich "sociology of knowledge" of race around the 1927 flood. Ida B. Wells-Barnett and W. E. B. Du Bois spoke in front of crowds and wrote commentaries in the *Chicago Defender* and *Crisis*. Black ministers denounced mistreatment from the pulpit on Sunday mornings and took up collections for survivors. The NAACP wrote letters to the secretary of commerce and head of relief operations, Herbert Hoover, imploring him to ensure black survivors were treated fairly. Self-described "Creoles of color" migrated from Louisiana to Texas, expanding the idea of race and migration. And blues musicians and literary writers used the flood as a window into various dimensions of race and environment through creative artistic expression.

We normally think of diaspora as the movement of people away from an ancestral homeland while maintaining a physical or psychological connection to that homeland through tradition, culture, expression, language, and history. Scholars have written extensively about diasporic ties that link people and ideas across boundaries. This project takes a cue from Hasan Kwame Jeffries and Earl Lewis. Jeffries recounts the long battle for enfranchisement and political power in Alabama leading to creation of the 1967 Lowndes County Freedom Party and its slate of candidates running against segregationists in the 1968 election. He makes the case that the Great Migration pattern of movement from Lowndes County to California and other places created a "Lowndes Diaspora" in which migrants sent resources to support the local black freedom struggle.[37] Now living in the California land of *James* Crow (considered by migrants as the cousin of Jim Crow because, far from a utopia, segregation and racism were very prevalent in the west), they knew better than most the dangers of challenging segregation for those who remained in Alabama, this connection to place and experiential knowledge of race adjoining black communities thousands of miles apart. In his article "To Turn as on a Pivot: Writing African Americans into a History of Overlapping Diasporas," Earl Lewis posits that defining historical experiences of black communities in different parts of the country helped create "overlapping diasporas."[38] Though the history of Africans and African Americans from slavery to the present has never been monolithic, and there never has been such a thing as a singular black community, the pivot rests on a determination to develop and ask questions that show the interconnectedness of black communities and the reasons why people come to see themselves as part of a much broader collective identity, while living in separate and multidimensional black spaces. Describing the process of identity-making and diasporas within the institution of slavery, Lewis argues that "since, from the start, the slave population consisted of many peoples, something had to mold those who lived in a world of overlapping diasporas into African Americans. Racial slavery became the connector linking blacks to one another across different regional political economies, with greatly differing demographic profiles and opportunities for gaining freedom." The complexity of black communities and forces that connect them through various identities are part of how we understand diasporas.[39]

Building on Lewis's call to elevate the importance of diaspora in the writing of black history, or acknowledge the "permeability of boundaries and the multipositional nature of most human actors," I argue that the 1927 flood represents a distinct type of cultural diaspora where various expressions of race are connected to this specific historical event. Environmental disasters are often viewed as centralized historical events limited in space and time. However, black people and other minorities influenced American society long after the flood through various forms of cultural expression and social protest movements, extending the disaster's sphere of influence well beyond the period between March and August 1927 we normally associate with the disaster. My work differs from previous scholarship on the flood in my obsessive quest to write this history primarily from the perspective of those individuals able to provide a commentary of how the 1927 flood was understood and interpreted through the lens of race.[40] As a result, cultural commentators of the flood become essential for understanding the ways in which the environmental and racial landscape of the 1927 flood was framed for both survivors and nonsurvivors in the decade following the flood. Of more immediate importance during the flood were the messages of violence, peonage, forced labor, and the misuses of charity that became part of the underground railroad of information being spread to overlapping diasporic communities. Far from being a linear history of the 1927 flood, *Backwater Blues* utilizes sources culled from a variety of traditional and nontraditional historical archives, including the blues and historical fiction. While we must always be mindful of taking creative art forms at face value, I make the case throughout this book that cultural creative expressions often speak to black historical truths. Therefore blues songs like John Lee Hooker's "Tupelo" not only give artistic pleasure but can also provide a sense of cultural release through historical reminders of a painful past.

An underlying theme of *Backwater Blues* is the way in which African Americans defined the 1927 flood through a racial consciousness of nature. Through most of the twentieth century, assumptions about black environmental illiteracy have given rise to the widespread belief that African Americans rarely expressed thoughts or ideas about their surrounding environmental world. On the contrary, African Americans have a long tradition of intellectual narration and articulation of environmental landscapes that were only heightened during the 1927 flood. I make the case that historical commentary of the flood was rooted in the idea that race and nature were interrelated burdens; the perils of rain, wind, and water only exacerbated existing vulnerabilities of second-class citizenship. This was a sentiment given powerful meaning by Ned Cobb in the classic memoir *All God's Dangers*. Cobb provides a detailed account of his life in Tallapoosa County, Alabama, as a black farmer whose presence defied a planter caste system bent on keeping all black people under the ruling domain of Jim Crow segregation, successfully maneuvering through the many traps of sharecropping and tenant farming by wielding his economic independence in a racially caste-driven world where few black people accumulated wealth. Drawing on an uncommon memory and insightfulness honed by a lifetime's worth of experiences, Cobb gives us a lineage of his own family with tremendous detail while allowing readers to imagine the fortitude it took for a black man to survive and accumulate the wealth of things associated with whiteness. A black man who owned land, automobiles, horses, and mules was resented as uppity in the 1930s and risked violence at every turn. But Cobb, like so many other black people lost to history, was not intimidated and would defend his family and property with violent force if necessary. He became public enemy number one in Alabama after joining the communist-inspired local Sharecroppers Union and began organizing other tenant farmers and sharecroppers.[41] Cobb's knowledge of farming and husbandry was unsurpassed, and recalling the many perils of farming, which included floods, droughts, and boll weevil epidemics, he made the comment, "All God's dangers ain't white men."[42] The point Cobb makes is that black people have historically had to deal not only with racism but also with dangers arising from the environmental world—double burdens that have reinforced each other. Ultimately, the ways in which we understand the environmental world, particularly disasters, are imbued with fundamental questions of race and racial difference in American discourse and practice.

Blues is a sine qua non for thinking through important questions of race and environmentalism during the 1927 flood. Early blues emerged after the Civil War and particularly during the last two decades of the nineteenth century as an individual expression of experience in a world with many tribulations. During the late nineteenth and early twentieth centuries, blues singers were rarely paid, and as Amiri Baraka reminds us, it was universally understood that anyone could sing the blues who had lived in the world. Early blues was an intensely personal and private music, even though there was some standardization of lyrics and style. According to Baraka, "The music remained that personal because it began with the performers themselves, and not with formalized notions of how it was to be performed."[43] The personal nature of blues music shifted in the 1920s when musicians began recording for the first time. What were once personal reflections and deliberations of the surrounding world had by the 1920s transformed into a much more public and professional domain highlighting the shifting life experiences of African Americans. Through migration and introduction into a world outside farming and southern life, the intellectual currency and voice of blues changed the moment it entered the public sphere. At the same time, technological developments of the phonograph and radio also vastly extended the reach and influence of blues through the circuitous movement of people and ideas around the country. As millions of African Americans migrated from the rural South to urban centers during the Great Migration, so too did performers migrate to New York City, Chicago, Los Angeles, and Kansas City in search of recording industries. In this process they combined country blues with newer ideas informed by black life in the city, known as urban blues. As Clyde Woods describes, "The new and rapidly expanding recording industry extended the geographical range of the blues. . . . The establishment of an African American community of consciousness based on recorded blues and jazz was one of the most fundamentally significant and enduring mobilizations of this period."[44] The blues was becoming worldlier as an art form, burning inside the people traveling in Jim Crow trains and automobiles with worldly possessions packed in suitcases and bags, along the Great Migration's path to urban cities.

The recording era of the 1920s and 1930s transformed blues into a music that highlighted the universality of African American experiences, an important shift in two ways for understanding the groundswell of blues that emerged after the 1927 flood. First, it broadened the parameters of what blues musicians talked about. Second, a much larger group of listeners defined their experiences through blues entertainers. Recorded-era blues were less personal, commenting on group experiences, events, and crises impacting a much broader range of African Americans, including the 1927 flood, police brutality, migration, and discrimination faced by levee workers in federally funded levee camps. The 1927 flood was an event that gripped the entire nation for several months, and the peonage of African Americans in the Yazoo Mississippi Delta was a central part of the story. The magnitude and reach of the disaster became the framework of racial discourses for musicians and novelists, most of whom experienced the flood secondhand through survivors they met, black newspapers, or culturally via the firsthand stories that survivors told. War, disease, and environmental disaster were about the only events that might demand the entire nation's attention during this time period, so it makes sense that this most significant flood would draw the attention of blues singers making powerful commentaries on race.

To reiterate an earlier point, we can never forget that these were far from unencumbered expressions of racial protest, and the nature of the recording process lent itself to a certain obscurity of intent with recorded blues and songs sung in front of white audiences. Much of this complexity can be understood through recording companies' racially exploitative development of "race record" divisions in which they targeted urban listener markets they believed would become fascinated with "authentic" blues music. From the beginning of race records, but particularly by the 1940s, African Americans voiced displeasure over the term *race record* and the insulting advertisements employed by record companies. For example, some companies marketed country blues singers eating barbecue or sitting on front porches of shacks as the "real" blues musicians, pushing this type of image for consumer audiences over the reality of business-oriented blues men and women exhibiting a broad range of showmanship and performance that later musicians would emulate. The first blues to enter the professional and public domain in the late 1910s and early 1920s was known as classic blues. Cabaret singer Mamie

Smith, who originally signed with Okeh Records, recorded the first known classic blues songs in New York City on February 14, 1920. "You Can't Keep a Good Man Down" and "This Thing Called Love" were followed a few months later with "Crazy Blues" and "It's Right Here for You." The demand for "Crazy Blues" exceeded expectations, moving Okeh to establish a division called Original Race Recordings. Columbia, Paramount, Vocalion, Victor, and Decca quickly followed suit with their own version of the race record division with the hope of taking advantage of a new buying market.

Defined by their big voices backed up with large brass ensembles, classic blues singers were primarily women, many of whom had roots in the vaudeville circuit. The recording era made classic blues singers like Beulah "Sippie" Wallace, Clara Smith, Ida Cox, and Sarah Martin wildly popular when they traveled from town to town across the country. However, Gertrude "Ma" Rainey and Bessie Smith were the most widely known of all classic blues singers, elevating the professionalism and performance of blues on their way to becoming the first superstars of blues. Although classic blues singers dominated the early recording era, by the late 1920s the country, or "down home," blues era had begun to dominate the recording scene. If most classic blues singers were women, the overwhelming majority of country blues singers were men. Among the first known country blues songs were Sylvester Weaver's "Guitar Blues" and "Guitar Rag," recorded in October 1923, and "Papa" Charlie Jackson's "Lawdy, Lawdy Blues" and "Airy Man Blues," recorded in August 1924. Some of the best-known early recorded country blues singers include Charley Patton, "Blind" Lemon Jefferson, "Mississippi" John Hurt, Alonzo Lonnie Johnson, "Texas" Alger Alexander, Charles "Cow Cow" Davenport, and "Sleepy" John Estes. Many of these early country blues singers recorded songs on the 1927 flood, as did Bessie Smith and Beulah Wallace from the classic era. Music scholar Eileen Southern describes the terms *down home* and *country* as being emblematic of a style or spirit of blues, not necessarily a place, as singers performed in both rural and urban settings, and some "down home" singers did not grow up in the South.[45] Further, such terms represented the politics of race records and not those of blues singers themselves. According to historian Davarian Baldwin, "It was partially the record 'industry's desire not to confront the image of the slick city black' that encouraged a shift to the marketing and promotion of the down home blues music genre. While the blues explosion of 1920 showcases the ability of the 'Negro market' to influence the production decisions of record companies, we also see corporate power's ultimate ability to limit the market to a particular kind of blues image. The rise in down home blues and music ministers complete with 'down-south' and even plantation images did not necessarily reflect black marketplace demands as much as it did white interests."[46] The artificiality of such terms and how they came into existence represents an important narrative for understanding the meaning of race records.

Backwater Blues deals solely with the negotiated recorded songs that entered the public sphere and the intellectual criticism and ideas that blues musicians disseminated throughout the world.[47] It is quite possible, if not understandable, that blues musicians sang differently in black spaces as opposed to recording centers in New York and Chicago, the recording terrain being a constant negotiation between entertainers and industry. In his work on blues as ideology and vernacular, Houston Baker suggests that "an ideological analysis of expressiveness as a commodity should take adequate account of the defining variables in the culture where this commercialization occurs."[48] Baker makes clear that even though blues singers may have changed words and meanings depending on the audience, this dynamic should not be perceived as diminishing the value of the blues; instead, it shows blues singers' awareness and acuity, their ability and willingness to navigate the world of business and commercial recording. Recorded blues were complex and intellectually metaphorical portals into the thoughts and imagination of blues musicians, although they were certainly cognizant of what they sang in private or in front of black and mixed audiences, and what entered the public sphere.[49] Recorded blues singers subverted the dominant image of "authentic" blues singers of the era as sitting barefoot on the front porch of sharecropping cabins with straw hats. The point is they were entertainers and commentators, and we must fully grapple with the richness of their dual identities.

When analyzing songs, I primarily use two or three lines of blues songs rather than writing out the entire song. I do this to keep from bogging readers down with lengthy quotes of music in the middle of the text, while still drawing attention to what I think is important. Further, blues songs often have many different themes going on simultaneously, and I want to focus the reader's attention on what is important for *Backwater Blues.* The majority of songs I analyze employ the traditional AA'B format borrowed from work songs. Normally this three-line verse consists of two identical lines followed by a third line that provides an explanatory framework. The explanatory framework comes in the form of irony, humor, a theoretical or intellectual position, or an instrumental response. The first two lines often pose a problem, and in the traditional call and response format the third line is used to answer or interpret that problem. For example, Texas Alexander's "Levee Camp Moan" employs this format when he sings: "They accuse me of murder, I haven't harmed a man; they accuse me of murder, I haven't harmed a man; they even accuse me of forgery and I can't write my name."[50] Although songs vary in length, the twelve-bar structure consisting of three lines with four bars each is most common. As a social theory of analyzing blues music I draw on the work of many scholars, including Clyde Woods's theory of a "blues epistemology." Woods describes this idea of blues as a working-class expression of culture and sophisticated intellectual countermovement against the surveillance and oppression imposed by a plantation-owning southern white power structure. In the absence of safe dominant forms of political expression, the "blues epistemology" of cultural resistance and healing was a way for African Americans to comment on and voice opposition to the world around them.[51]

The blues represents a driving force in this project. Sometimes they are the primary mode of analysis and other times they operate behind the scenes in defining the experiences of black people during the flood. Both classic and country singers used the national imagination and fascination with the 1927 flood as a way of documenting a traumatic historical event while simultaneously expressing individual and collective group experiences. Well over fifty blues songs were recorded on the 1927 flood, reflecting not just the classic and country eras but different regional styles that included Delta blues, urban blues, Piedmont blues, Texas blues, and gospel blues. While I do not distinguish between regional variations in this work, differences can be heard in the singing style, instrumentation, and bar structure of different regions. It is important to remember that it was not uncommon for musicians to borrow lines from earlier songs or provide personal interpretations to previously recorded songs.[52]

As blues provided moments of intense clarity and creative expression for social truths, so too did the *blues voice* of Richard Wright as he created two short fiction stories on the 1927 flood.[53] For the purposes of this work, a blues voice is the venue and ability to vocalize through protest, consciousness, words, sounds, vernacular, meaning, pauses, sighs, and expression the varied individual and collective experiences of the 1927 flood. In this sense, Richard Wright's flood stories serve a function similar to that of the blues in the way they "signify" experience, coming through as an explanatory framework of literary and creative expression. In her description of Richard Wright's "12 Million Black Voices," Farah Jasmine Griffin argues that at key points in the text Wright essentially becomes a blues singer. "The land we till is beautiful.... Our Southern springs are filled with quiet noises and scenes of growth." For Griffin, "Wright establishes not only the connection between black people and the South, but also his own connection with the people by using the pronoun 'we.' At this point in the narrative, he becomes a blues singer, sharing in the experiences of black Southerners about whom he writes. The book is a kind of blues performance in itself, expressing the humanity of black people in the face of racial and economic adversity."[54] *Backwater Blues* builds on this analysis by integrating the largely marginalized literary texts of Richard Wright's two flood stories into the broader historical narrative of the 1927 flood. Though Wright rarely uses the pronouns "we" or "our" in his 1927 flood texts, the two stories are reflective of the blues in the way they present what Houston Baker calls a "life-crisis of black identity." The life crisis presented by Wright transforms his language into a unique blues voice symbolized by a blues universality of experience. Taken together, the blues and Wright's blues voice provide a much clearer window into various social truths of experience for black people during the 1927 flood.

Chapter 1 introduces the blues as a universal theory for reevaluating the social experience of black people during the 1927 flood, focusing specifically on the meaning of citizenship and displacement. Chapter 2 redefines the importance of Richard Wright's protest literature and environmental blues voice through two short stories he published on the 1927 flood. Wright published "The Man Who Saw the Flood" and "Down by the Riverside" in response to what he defined as the historical mistreatment of black people under the ruling thumb of Jim Crow. Wright was a literary giant and astute intellectual who creatively used the written word to voice historical experiences of race; few remember that he commented on the 1927 flood through his fiction. Wright's fascination with the 1927 flood suggests the disaster was still a powerful metaphor for race in the 1930s; and like the blues archive, historical fiction can be important to the historical record when situated in conversation with other narratives.

Chapter 3 situates the 1927 flood as a turning point in the nation's consciousness of responding to an American disaster, occurring in an era when environmental disasters were largely considered local problems to be dealt with by local governments.[55] As the country transitioned from a period of war to peace after World War I, Americans were yet again asked to demonstrate patriotism through relief, reflecting broader narratives of postwar militarism in American society.[56] American environmentalism took on ideals of militarism in postwar America, framing everything from the use of insecticides to the public's civic responsibility after an environmental disaster. As part of a nationwide call to arms, the flood was richly defined with metaphors of war and military engagement; flooded landscapes were not simply places of destruction, but battle zones and combat fields pitting humankind versus the Mississippi River. Importantly, questions of self-help and racial notions of charity took shape within this context of environmentalism, militarism, and relief, as African Americans across the country were bombarded with the same patriotic appeals for money as white Americans while also hearing from black-operated newspapers of slavery-like conditions inside Red Cross relief camps. Particularly for black people who migrated from the South or had intimate knowledge of the region's customs, it was not difficult to believe stories of mistreatment. Their "duty" as citizens was precluded by racial status, and so during an era of self-help and racial uplift African Americans found alternatives for charity that did not include the American Red Cross.

Chapters 4 and 5 frame the *flood diaspora* beyond the actual flood in both time and space by looking at the influence of the disaster on migration and labor. An important migration narrative of the 1927 flood is represented by the little-known yet distinct migration pattern between Louisiana and Texas that predated a similar trajectory seventy-eight years later during Hurricane Katrina. An influx of self-described Creoles of color migrated from

Southwest Louisiana to Houston, helping build the neighborhood known as Frenchtown. The neighborhood was originally settled by Creoles of color in the early 1900s, but the wave of migrants displaced by the 1927 flood significantly shaped the neighborhood's vitality and presence in the oil-rich and growing energy capital. Because of their complexion, patois, and staunch Catholicism, Creoles of color often occupied a middle ground of Houston society, not fully accepted by either black or white communities. They were, on the other hand, fiercely loyal to their ethnic distinctiveness, not necessarily seeking justification from a binary racial identification in a city where Jim Crow norms saw only black and white. Their presence complicated the racial hierarchy of Houston in the 1920s and 1930s, and the evolution of a blended neighborhood showed the ways in which the 1927 flood influenced the nation beyond borders and backwaters.

The final chapter of this book focuses on the central role of the National Association for the Advancement of Colored People (NAACP) in exposing the mistreatment of African Americans during the 1927 flood, setting the stage for what was in many ways a much larger and prolonged battle over the rights of levee camp workers during the New Deal. The 1928 Flood Control Act was passed in response to the 1927 flood and the subsequent realization of the need to construct and reinforce levees throughout the Mississippi Valley. The result was a federally funded levee construction program between 1928 and 1933 that the NAACP would call the Mississippi Flood Control Project (MFCP). Accusations of wage discrimination and violence surfaced immediately, and the NAACP, less than two decades since its inception, quickly stepped into place to protect black workers. Primarily focusing on workers in Mississippi, Arkansas, and Louisiana, the NAACP publicly disclosed an inherent hypocrisy of the federal government's refusal to protect black levee camp workers on a project infused with federal dollars, eventually pushing for their inclusion under New Deal labor laws. Levee camp life was also a theme of blues musicians who posited an intellectual and universal experiential framework for black labor.

Throughout the following pages I primarily use the terms *environment* or *environmental disaster,* rather than *nature* or *natural disaster. Environmental disaster* is a broader term that encapsulates the totality of a flood event including both the human and nonhuman world. A wealth of recent literature argues that there is no such thing as a purely "natural" disaster devoid of human culpability, taking as common knowledge the unnaturalness of natural disasters.[57] The ideological construction of nature and natural disaster represented by the elements of wind, rain, heat, and water still has a tendency to operate outside human recorded history by minimizing the value and importance of human decision-making in the creation of suffering. In his *Organic Machine: The Remaking of the Columbia River,* historian Richard White makes the connection between the human and nonhuman world for thinking about environmental history: "I mean to do more than write a human history alongside a natural history and call it an environmental history," he writes. "This would be like writing a biography of a wife, placing it alongside the biography of a husband and calling it the history of a marriage. I want the history of the relationship itself."[58] In making the case for a more comprehensive and interrelated history of race and environment, it is essential to understand why charges of environmental inequity we commonly associate with late twentieth-century politics have roots in an earlier period. *Backwater Blues* makes the case that environmental disasters provide some of the most telling and revealing snapshots of our racial fabric across time, offering an invaluable lens into the meaning of race, citizenship, and the environmental world.

1 Down the Line

Blues Brilliance, Displacement, and Living under the Shadow of Levees

> Well, in the old days, you see, you weren't allowed to express your feelings all that much. A lot of stuff was bottled up inside. . . . You can't explain it in a conversation so the best way to do it is to sing.
>
> —Bluesman Cash McCall

> We who are under the lash . . . pray God daily that the way may open for us to leave these terrible conditions.
>
> —Letter from an unknown survivor of the 1927 Flood to the *Chicago Defender*, July 16, 1927

The blues serves as an important theoretical counternarrative to the historical archive and how historians make sense of the 1927 flood through "traditional" sources. For many reasons, traditional archives obscure more than they reveal about black social realities during the 1927 flood. A dearth of first-hand sources from black people precludes tying archives to a materiality of experience. Moreover, we have very little of black people's own words in the form of letters, diaries, oral history, circulars, census records, and other archival sources from the flood. This is not to say important sources do not exist. Black leaders, institutions, and newspapers were vocal throughout the ordeal, but the materiality of black people's experience is still largely lost to us. By "materiality" I mean the personal recollection of the day a local levee broke or the time of day floodwaters first rolled across fields onto their porches, how long and hard it rained, and the smell of mud and dead animal carcasses. What was their personal experience inside a Red Cross relief camp or the rationale behind migration to Chicago or Houston? Were they already looking to migrate like the million that preceded them, or was it a realization that life after the flood would be even worse? Even the much-used Works Progress Administration source materials yield few results. Much of how we account for black people is through reductionism, where the totality of black experiences might be reduced to how many people were housed and fed by the American Red Cross or immunized by public health departments. The archive presents at best a temporal space of knowledge around the 1927 flood.

A high rate of illiteracy among African Americans in the 1920s, itself a legacy of slavery and lack of citizenship, accounts for only a surface understanding of the limited archive.[1] Equally important was the violence toward and surveillance of black people in southern states and the way it undermined their ability to safely articulate experiences in public spaces. An open expression of black resistance to white hegemony (either oral or written) during this period in the Yazoo Delta often met with violence and death. Concomitantly, when black people wrote letters to newspapers they often did so anonymously, as they understood all too well the lethal penalties for outspokenness on racial matters.[2] As a result, even the small nuggets of anonymous truth provided by the historical archive unearth as much about the actualization of blackness in the 1920s as it does the 1927 flood. The anonymous letter to the *Chicago Defender* that appears in the epigraph of this chapter is a prime example. Not only does it express outrage at being mistreated and a desire to leave a land of bondage, it also takes into account the peculiarity of blackness during the flood. Like a blues verse, "we who are under the lash" marks a collective black identity as the universal suffering group. The survivor never specifies what he or she is under the lash from exactly—the environment, racism, or both. "Under the lash" is also telling because of its historical reminder of slavery, when the whip was constantly employed to subjugate Africans and African Americans. Because of the letter's succinctness and lack of information, we can only speculate about who wrote the letter. Was the writer male or female? Where exactly did she or he reside during the 1927 flood and did he or she live in a Red Cross relief camp that informed the experiences? Not only does the presence of the letter reject ideas of illiteracy, but the tone perhaps implies a middle-class status undermining most treatments of flood survivors that assume black victims were always poor sharecroppers. Indeed, the chief reason we have so few accounts from black voices is that many feared white retaliation by going on the historical record, a hard reality facing survivors, regardless of status or class.

The fearful reality for black flood survivors still does not fully account for the limited archive. Archives are ideological creations with their own set of arguments and racialized discourse wedded to the recent emergence of social history. Legislation in the 1960s was successful in tearing down overt discrimination in American society through the Civil Rights and Voting Rights Acts. The 1960s also witnessed a significant push for establishing African American history / studies programs in predominantly white colleges and universities and advancing a more inclusive type of historical narrative. The training of more black scholars and the general trend toward social history as an integral part of historical research by the mid to late 1970s pushed the historical field as a whole to think more critically about people who had been left out of historical narratives, including minorities and women. The 1927 flood represents a limited ideological archive because in the decades leading up to the civil rights era and beyond the experiences of black flood sufferers remained largely invisible to most archives. Very little attention was paid to documenting black flood survivors in the form of correspondences or oral history, leaving historians to piece together black experiences through small nuggets and reading between the lines, so to speak, of correspondences about black people, statistical analyses, and parochial federal documents. The importance of blues and other black art forms in representing black realities becomes clear. Such mediums offer valuable cultural perspectives that are otherwise unavailable to the historian.

The 1927 flood inspired the richest groundswell of recorded blues after a specific environmental disaster in history. This chapter resituates blues as part of the 1927 flood's historical narrative, serving the dual purpose of creating memory around the disaster in the 1920s and 1930s and archiving those stories for the historian. The blues was not necessarily political, but the creation of songs served the purpose of a political and historical act addressing what some black flood survivors still living in the South could not express safely, what black people familiar with the South knew to be true even if they no longer resided there, and what people outside the South perhaps had little awareness of. As literary scholar Cheryl Wall reminds us, "Blues is the music that represents a past that is there, even if one is not conscious of it. . . . Music is also a metaphor for the unspeakable: what cannot be said both because it is too painful or dangerous to express in words and because no one could hear or understand the words if they could be found." In Toni Morrison's *Beloved,* Wall describes how the character Paul D remembered the pain and trauma of his enslavement: "Sang it sometimes but I never told a soul."[3] The music is a salve, a coping mechanism that allows one to face human atrocity. Culturally speaking, blues gave voice to the pain of black life in ways that no other medium—save perhaps gospel—could. Close scrutiny of blues music in response to the 1927 flood provides crucial insights into the untold story of black survival and loss.[4]

The blues can be read as a counterhegemonic force or corrective impulse that sets the record straight, so to speak, about what the 1927 flood and broader environmental world meant for black folks at the time. To be sure, the 1927 flood was not the unifying or patriotic moment for black people in the way the federal government and Red Cross framed it for the nation. Indeed, the blues makes the argument that the flood, unlike any other national moments in recent memory, revealed the Yazoo Delta's inhumane treatment of black people. Early twentieth-century contemporary narratives of environmentalism suggest that black people rarely, if ever, commented on the environmental world in any meaningful way. The blues (voice) proves otherwise. Environmental issues ranging from boll weevils, floods, droughts, and tornadoes are featured subjects in blues music.[5] Considering the extent to which black people depended on agriculture to survive, it is hardly surprising that their sentiments about the environment and their racial subjectivity emerge in this tragic and comic blues medium.[6] For example, both black and white farmers were made painfully aware of the loss resulting from boll weevils, which entered the United States in massive numbers via Mexico in the 1890s. Weevils are small insects that attach to young balls of cotton, destroying their potential to reach maturity; by World War I boll weevil infestations had reached epidemic status in Louisiana, Alabama, Georgia, and Florida, causing severe financial damage. Expressed in the following blues lyric, the reality of black sharecroppers was to deal with both race and environment: "The white man he got half the crop, boll weevil took the rest;

I ain't got no home."[7] Environmental disasters were particularly disastrous for black families because they left them with few alternatives in the midst of an already limited economic existence.

This chapter focuses on the themes of displacement/homelessness and citizenship that emerge as a palpable blues explanatory framework on the 1927 flood. Blues singers frequently struck the tension-filled chord of movement and uncertainty of place by highlighting the ways in which race often superseded everything in the environmental world. At the same time that black people were pushed "down the line" and displaced by the flood, Yazoo Delta planters were reinventing ways to control black movement so as not to lose a valuable workforce. As a result, technology became an ever-present force in the lives of Yazoo Delta residents. The reality was that everyone within the Mississippi River's reach lived under the shadow of levees and feared being pushed down the line by the failure of massive levees; far from being apolitical technological structures, levees instead represented social and cultural constructions of race and class during the disaster.[8]

Finally, the blues archive complements other ways of knowing about the 1927 flood, providing a fuller account of the historical record. There are moments when specific historical experiences of black survivors, unearthed by historians only decades after the flood, were already explained and contextualized by the blues archive. It is important to tie these overlapping narratives of race and environmentalism together in a way that helps us create, in the words of Angela Davis, "a patchwork social history of black Americans during the decades following emancipation."[9]

Known as the "Empress of Blues," Bessie Smith was born on April 15, 1894, in Chattanooga, Tennessee. By 1912 she had already left home and was traveling with a blues troupe headed by Gertrude "Ma" Rainey. Smith was one of the first classic blues singers to sign a deal with Columbia Records, recording "Down Hearted Blues" in 1923. It was a commercial success, selling close to a million copies while helping make her the most well-known classic blues singer of the era. Her deep, rich, tonal voice captivated audiences in the 1920s and 1930s, propelling her to stardom along with Rainey. On stage, Smith's extravagant personality and wardrobe were unparalleled, and off stage the business intelligence she exemplified would be emulated by blues musicians long after the automobile accident that took her life in 1937 on a rural Mississippi road.[10]

Like other blues singers, Smith's explanations of the world around her were partly informed by personal experiences. In early 1927 her touring band was traveling by train in the South when they encountered a major flood. It remains unclear whether this flooding had anything to do with the 1927 flood; nonetheless, the water was enough to temporarily halt their travel. Smith's sister-in-law Maud Smith recalled the ordeal years later: "We came to this little town, which was flooded, so everybody had to step off the train into little rowboats that took us to where we were staying."[11] Not only was the train segregated, according to custom, but the housing of blacks and whites was also segregated. Whites were taken to a local theater for safety while blacks were taken to the top floor of a local funeral home. Smith was less than thrilled by the arrangement and informed those around her that "no, no, I can't stay *here* tonight."[12] But this was 1927 in the Deep South and she, like the other black people she encountered, had fewer options than whites during this period of calamity. It made no difference that she was the Empress of Blues. Inside the funeral parlor, hearing stories of beleaguered and marginalized black folks trapped in a racial caste system hell-bent on keeping them oppressed, and having little protection from the environmental world, Smith began the process of formulating the backwater blues.[13]

When Smith returned home to Philadelphia she immediately drafted a version of "Backwater Blues," which was released for the public in February 1927. By the time "Backwater Blues" hit the airwaves it had been raining consistently for months in many states, but the idea of an epic flood had yet to take shape in the imagination of most Americans. National newspapers were preoccupied with other national news, and the federal government was still a month away from mobilizing resources in response to the flood. The timing was nothing short of perfect for Bessie Smith, if not a bit prescient. A month after the release of the song a new spring flood, this one more powerful than any before it, was shifting the public's consciousness, making "Backwater Blues" a powerful representation of what individuals and groups were experiencing.[14]

"Backwater Blues" is a song exclusively about race and nature. Sung in the traditional AA'B format, the song opens with a grim description of rain for five days producing an ominously dark sky. The hook in "Backwater Blues" that provides the meaning, commentary, critique, or evaluation is always about displacement. "I woke up this morning, can't even get out of my door; there is enough trouble to make a poor girl wonder where she want to go." The song concludes with the warning, "It thundered and lightenin'd and the wind began to blow; there were thousands of poor people didn't have no place to go."[15] Smith's words make sense in the aftermath of her own experience of being displaced by a flood and hearing the stories of other black people in that funeral parlor just a month before. It also struck a chord with poor African Americans displaced by the flood and shepherded into Red Cross camps like cattle, their movements watched by white planters, the police, and the Mississippi National Guard.

By late March the federal government and entire nation slowly began to take notice of what was occurring in the Mississippi Valley. This was not like an earthquake or tornado that struck quickly and violently. Instead, the 1927 flood was a slow-moving disaster that built up to a crescendo over time as levee after levee began to fail during the spring. No single backwater flood created as much damage and contributed to the imagination and memory of the 1927 flood as the Mounds Landing crevasse. The Mounds Landing levee protected farmlands and cotton-producing areas in the heart of the Yazoo Mississippi Delta, including Cleveland and the powerful cotton capital of Greenville. When the levee finally gave way on Thursday, April 21, it created a crevasse of epic proportion, summed up in a telegram from an Army Corps official in the region to General Edgar Jadwin, head of the corps: "Levee broke at ferry landing Mounds Mississippi eight a.m. Crevasse will overflow entire Mississippi Delta."[16] This was not the first levee break, nor would it be the last, but the Mounds Landing crevasse significantly shaped the 1927 flood because it demanded intervention from the federal government. Remarkably, the Red Cross claimed only two people died during the crevasse. The Mississippi National Guard reported only that no guardsmen were killed. While we have no official account of how many perished during the break, the death toll among blacks was likely underreported, and telling of how blacks remained largely invisible in the official records of the flood.[17]

According to eyewitness accounts it sounded like the detonation of a bomb as the entire Mounds Landing levee catapulted forward. The crevasse pushed floodwaters onto the landscape covering an area an astonishing fifty miles wide and one hundred miles long; in places the water was twenty feet deep. Floodwaters swept some people away never to be seen again, while others hung precariously to life in trees, on rooftops, and in attics. People took refuge wherever they could (and if they were black, anyplace they were allowed and was safe). The Mississippi River flowed with such tremendous force and height that tributaries like the Ohio and Missouri Rivers could no longer flow into the larger body of water. In some cases these tributaries actually began flowing backward because of the Mississippi River's current, providing yet another definition of backwater.

Fred Chaney, who was white, survived with his family for several days in a boxcar after escaping floodwaters in Washington County, Mississippi, about fifteen miles from Greenville. They were desperately trying to make it to Greenville, where they heard people were receiving food and supplies on the top floors of downtown office buildings, but floodwaters rose so quickly they could only reach a nearby rail yard. Here they found a number of black and white survivors living inside boxcars.[18] The socialization of race informed why black families took refuge on one side of the rail yard and white families on the other. This was custom and expected; no amount of floodwater could wash away the lines that separated black from white.

After a few days, floodwaters were beginning to lap across the inside of the Chaney boxcar, causing the family to relocate on top of the boxcar, exposed to the elements. The Chaneys still had food, so they were in better shape than others. Not long after moving to the boxcar's top they heard the screams of a white man hanging precariously from a tree branch not far away. They didn't know how he got there or how long he had been holding on, but they were certain floodwaters were too deep and current too powerful for him to survive long trying to swim. The only chance for rescue was to find a boat, which Chaney and his family did not have. On the other side of the rail yard, where African Americans were living, they noticed that someone did have a boat, a man by the name of Michael. Chaney demanded that Michael bring his boat to the other side of the freight yard and commandeered the vessel for a rescue attempt. We don't know who Michael was, whether he objected to the request or felt he had no other choice, but refusal might have lead to repercussions down the road for him and his family. The boat was old and unstable, and Chaney feared it might not stay afloat long enough for a rescue. It stayed afloat long enough for the two men to put together an impromptu rescue with Michael's boat, which had the biblical verse *The Spirit of God is Upon the Waters* inscribed on one side and *Noah's Ark* on the other.[19]

The day after the Mounds Landing crevasse, President Calvin Coolidge appointed Secretary of Commerce Herbert Hoover as chairman of relief operations in the Yazoo Mississippi Delta, giving him authority over the American Red Cross and the power to mobilize segments of the American military. Red Cross supplies were locally funneled through citizens and relief committees. Hoover held firm to the philosophy that local needs were best understood by local citizens and that the American Red Cross should not encroach on local customs and beliefs; it provided resources but refused to insist on how they would be distributed. William Alexander Percy, the son of influential banker and former Mississippi U.S. senator Leroy Percy, was placed in charge of relief supplies in Greenville, Mississippi. The Percy name held tremendous influence in the Yazoo Delta region, representing land barons and politicians.[20] Close to two hundred thousand people lived in the Yazoo Delta region during the flood, and most were either temporarily or permanently displaced from their homes. Over a five-month span, some seventy thousand survivors resided in Red Cross relief camps while close to ninety thousand were assisted by the Red Cross in personal homes, hotels, boxcars, and buildings. Countless other blacks and whites fled the Yazoo Delta never to return. The Red Cross operated 154 relief camps in the seven states flooded during the disaster, the vast majority of inhabitants being poor blacks.[21] The immediate aftermath of the disaster exposed the ways in which issues of race and power were embedded within the process of charity and relief, revealing these tensions as everyone attempted to make sense of the transformed environmental landscape. Aerial shots of flooded landscapes by the military, Mississippi River Commission, and Illinois Central Railroad were common. Photographers commonly employed an ideology of documenting and reproducing (Figure 1) aerial images that showed the flood blurring landscapes below.

The Percys and other white landowners around Greenville forced as many black flood survivors as possible into these Red Cross relief camps so they

FIGURE 1. This aerial shot of Arkansas City, Arkansas, shows backwaters spread wide across the landscape. Red Cross tents are lined up for miles on the levee. Photograph by the United States Army Air Forces, May 5, 1927. Courtesy of the National Archives and Records Administration.

could better prevent migration and have a readily available labor supply when the waters finally receded. Differences between the mostly black Red Cross relief camp in Greenville and the mostly white camp in Vicksburg show not only differences in space and quality of camp life but also how much the plantation bloc was wedded to policing blackness. The Vicksburg camp was in much better condition because Vicksburg was largely spared by the flood. White flood victims were also more likely to receive Red Cross assistance in homes and downtown office buildings in places like Greenville, while black survivors, from beginning to end, could not expect help from the Red Cross unless they entered one of the relief camps.[22]

Alice Pearson's "Greenville Levee Blues," recorded in July 1927, provides a window into the experiences of black people in Greenville. The specificity of this song sets it apart from other songs in the 1927 blues archive. Pearson had a brief recording career, recording only one session (with Paramount

Records in Chicago), and seemed to be especially interested in questions of nature. Three of her early songs, "Greenville Levee Blues," "Water Bound Blues," and "Memphis Earthquake," dealt specifically with environmental disasters, and other scholars have suggested that Pearson lived near Greenville during the 1927 flood.[23] The first two stanzas set a tone similar to Bessie Smith's "Backwater Blues." "I woke up this morning, couldn't even get out of my door; the levee broke and the town is overflowed." Her most incisive commentary comes in an overt critique of citizenship and blackness in Greenville. "People (living) on the levee, sleeping on the ground; I want to tell everybody that Greenville's a good old town."[24] When Pearson uses the term "good old town" she doesn't mean it as a positive term. Instead she is highlighting the oppressiveness and racial experiences of living in Greenville and, in particular, what it meant to be displaced in this racial landscape of vulnerability. The Greenville Red Cross camp was physically located on top of the city's levee because it was the highest point, but by mid-April it was in such horrific condition as to make the space basically unlivable. It was unbearably hot and muggy during the day, cold and windy at night, and the persistent rainfall and floodwaters washing up against the levee made the camp a slippery mud hill; because Red Cross tents were in short supply some people slept unprotected on the levee, exposed to the elements. Pearson's words represent a historical truth for displaced black people who lived on levees and slept on the ground in Greenville, and whose movements were controlled by a "good old town" network.[25] Figure 2 shows similar conditions in the Yazoo City, Mississippi, Red Cross camp where the background environmental landscape can be read as a public health document. Poor diet, rainy and cold conditions, and small pockets of stagnant water elevated the risk for disease inside many Red Cross camps.

It was clear from the beginning of the relief process that William Percy wanted to wield as much power over black flood survivors as possible. Demonstrating white paternalism, he later wrote in his memoir that "none of us was influenced by what the Negroes themselves wanted: they had no capacity to plan for their own welfare; planning for them was another of our burdens." [26] The Greenville levee was in such bad shape that Percy contemplated moving African Americans to Vicksburg, an unpopular decision among his father and other planters. Even though there was widespread fear

FIGURE 2. Black survivors in a Yazoo City Red Cross camp. Close attention to the surrounding landscape shows an extremely muddy and unhealthy environment in which survivors lived for months. Photograph by the Illinois Central Railroad, May 13, 1927. Courtesy of the National Archives and Records Administration.

of disease, including malaria, yellow fever, tuberculosis, and pellagra, on the Greenville levee, planters protested the move by arguing that blacks might easily elude the surveillance of landowners and escape if taken out of the immediate vicinity. The move was successfully blocked by planters who appealed to the elder Leroy Percy over the son with the specific intention that black workers—whose importance was only tied to their labor—must not be allowed to move freely lest the region's future prosperity become imperiled.[27]

Efforts to undermine movement were painfully connected to the reinscription of power over black bodies through labor. When Alonzo "Lonnie" Johnson recorded "Broken Levee Blues" in 1928, African Americans throughout the diaspora heard about forced labor in Red Cross camps through word of mouth and black newspapers. Johnson also confronted listeners with this reality through blues. Born in New Orleans in 1899, Johnson was no stranger to heartache. He accompanied his vocals and topical subject material with unique skills on the guitar, banjo, violin, and kazoo, making him a very popular performer at home and overseas. While he was touring Europe, most of his family was wiped out by the Spanish influenza epidemic of 1918–19. "Broken Levee Blues" is rare in its direct and unflinching appraisal of forced labor during the flood. "The police run me from Cairo, all through Arkansas; they put me in jail behind those cold iron bars. The police say work right or go to jail, I say I ain't totting no sacks; I won't drown on that levee and you ain't gonna break my back." Johnson paints a treacherous social existence in which black survivors faced displacement from nature and harassment from police and authorities. Black men were pressed into backbreaking labor and Johnson articulates what some felt: they would rather face imprisonment and death than be placed in a situation resembling slavery.[28]

Black bodies were desired not only to secure and fortify vulnerable levees around Greenville and throughout the Yazoo Delta but also for unloading Red Cross relief supplies. Blacks were forced to unload supplies at gunpoint in Greenville and threatened with death if they tried to leave or refused work. If a local white person needed help clearing land or unloading supplies, any black person inside or outside a relief camp could be conscripted. William Percy issued a work demand for the Greenville area giving whites authority to force African Americans not residing in Red Cross camps into whatever work whites wanted done. "All Negroes in Greenville outside of the levee camp who are able to work should work. If work is offered them and they refuse to work they should be arrested as vagrants. Names and addresses of those refusing to work should be telephoned to police headquarters." Stories circulated of black people being pulled out of their homes and off the street at gunpoint and physically taken to the levee.[29] One unknown African American man was shot and killed by police after refusing the demand of local whites who were going house to house looking for laborers. As it turned out the man had already worked close to twelve hours on the levee earlier that day and had just returned home. He was killed after refusing to go back.[30]

In Mississippi the National Guard was activated to patrol Red Cross camp perimeters and control the movement of African Americans. If a black person worked as a sharecropper before the flood, he or she had to provide the name of that landowner before entering a relief camp and receiving food. Black people who did not work for a white person still had to be vouched for by a white person. Every black family, single man, woman, and child, had to be vouched for by a local white person to receive food and shelter, without exception.[31] Any black person caught living outside the Greenville relief camp without suitable explanation was arrested. Movement surveillance was largely achieved through a tag system reminiscent of the slave codes used during slavery and the black codes during the post-Reconstruction era.[32] This tag included the person's name, who he or she worked for, and the person vouching for him or her. Even more insulting was the fact that this identification had to be visible at all times, and those who didn't have a tag or whose tag was missing could be jailed or forced to work on a levee detail. The intent of local white planters and politicians was clear in their desire to prevent migration and ensure the return of poor black field hands into the contractual conditions of peonage existing before the flood.[33] These ideas were perhaps best voiced in a letter from Curtis T. Green, commander of the Greenville National Guard, to the NAACP's Walter White. Green wrote, "We do not propose to have it [the Delta] stripped of labor." Green decided blacks should be controlled and kept in place until floodwaters receded and individual planters could come and find "his niggers . . . no man being allowed . . . any other but his own niggers."[34] Writing on postbellum exercises of freedom and terror in the nineteenth century, Saidiya Hartman asserts that "in the context of freedom, the need to re-impose black subordination was no less pressing and was actualized not only through forms of legal repression and punishment but also through the inculcation of rules of conduct."[35] Any type of actions by African Americans that did not coincide with what former slaveholders were accustomed to was seen as insolent behavior. In postbellum nineteenth-century America, particularly the South, former slaveholders reinscribing subordination often meant restricting the mobility and movement of African Americans across the southern landscape and thus limiting the freedoms associated with economic independence. In the early twentieth century as well, moving about freely was one of the many ways black people asserted their citizenship; the restriction of movement was an abhorrent abridgment of citizenship rights commented on in sermons, work songs, and the blues.[36]

As much as black people knew what it meant to enter one of these camps, in many ways they had no choice. Not only did the threat of jail and violence hover over them, but the more pressing concerns of starvation and disease significantly limited their options. Destroyed crops and flooded stores left them with virtually no other way to secure food, while parents also had to worry about feeding children. Black people were not allowed in the white spaces where the Red Cross was taking care of white flood survivors; planters like the Percys had a vested interest in keeping the Red Cross from providing resources to black survivors outside of camps. Hunger tied to disease was not an unusual experience for black residents in the Yazoo Delta, living in abject poverty and a constellation of peonage and poor health since Reconstruction. Still, the African American *Louisiana Weekly* framed the fear of pellagra and other diseases as a "new menace" among survivors.[37] The fear was not without merit. Pellagra had long been endemic to the Yazoo Mississippi Delta region as an illness associated with poverty. The etiology of pellagra is a poor diet lacking essential nutrients found in fresh meats, vegetables, and milk—the antithesis of the average poor southerner's diet of fatback, cornmeal, and molasses. Symptoms of pellagra were known as the "Four D's," consisting of dermatitis (skin lesions), diarrhea, dementia (or mental defects), and, if left untreated for an extended period of time, death.[38] Pellagra was still a mysterious disease in some medical circles in 1927, particularly among those who held tightly to the reductionist ideology of a microbe-centered base for diseases in the germ theory era. The numbers were telling, however: approximately one hundred thousand people in the southern states alone died of pellagra during the first four decades of the twentieth century. African Americans suffered at least a two-to-one morbidity rate from pellagra compared to whites, as they did from almost every other disease during the era.[39] An impending fear after the 1927 flood was that breakdowns in food production, consumption, and transportation would leave the region vulnerable to pellagra outbreaks, as happened after the Mississippi River floods in 1912 and 1922.[40] In the Yazoo Delta, African Americans suffered higher morbidity and mortality rates than whites from typhoid, cholera, tuberculosis, dysentery, pneumonia, rheumatism, influenza, premature birth, accidents of labor, and almost every other disease. Many went from cradle to grave without ever visiting a physician, highlighting Talcott

Parsons's theory of a "sick role."[41] By the 1920s there was only one hospital bed for every 1,941 black patients nationwide, compared to one for every 139 white patients.[42] Poverty, squalid housing, unsanitary living conditions, poor diet, the stress of racism, and overworked bodies made up the social landscape African Americans negotiated before, during, and immediately after the 1927 flood.[43]

In Greenville, African Americans found it exceedingly difficult to secure common necessities outside the matrix of charity and relief tied to the American Red Cross.[44] Across flooded landscapes black survivors sent letters to the *Chicago Defender, Pittsburgh Courier, Baltimore Afro-American,* and other black newspapers asking for help. One anonymous letter printed by the *Defender* informed readers that blacks were "made to work like a dog under a gun and club and tagged like a bale of cotton."[45] Another survivor wrote to Walter White of the NAACP, "Thousands of us will choose death by starvation rather than enter another camp."[46] In Vicksburg black people opened their doors to assist displaced victims while other black survivors drew inspiration from a legacy of maroon communities in Brazil, Jamaica, and the United States by temporarily surviving in swamps and forests to avoid the controlling arm of the Red Cross, the National Guard, and local planters.[47]

Blues musician Charley Patton captures the mood and sentiment of the black experience in Mississippi during this era. Patton was to the male-dominated country blues era what Bessie Smith was to the classic era. Of all country blues singers none was as popular as Charley Patton, known as the "King of the Delta." Born in Hinds County, Mississippi, sometime between 1887 and 1891, Patton influenced a generation of Delta guitar blues artists, including Son House, Howlin' Wolf, Robert Johnson, Muddy Waters, and John Lee Hooker. Patton's signature voice was rough and coarse in a way that became identified with the Delta blues itself, and his showmanship on stage was unmistakable—playing guitars behind his back and between his legs before crowds. Indeed, his voice was so rough that occasionally it is difficult to discern words in some of his songs.[48] His topical songs were known for their expression of life within the Yazoo Delta, particularly such songs as "High Sheriff Blues," which describes life inside Mississippi Delta prison camps. Patton recorded two separate parts of a song called "High

Water Blues" about the 1927 flood, and interviews place him, like Alice Pearson, near the disaster. The driving hook in part 1 is the "line": "Backwater done rose around Sumner, drove poor Charley down the line; Lord I tell the world the water done jumped through this town." The image of being "driven down the line" and backwater actively moving through the environmental world is a powerful description of an actual experience that implies displacement or mobility, in this case floodwaters forcing Patton "down the line" to leave his home. But nature is not the only thing driving Patton down the line: "Lord the whole round country, man is overflowed; I would go to the hill country but they got me barred."[49] "Hills" (or hill country) is a term that occasionally shows up in flood blues songs and can be interpreted to describe movement to safer ground. It is a metaphor; there are not many hills in the Yazoo Delta, but Vicksburg or Memphis might be considered the hill country in terms of escaping the flood's immediate path. Peonage conditions, forced labor on levees, and tag systems all restricted movement of black people into certain spaces. Patton is claiming the right to move freely across the landscape to a place of safety, to move without being forced into a charity camp that was really a labor camp. Bluesman George Carter also picked up the limited social existence and options for black people after the flood in "Rising River Blues." "Rising river blues running by my door, it run sweet mama like it haven't run before; I gotta move in the alley, I ain't allowed on the street; These rising river blues sure have got me beat."[50] His critique of segregation, citizenship, and the marginality of what an alley represents is unmistakable. George Carter was an alias of Thomas Dorsey, best known as a pioneer of gospel music. It was not unusual for record companies during the era to change the name of blues singers already under contract with another company so they could also record the singer. Some musicians, like Dorsey, took aliases so they too could take advantage of recording with more than one record company at a time.

Living under the Shadow of Levees

The 1927 flood is fundamentally a story of worthiness and unworthiness in a powerfully racialized society. Charity, displacement, and race-based peonage were powerful markers of social worth in 1927. But we can also see markers of social worth embedded within a part of the flood that is not as easily accessible. The artificial construction of massive levees, including the one involved in the Mounds Landing crevasse that set the federal government in motion, was blamed for creating the suffering that black and white Mississippians experienced. Levees were not simply structures of concrete, wood, and dirt, disconnected from social history, and their construction and presence were far from a disentangled social theory of decisions by engineers and politicians regarding flood control. The control of the Mississippi River and construction of levees was about more than the United States Army Corps of Engineers. Levees were designed to protect people and the Yazoo Delta cotton-growing economy. But the process was not unilateral; people physically and psychologically fell through the gaps of levee coverage, a point that emerges in the blues archive. Still, how might we take note of 1927 technology and the ways in which it shaped life? In his classic work *The Whale and the Reactor: A Search for Limits in an Age of High Technology,* social theorist Langdon Winner asks whether "artifacts have politics" and how we might imagine culture, politics, class dynamics, and race within the theoretical and practical development of technological systems. "At issue is the claim that the machines, structures, and systems of modern material culture can be accurately judged not only for their contributions to efficiency and productivity and their positive and negative environmental side effects, but also for the ways in which they can embody specific forms of power and authority," Winner writes.[51] Ultimately, people made choices about levees, deciding when and how to build them, the appropriate height and width, and whether certain communities would be protected. The failure of levees was not simply happenstance, an occurrence devoid of human culpability, but rather demonstrated the power certain groups held over other groups in the shaping and creation of suffering.

New Orleans during the 1927 flood represents a powerful marker of social worth, pitting country against city, and urban metropolis against rural hinterland. From its founding by Jean-Baptiste Le Moyne, Sieur de Bienville, in 1718 as the French capital of Louisiana, it was a vulnerable environmental landscape. Surrounded by the Mississippi River and another body of water later named Lake Pontchartrain, the French capital was called L'Isle de la Nouvelle Orleans.[52] Bienville and the settlement's boosters hoped that New Orleans would become the most important city in the South and the commercial gateway to Europe and the Atlantic world. What the physical landscape of New Orleans provided in spatial location as a commercial gateway it also took away as a uniquely vulnerable environment, becoming a city in the middle of a fishbowl surrounded by fifteen- to twenty-foot-high levees.[53] As the height and breadth of levees continued to grow, the vulnerability of living under its shadow was not lost on residents and visitors to the region. In New Orleans, elevated levees and the Mississippi River that flowed behind them provided a heightened sense of insecurity. T. L. Nichols visited New Orleans in the late nineteenth century and described the unsettling environmental landscape, juxtaposing the low-lying landscape of New Orleans surrounded by water with the massive levees that protected the city. Making a conscious connection between the river and the artificiality of technology, he wrote that "hundreds of ships and steamers were floating far above the level of the streets—as high, indeed as the roofs of the houses in the back streets of town." For some, the sight of commercial ships floating high above their heads was unnatural and surreal, even ghastly, while others questioned the ability of artificial levees to keep floodwaters out of the city. John Hammond was jarred by the size of levees when he visited the city in 1916, noting in his writings how seemingly inconsequential the levees were in relation to the Mississippi River, "a mound of earth that somehow made me think of the Pyramids." After climbing the levee and seeing the Mississippi River's power, he describes his impression: "The city lay back of me, far beneath the level of the mighty river upon whose brink I stood. It seemed so easy for the river to dash away the barrier of earth, imposing as that had seemed a few minutes ago."[54]

Greenville residents had similar experiences. The sight of large steamers hovering above the city's physical landscape was not uncommon. In his book *Where I Was Born and Raised,* Mississippi writer and cultural critic David Cohn talks about the shadowing presence of levees surrounding the low-lying Queen City of Greenville in the early twentieth century: "In the springtime when the waters of the river are high against the levees, [residents of Greenville gaze] at the yellow flood and ponder the possibilities of disaster." Cohn's description of elevated artificial levees surrounding Greenville is equally powerful when situated within a theory of vulnerable landscapes and levee construction. Cohn paints Greenville, like New Orleans, as a defenseless city where "steamboats on the swollen stream pass high above the level of the earth like monstrous birds in slow flight."[55] Artificial levees had grown into massive technological structures that could have a pervasive, even intrusive, presence in the lives of Yazoo Delta residents. Levees designed to protect the economy and protect human life were, at times, transformed into mechanisms for the creation of suffering that became part of living under the shadow of levees.

For New Orleanians during the 1927 flood, the vulnerability of living under the shadow of levees was a reflection of the built environment and manipulation of technology. New Orleans politicians and businessmen, including the recently elected Democratic mayor Arthur O'Keefe, considered the Crescent City the most important economic city of the South. As floodwaters barreled down the Mississippi River and its tributaries toward New Orleans in late March, correspondence between city, state, and local officials reflected an adamancy that a flooded New Orleans would be disastrous for the region, if not the entire nation.[56] The business-friendly *Times-Picayune* hoped to quell fear within the city and the rest of the world about the city's impending crisis. One headline read, "Safety Assured in New Orleans: Merchants and Residents Concerned over False Reports about City." The article opened by noting that "New Orleans is and has been doing business as usual. Residents and merchants are pursuing their vocations and avocations without interruption. The levees surrounding the city are intact and not one drop of flood water from the river has touched the city and no such intrusion is expected."[57] This proved to be false bravado; city leaders did not have complete faith in the levees surrounding the city. Instead, behind closed doors, city officials gathered support for a plan to ensure that vulnerable New Orleans would be safe from the flood.

On Good Friday city officials initiated a new civic organization called the Citizens Flood Relief Committee (CFRC), composed largely of the city's business elite. Its primary goal was to protect the valuable waterfront and commercial interests of the city. Their biggest fear was that a tarnished image would keep visitors and investors from the city even if floodwaters stayed clear.[58] O'Keefe and Marcel Garsaud, New Orleans's dock board manager, presented a resolution to the Mississippi River Commission (MRC) to destroy the levee at Poydras, twelve miles downstream, flooding the New

Orleans hinterland parishes of Plaquemines and St. Bernard. This would have been unthinkable before, but now the future of New Orleans was at stake. Historian Ari Kelman describes the MRC's initial reaction to this idea as "chilly," primarily because such an action would effectively "jettison decades of policy and admit culpability in raising the river."[59] At the same time, CFRC delegate James Thomson met with President Calvin Coolidge, Edgar Jadwin of the Corps of Engineers, and Secretary of War Dwight Davis in Washington. Somewhat reluctantly, all parties agreed to the proposal, with the contingency of a 100 percent reimbursement of adjusted claims filed by displaced residents of the proposed blast. The vast majority of the ten thousand residents were the Acadian descendants of ancestors who had migrated from Nova Scotia over a century before and worked in the Louisiana fur-trapping industry.[60]

On Tuesday, April 26, Democratic Louisiana governor Oramel Simpson signed the order to cut the Poydras levee, setting the stage for one of the more baffling moments in the history of environmental disasters. Residents of the two doomed parishes had three days to collect their belongings and leave for what was supposed to be a temporary displacement. For most, the displacement was anything but temporary.[61] They refused to go quietly into the night; armed citizens in St. Bernard and Plaquemines Parishes began patrolling the Poydras levee, showing they were willing to use violence to protect their property and livelihood. On a few occasions shots were fired by patrollers as a warning to unknown individuals coming too close to the levee, and in a well-publicized incident shots were even fired near Secretary of Commerce Herbert Hoover. When rumors circulated that the angry residents from St. Bernard and Plaquemines were planning to sabotage New Orleans's levees in a preemptive strike, New Orleanians took no chances and formed their own round-the-clock armed levee patrols, calling in the National Guard to provide additional protection.[62] Moving day was April 26: residents drove and walked out of the parishes in what one observer wryly described as an "endless caravan which streamed out of the doomed area."[63] Those displaced would be temporarily housed at an army base inside New Orleans city limits, one floor for blacks and another for whites. People were forced together by the actions of others, but racial customs and norms were nonetheless maintained during this human-made disaster.

Three days later, during the early morning hours of April 29, officials blocked entrance into the two parishes while military planes flew above looking for last-minute evacuations. Reporters, journalists, and interested bystanders gathered at the Caernarvon levee twelve miles away from a portion of Canal Street at high noon; some traveled across the country to witness an event likened to a strategic military maneuver that would spill floodwaters over an estimated seventy thousand acres of economically viable Louisiana landscape in a visually fantastic show of human's control over nature. The end result was successful, but the show itself was rather pedestrian. It took three separate blasts until a fifteen-foot-wide stream of water finally began to emerge from the levee, hours after the first blast. It was perhaps disappointing to those whose lives and livelihoods had not been destroyed in an instant. As one witness observed, "There was to be a mighty wall of water suddenly unleashed, Niagara-like, ripping, tearing all before it;

FIGURE 3. The human-created levee crevasse near Caernarvon, Louisiana. Notice the spectators near the blast. Photograph by the United States Weather Bureau, April 29, 1927. Courtesy of the National Archives and Records Administration.

whirling down toward the Gulf of Mexico like the onrush of Attilla's horde of Huns. Was there? There was not."[64] One thing did fantastically explode with the Caernarvon crevasse—the much-maligned "levees only" policy. The dirty secret had once and for all been brought into the open with this act, and no longer could the Corps of Engineers and the Mississippi River Commission deflect the criticism that a narrowly conceived policy of flood control had brought such pain to thousands of people. One of the few lasting images (Figure 3) of the event shows the act of human-created suffering with a trickle of floodwater coming through the levee.

The numbers were staggering. Close to ten thousand people were displaced, and 70 percent of the region's muskrat population was destroyed. It took several years for the muskrat population to come back and even longer for the trapping and fur pelt industry economy to recover. Muskrats are nocturnal creatures, and the blast forced them out of their natural habitat and routine. Those not among the hundreds of thousands that drowned eventually perished from overexposure to sunlight.[65] The return of a viable trapping industry was significantly hampered by a depleted muskrat population and bureaucratic obstacles put in place to deny paying 100 percent reimbursement. Settlements proved more costly than the city anticipated, and lawyers for the CFRC found loopholes in settlement agreements to enable the CFRC to withhold payment. The CFRC agreed to bear the cost of housing and feeding victims displaced from the blast while temporarily residing in New Orleans, but it also deducted food allotments from final settlements. Over $35 million in claims was quickly reduced to $2.9 million by CFRC lawyers, and most of this amount went to the Acme Land and Fur Company.[66] Most of those displaced received somewhere in the range of $300, while others received nothing. Rather than face uphill and costly court battles they could little afford, St. Bernards and Plaquemines Parish residents accepted meager payments for their suffering and began the slow process of rebuilding their lives from scratch. Most would never recover.[67]

This was far from the only moment when social worth was defined through levees during the 1927 flood. The blues provides an aperture into that which is difficult to verbalize, forgotten, and best never remembered. Classic blues singer Mattie Delaney echoes this sentiment in "Tallahatchie River Blues." "Tallahatchie River Risin', Lord it's mighty bad; some peoples on the Tallahatchie done lost everything they had. The people in the Delta wonderin' what to do; they don't build some levees, I don't know what became of you." A tributary of the Mississippi River, the Tallahatchie River is also known as the site where Emmitt Till's body was found in 1955 after being savagely beaten by white men near Money, Mississippi, for allegedly whistling at a white woman.[68] "Tallahatchie River Blues" suggests that, even before the flood, not every community enjoyed the same measure of defense from levees. Uniformity of levee construction under the Mississippi River Commission and Corps of Engineers was still not a reality by 1927, and gaps continued to plague the coterminous levee system throughout the Yazoo Delta.[69] Levee construction and repair work was a never-ending process. For instance, the Riverton levee in Bolivar County, Mississippi, was initially completed in January 1883. Over the course of three decades the levee had so weakened from water washing against and underneath the structure that by 1919 the local levee board of commissioners targeted the Riverton levee as an area desperately in need of revetment and extension work. They justified the work by saying the weakness of this particular levee might place the entire region in peril. Flanked by important cotton-producing regions in the Delta, including Rosedale two miles away and Greenville thirty-five miles away, a weakened Riverton levee put countless lives at risk and had significant economic ramifications for planters.[70] "Tallahatchie River Blues" reified the meaning of vulnerability for people who depended on levees to provide protection but also understood how their security might be tenuous. This was the historical truth Mattie Delaney spoke of. Even if the corps was perhaps alone in its steadfast belief in the levee system leading up to the 1927 flood, others clearly had a more polysemous faith.

Sippie Wallace made a much more concrete analysis of the vulnerability and unnaturalness of levees. Born Beulah Thomas on November 1, 1898, in Houston, Texas, she was one of the more commercially successful Texas R&B singers of the 1920s. On May 6, 1927, during the height of flood displacement and relief operations, Wallace recorded "The Flood Blues." "They sent out a law for everybody to leave town; but when I got the news I was high water bound. They dynamite the levee thought it might give us ease; but the water still rising do you hear this plea?"[71] The social critique described in the song is of an experiential truth. It is a cruel reality that a levee crevasse that destroys one community might result in the safety of border communities downstream. Pressure placed on levees throughout a contiguous stretch is lessened when a crevasse occurs at one specific spot in the system, even if floodwaters might spread across the landscape as backwater. The severity of Mounds Landing in 1927 was rare as most breaks did not cover that much ground. In most cases neighbors breathed a little easier if they heard of breaks in nearby communities, but people also did a little more than wish bad luck on neighbors. Rumors of residents deliberately sabotaging the levee of a neighboring community with dynamite under the dark of night were taken seriously. Indeed, by the middle of April armed citizens in Arkansas, Louisiana, and Mississippi patrolled levees day and night to prevent such attacks, with friends, neighbors, and bordering states suspicious of each other's activities and motives at every turn.[72]

Rosemary Howe Scioneaux experienced this firsthand in Southern Louisiana. Her family lived near Donaldsonville, thirty miles from Baton Rouge, and though she was just a child at the time she would later recall how the adults were terrified that the levee would not hold.[73] They were afraid of something more than nature. They were also afraid of neighbors who might sacrifice the area around Donaldsonville to save themselves, which was just as much part of her memory of the disaster as the flood itself. "People who lived south of Donaldsonville set up patrols along the levee," Scioneaux recalled years later. "They were afraid the people in Gonzales would dynamite the levee on our side."[74] Scioneaux's parents and other adults measured the river every day, hoping flood levels would decrease, but when it remained high they hardened themselves to remain vigilant against their own neighbors and friends. On Good Friday, Scioneaux asked her mother what they would do if the levee broke, to which her mother quipped sarcastically but also seriously, "Get a raft and hang on." A few days later the river's depth decreased significantly in Donaldsonville. As it turned out, the levee near Morganza, Louisiana, west of their community, had failed.[75] Scioneaux's family was safe, but only at the expense of a neighboring community.

Seven months after "Backwater Blues," Bessie Smith recorded another song, "Homeless Blues."[76] By now the flood had been seared into the American imagination through patriotic appeals for money that cast the disaster as the greatest of its kind in history. Red Cross camps were still in existence and hundreds of people remained homeless, but for most Americans the autumn of 1927 brought a semblance of normalcy. Coverage of the flood was lessening in newspapers and slowly the country was moving away from its disaster consciousness. Nonetheless, "Homeless Blues" was a reminder of what thousands of people had recently experienced and many were still dealing with. Wounds of the disaster were still fresh in the public imagination when Smith's second song, this one less prescient but equally forceful, hit the airwaves in September 1927. As cultural theorist Farah Jasmine Griffin describes "Homeless Blues's" infinite wisdom, it was direct in its critique of the Mississippi River and the limits of black citizenship.[77] "Oh Mississippi River, what a fix you left me in." When Smith sings the line "Hungry and disgusted, no place to lay my head," she is indicting both the Mississippi River for creating the initial suffering and American racism for prolonging the pain. At one particular juncture she suggests that death is perhaps preferable to being homeless and without protection, setting the stage for a final critique. She concludes "Homeless Blues" with a scathingly metaphorical critique of the limits imposed on African Americans in the South and their desire to escape a limited life. "Wish I was an eagle, but I'm just a plain old black crow; I'm gonna flap my wings and leave here and never come back no more."[78] As Griffin argues, the dichotomy of an eagle versus a crow is telling; the former represents freedom and the very meaning of citizenship and the latter a stark reminder of everything the eagle is not. An "old black crow" is taken from Jim Crow, the term used to describe an American apartheid system of segregation.[79] The last line of "Homeless Blues" critiques the South in the same way millions of African Americans did. One by one, individually and collectively, black people left the South in a mass exodus known as the Great Migration. There was never just one reason they decided to migrate. Sharecropping, violence, education, health, freedom of movement, and social and kinship networks all played varying roles in migrants' decision to leave. Bessie Smith's particular critique in "Homeless Blues" posits the importance of environmental disasters alongside the limited social existence of Jim Crow's inhumanity in that decision-making consciousness, a limited social existence Richard Wright would also pick up in constructing his own blues voice on the 1927 flood.

2 Burning Waters Rise

Richard Wright's *Blues Voice* and the Double Environmental Burden of Race

Truth eternally thrusts itself as the highest handmaid of imagination, as the one great vehicle of universal understanding.

—W. E. B. Du Bois

When the flood waters recede, the poor folk along the river start from scratch.

—Richard Wright

In June 1926, one year before the 1927 flood spilled across the Yazoo Mississippi Delta landscape, W. E. B. Du Bois delivered a speech at the twelfth annual Spingarn celebration honoring Carter G. Woodson; the speech was later published in *Crisis* magazine as "Criteria of Negro Art." Already a towering figure in the field of sociology, Du Bois inserted himself squarely into a debate that had existed at least since the beginning of the Harlem Renaissance: whether black art should or could be used as a form of racial propaganda. "What have we who are slaves and black to do with Art?" Du Bois asked. For Du Bois the beauty of black art in all its forms could not be separated from certain intrinsic and historical truths of blackness and the need to express individual and universal racial experiences through creativity. The black artist, Du Bois insisted, is compelled to speak the truths of slavery and racial injustice using the creative mechanisms at his or her disposal. "Thus all Art is propaganda and ever must be," Du Bois wrote.[1]

Du Bois reminds us that creativity in all forms is most often an engagement of personal truths; that it makes sense for people to write from the template of their own historical reality. He also makes the case that black people must use all forms of truth-telling available to them at the time, from social science to creative art, in demanding freedom and righteousness. "The apostle of Beauty," he laments, "thus becomes the apostle of Truth and Right not by choice but by inner and outer compulsion."[2] Black artists have often felt compelled to construct narratives of universal truth through historical fiction, poetry, artwork, and blues. I follow Du Bois's lead by arguing that black artistic creativity, particularly in the absence of archival records, provides important ways of understanding the 1927 flood. This chapter deals in particular with the historical imaginative literature of Richard Wright, which encompasses a blues voice of explanation around the social dimensions of disaster, in essence performing a function similar to that of the blues by explaining to the world what many black people during the disaster could not publicly vocalize through their own voices. As blues provided moments of intense clarity and creative expression for social truths, so too did the blues voice Richard Wright created through his two short flood stories.[3]

I construct these narratives around two basic premises. First, historical fiction helped shape a counterdiscourse around the 1927 flood. By the early twentieth century, environmental thought was central to the Western intellectual tradition. Yet very few mainstream environmental writers of the time gave serious consideration to questions of race and how nonwhites engaged intellectually, socially, and culturally with the environmental world. From the writings of black intellectuals of the era, especially during the Harlem Renaissance, oppositional tactics emerged for evaluating and describing the environmental world that black people inhabited. Rather than simply observing a passive or sublime "nature," black intellectuals often connected the beauty of nature with racial protest. As Paul Outka argues, "While moments of genuine natural appreciation emerge for the first time in African American texts from this period, they certainly do not describe an embrace of natural experience in anything like the ways white people valorized sublime or pastoral experience."[4] For Outka, race and nature represent a "series of paradoxes" where black intellectuals and writers appreciate the beauty of nonhuman nature for what it's worth, but also detest the traumatic violence against black bodies within those same spaces. "The connection with the land recorded in the Harlem Renaissance remained dangerous and painful, making nature a locus of vulnerability as well as comfort and homecoming, simultaneously an intensely political and historicized site of suffering and oppression."[5] Richard Wright's texts on the 1927 flood represented a self-conscious literary counter-narrative and oppositional framework to the broader discourse of environmentalism of the time, and more specifically, posited that race represented an added burden for African Americans during the flood.[6] For Wright, the environmental world was active rather than passive or serene—where the terrors of racism exacerbated conditions of nonhuman uncontrollable nature.

Second, an uneasy reality brought home by Hurricane Katrina and other environmental disasters over the last century is that the social dimensions of disaster are not new. What we now think of as the environmental (in)justice issues of Hurricane Katrina taking shape from a movement that began in the late 1970s and early 1980s actually found a voice among a cadre of early twentieth-century black intellectuals, artists, and novelists that included W. E. B. Du Bois, Zora Neale Hurston, Ida B. Wells, Richard Wright, and many others.[7] Collectively these writings suggest that black people have long suffered from both the environmental world and the sociocultural environment of race. Tornadoes, hurricanes, and floods are not just moments of environmental crises; they are a particular kind of racial event. Commentators of these moments in the twentieth century, from Zora Neale Hurston and W. E. B. Du Bois to Bessie Smith and Richard Wright, understood that disasters largely exposed divisions between rather than united groups of people based on race. Dealing with the wrath of nature was hard enough; dealing with the wrath of nature alongside race and racism made for a double burden that, in many instances, African Americans alone shouldered. The limits of citizenship and "othering" of black people within environmental landscapes has historically been most visible during the same crises framed to a broader public as unifying, making the materiality of experience that much more difficult to see.[8]

As a way of briefly framing how broader ideas of race and nature have taken shape over the last century, we might begin with historian Frederick Jackson Turner's 1893 essay on the myth of "wilderness," and what environmental historians like William Cronon have described as the romantic conceptualization of "un-fallen nature."[9] In short, Turner's intellectual thesis of wilderness suggested that, by roughly 1890, a much more modernized and industrialized America was suffering from the trappings of civilization and refinement; and a fading American frontier was resulting in the disintegration of early American republic ideals of rugged individualism on which the country was founded. It was only by returning to a simpler frontier that the country might reinvigorate "democratic" institutions and creativity that characterized the early republic. The frontier was intended to represent the very essence of American national identity built on the hard work of free and uninhabited land and spaces constructed as "wilderness"; on the backs of which supposedly stood America's principles of democracy and individualism.[10] The idea of wilderness as a "virgin" physical and cultural landscape necessarily extracted the presence of aboriginal groups in the process of making it free, uninhabited, and a place worthy of admiration and sublimity. Historians such as Roderick Nash and William Cronon describe a very different frontier—one marked by extreme cultural and physical violence against Native Americans forcibly removed from the lands they inhabited for centuries before European arrival.[11] As Cronon reminds us, "The removal of Indians to create an uninhabited wilderness—uninhabited as never before in the human history of the place—reminds us just how invented, just how constructed, the American wilderness really is."[12]

The myth of wilderness as a place of untouched spoils was deeply rooted in the origins of early twentieth-century conservation theory, particularly the federal protection of untouched parks and pristine nature worthy of admiration for tourists. Such reimaginations of nature could take shape only as the experiences of racial others were violently absented from the landscape.[13] John Muir and Henry David Thoreau describe nature as places that might simultaneously be awe-inspiring, sublime, fearful, and divine, but ultimately must be protected to remain authentically natural. These ideas make up the national preoccupation with protected natural parks and "wilderness" in the United States, particularly the belief that tourists in these spaces were "seeing their nation in its pristine, original state, in the new morning of God's own creation."[14] Nature was defined as the place where human beings were not, and if they were it was only as the occasional white middle-class leisurely sojourner in previously untouched landscapes.

Indeed, one of the many problems of the wilderness myth and intellectual ideas of nature and the environmental world is that people who worked on the land by force or necessity are often left out of narratives. Enslaved Africans and African Americans who developed highly effective practices of rice cultivation in the South Carolina Low Country through the process of trunk-minding are largely ignored in writings about the environmental world.[15] So too are black farmers and sharecroppers who yielded bumper crops despite droughts, high waters, boll weevils, and debt peonage.

Race has also been largely written out of leisure. The ever-present reality of exclusion often prevented blacks from participating in certain leisure activities associated with nature during the twentieth century.[16] From California to Florida during the era of Jim Crow, beaches, resorts, and parks were racially segregated and black people found themselves locked out of nature's resources; particularly those associated with water. Battles to desegregate access to beaches could be as vitriolic as those to desegregate lunch counters in Alabama, housing in Chicago, and schools in Topeka, Kansas. When the 1919 Chicago Race Riot began because a black boy crossed an imaginary racial line while swimming, it reflected what was widely considered a commentary on race, but rarely considered an issue of race and nature, even though the key to the moment was access to nature.[17] During segregation the consumption and enjoyment of water was normally considered a valuable and universal good, except when access to public beaches was defined by race, or when high-pressure water was used through fire hoses against civil rights protestors in Birmingham and other places in the 1960s.[18] The experiences of poor people and people of color, as well as critiques of such experiences—through art and social science—of what the environment (racial discourse and elements of "nature") means to them remains an important part of social history.

African Americans have long expressed their relationship with the environmental world through the cultural mediums of blues, paintings, speeches, and experiential knowledge of landscapes passed from generation to generation, providing what African American ecoliterary scholar Kimberly Smith also defines as an important counternarrative against black environmental complacency. "Contrary to conventional wisdom," she argues, "black Americans have not been indifferent to environmental values; there is, in fact, a rich tradition of black environmental thought. Du Bois and many other black writers—including Henry Bibb, Martin Delany, Frederick Douglass, Booker T. Washington, George Washington Carver, Alain Locke, Jean Toomer, and Langston Hughes—had a great deal to say about how slavery and racial oppression affected black Americans' relationship to the land."[19] So too did Ida B. Wells-Barnett and Zora Neale Hurston. Turn-of-the-twentieth-century African American environmental thought was greatly influenced by the history of slavery and racism embedded within landscapes defined as "natural." The collective memory of a group toward nature is measured in part, Smith argues, by the "justice or injustice of their social arrangements."[20] Individual and collective historical experiences frame the lens through which black people have explained the environmental world around them, including disasters. Unlike mainstream environmental writing of the early twentieth century, black commentators employ a historical rhetoric of universal racialism and politics of protest to explain the meaning of their environmental world. In his 1925 work *The New Negro: Voices of the Harlem Renaissance,* Alain Locke suggests that part of what separates black artistic and literary traditions from other traditions is an almost obsessive connection between creativity and group historical experience.[21] Like the blues, writers often felt compelled to write from a template of "we" as justification for the individual and collective experience.

There are many different ways that historical fiction can help us write about the past. Lawrence Buell reminds us of this interdependence between literature and history as novelists have inserted themselves into everything from nineteenth-century yellow fever epidemics in New York and Philadelphia to twentieth-century rural environmental and agrarian landscapes of the South. Buell also makes a connection between social activism and literature when he describes the intense moment Hull House founder Jane Addams remembered: "In my first view of the horror of East London I should have recalled De Quincey's literary description in *The English Mail Coach* of a case of absorption in literary meditation rendering the persona incapable of preventing an accident in real life."[22] Addams may have been surprised to think about a work of fiction when confronted with poverty, but imaginative literature can profoundly influence how we think about historical moments.

Few works of imaginative literature have so significantly shaped our interpretation of an environmental disaster like John Steinbeck's Dust Bowl–inspired *Grapes of Wrath*. "No other novel of the thirties," says Dust Bowl scholar Donald Worster, "had anything like its national impact; it taught an entire reading public what to think about the Okies and exodusters, and it would endure, for all its aesthetic and analytical faults, as one of the great American works of literature."[23] Worster might be correct in elevating the novel to the pinnacle of sales and mainstream popularity in the 1930s and 1940s, but *The Grapes of Wrath* is only a small part of how we might think through literary creative expressions of environmental disasters.

The environmental writings of Richard Wright, particularly his two short stories, "The Man Who Saw the Flood" and "Down by the Riverside," were among the first written texts explaining the 1927 flood as a racial and environmental event. As way of providing additional context, I also employ Zora Neale Hurston's classic *Their Eyes Were Watching God* to help illustrate the way both writers used an environmental world that, compared to writers like Thoreau, John Muir, and southern writer William Faulkner, was more active, aggressive, and revolutionary than passive, sublime, and demure. For Hurston and Wright, nature reflected central questions of race, revolution, and the desire for citizenship and humanity in a powerfully inhumane world.

Richard Wright's Flood Blues

Richard Wright developed his world-explanatory framework and blues voice in much the same way as Bessie Smith and Charley Patton: by individual experiences shared with the world through creative expression. Richard Nathaniel Wright was born September 4, 1908, on Rucker's Plantation near Natchez, Mississippi. His father, Nathaniel, was illiterate and worked as a sharecropper and sawmill worker in the area, and similar to so many other poor black folk in the region, Wright's family knew the struggles of sharecropping and poverty in the deepest South and the power behind asserting their citizenship through mobility. His childhood is the reason why poverty and oppression played such a prominent feature in his writing and poems during the 1930s.

While his explanatory framework was being honed by the powerfully southern world surrounding him, Wright's mother, Ella Wilson Wright, provided the initial support for his artistic expression. An educated woman and schoolteacher in Mississippi, Ella Wright pushed Richard and his younger brother Leon to excel in school and showed them the power of words to transform the human condition. The family moved to Memphis around 1914, when Wright was just six years old, but he would constantly travel back and forth between Memphis and parts of Mississippi visiting and living with relatives. Not long after moving to Memphis, Wright's parents separated and his mother was forced to take several odd jobs to make ends meet while Richard and his brother temporarily lived in a Memphis orphanage. When Ella Wright fell ill a few years later, she moved the family to Jackson, Mississippi, to live with her parents.

Over the next few years the family moved several more times between relatives in Natchez and Jackson, as well as in Elaine, Arkansas. Wright attended numerous schools during this transitional period but completed the ninth grade in Jackson in June 1925. He had published his first piece of literature the year before and was attending high school before he had to leave Mississippi to find employment in Memphis. Biographers of Wright suggest he was around seventeen years old when he permanently left Jackson, working as a dishwasher and at an optical company in Memphis while studying contemporary American literature during his free time.[24]

Biographers also place Richard Wright in Memphis during the 1927 flood, and he likely heard about it firsthand from relatives and friends residing in Mississippi and Arkansas, significantly shaping his evaluation of the disaster. Dealing with the environmental world was not anathema to Wright's personal sensibilities, living as he did alongside the Mississippi River and its tributaries for much of his early life. His immediate and extended family likely dealt with Mississippi River flooding in the past and understood the environmental perils of farming that included floods, droughts, and the boll weevil. Wright expressed this strong connection between labor and environmentalism in "The Man Who Saw the Flood" in a way that demonstrated personal experience with both the 1927 flood and the complicated history of sharecropping. In both of Wright's flood stories there is very little mawkish sentimentality about southern folkways and life; instead, he pays very close attention to how race hardens attitudes about environmentalism and vice versa.[25]

By December 1927, just months after the flood's peak in the Yazoo Delta, Richard Wright had migrated to Chicago in pursuit of a place more suitable for his increasingly left-wing politics and writing. The Great Migration was in full swing, and along with other kindred souls he migrated out of the South in search of freer spaces and opportunities for economic and professional advancement. By some accounts the Harlem Renaissance was slowly grinding to a halt, but Wright found in Chicago a wealth of writing and political groups made up of ex-southerners, northerners, and Caribbean immigrants that formed the backbone for much of his writings.[26]

Heavily influenced by the potential to critique industrialism and capitalism through nature, Wright's early writings served the dual purposes of autobiographical observations and racial protest. In particular, his imageries of water and fire were far from sublime, but instead a powerful motif representing displacement, movement, protest, and violence—a part of Wright's political consciousness growing up alongside the Mississippi River. He published at least three short stories on environmental flooding, including an early work called "Silt." A 1934 poem called "Everywhere Burning Waters Rise" published in the *Left Front* shows Wright's naturalistic employment of fire, which became a recurring motif in his later writings. He clearly demonstrates the influence of communism in this poem of revolution, while at the same time using metaphors of urban and rural environmentalism. For Wright the roots of revolution are "everywhere, on tall and smoke-less stack pipes, on the empty silos of deserted farms." Revolution can be observed through "tenemented mountains of hunger, in ghetto swamps of suffering, in breadlined forests of despair, on peonized plains of hopelessness." Later in the poem he writes, "Thousands are surrounding food-stores storming, storming, rising red rivers are flowing, till on the lowlands of starvation meeting and swelling to a roaring torrential tide, and becoming strangely transformed into waters of fire and blazing their way to the foaming sea of revolution." Wright also uses the metaphor of fire to describe lynching in *Uncle Tom's Children* and the limits of black citizenship in *Native Son* and *Black Boy*.[27]

Both "The Man Who Saw the Flood" and *Uncle Tom's Children* (which was of course a play on Harriet Beecher Stowe's pre–Civil War *Uncle Tom's Cabin*) represented historical actors and figures in protest, active rather than passive in the face of racism. In an April 1938 review of *Uncle Tom's Children* in the *Saturday Review of Literature,* Zora Neale Hurston wrote, "This is a book about hatreds. Mr. Wright serves notice by his title that he speaks of people in revolt, and his stories are so grim that the Dismal Swamp of race hatred must be where they live."[28] Harlem Renaissance writer Countee Cullen similarly wrote in the *African* that "Uncle Tom's Children . . . are not chips off the old block, and barely recognizable as the offspring of their famous, but hardly admirable forebear. These children are after what belongs to men; they want happiness, better homes, better economic conditions. They still find the getting hard, but (here the blood is different) they are willing to fight. These Negroes are different; there is in them something of what must have been in the first African slaves, something of the fine, healthy anger that saw in death a brighter destiny than slavery."[29] Ralph Ellison suggested that *Uncle Tom's Children* "represents one of the few instances in which an American Negro writer has successfully delineated the universals embodied in Negro experience. . . . They are three-dimensional people, possessing an emotional and psychological complexity never before achieved in American Negro writing . . . overcoming the social and cultural isolation of Negro life and moving into a world of unlimited intellectual and imaginative possibilities."[30]

"The Man Who Saw the Flood" first appeared in a rather short-lived but very prominent communist journal called *New Masses* in 1937. The story is ultimately about one black family's struggle to survive immediately after the 1927 flood, but the explanatory framework Wright provides for understanding this struggle comes through hunger, immobility, and the impossibility of sharecropping. In a certain sense the story is more about the "ethics of Jim Crow" rooted in second-class citizenship and race than about the storm that serves as the backdrop for his criticism.[31] The story begins with the return of a poor black sharecropping family—Tom, his wife, May, and their child, Sally—to their small cabin. "At last the flood waters had receded. A black father, a black mother, and a black child tramped through muddy fields, leading a tired cow by a thin bit of rope. . . . As far as they could see the ground was covered with flood silt."[32] Wright's blues voice comes through here as he describes the environmental landscape. Presumably the family had been displaced to a Red Cross relief camp, though Wright doesn't say this explicitly in the text. But he immediately taps into experiences of displacement and homelessness described by blues singers by putting into words how the meager sharecropping cabin was completely destroyed. Perhaps the family was lucky to still have a house; there was no sign of other houses in the area. There was also no sign of human or farm life and, as Wright describes, "over all hung a first-day strangeness." Wright pushes the text here to highlight the uneasiness of being displaced and the initial interaction with a landscape that is familiar yet distorted.[33] The steps leading up to the cabin are completely gone and high water marks in the house are over seven feet above the ground; their personal belongings scattered on the floor or missing. Wright has a penchant for using death as a symbol for black historical experience in what scholar Abdul R. JanMohamed describes as "death-bound subjectivity."[34] When Tom, May, and Sally entered their sharecropping cabin, "the floors swam in ooze. Like a mute warning, a wavering flood mark went high around the walls of the room. A dresser sat cater-cornered, its drawers and sides bulging like a bloated corpse. The bed, with the mattress still on it, was like a giant casket forged of mud."[35] Imageries of death among even inanimate objects serve the purpose of defining a dangerous social and environmental landscape.

Wright was not alone among writers to employ a racialized meaning of race and nature. Zora Neale Hurston used similar metaphors in *Their Eyes Were Watching God,* originally published in 1937. Born around 1891 in Eatonville, Florida, Hurston infused anthropology, folklore, and personal experiences into her writings, becoming one of the most powerful voices of African American culture during the 1920s and 1930s. In the book's final scene, a powerful hurricane rips through the Florida Everglades, or "muck," where main characters Janie and Tea Cake are experiencing a transformation in their personal relationship.[36] Hurston likely wrote this scene from personal memory after having recently survived one of the most destructive hurricanes to hit South Florida. In 1928 a devastating Category 4 storm known as the Lake Okeechobee Hurricane swept through the Florida Everglades when Hurston was residing in the Everglades Cypress Lumber Company near Loughman, Florida. Along with the 1900 Galveston Hurricane, Great Labor Day Hurricane of 1935 (also hitting South Florida), Hurricane Camille in 1969, and Hurricane Katrina in 2005, the 1928 storm remains one of the most powerful (in terms of wind force) in recorded history.[37]

Hurston was fascinated with the ability of storms to bring about social and environmental transformation while exposing the entrenchment of race. The environmental imagery is striking as the hurricane blurs boundaries between the living and dead, rich and poor. As literary scholar Cheryl Wall writes, "Instantly, the storm overturns the social hierarchy. The dispossessed Indians, not the propertied whites, are wise enough to seek higher ground. At least for the moment, divine power transcends temporal power."[38] Hurston is expressive in her description of wind and water not just as elements of nature but as agents of life and mercenaries of death. "Wind and water had given life to lots of things that folks think of as dead and given death to so much that had been living things," Hurston describes. "Water everywhere. Stray fish swimming in the yard."[39] As if possessed by the hurricane, nonliving objects take on living qualities, endangering the physical environment people traversed. On the other hand, things that had once been among the living, such as humans and animals, are transformed into inanimate objects—lifeless and floating in the water or swaying in the wind.

For Wright, "The Man Who Saw the Flood" can aptly be described as a narrative of hunger and sharecropping, issues that persistently show up in Wright's poetry and literature. Not long after the family returns home, Sally, the daughter, begins to complain of hunger, at which moment the story makes a pivotal turn in a way similar to the hook of a blues verse. This is the issue or problem the family must deal with, the "life crisis of black identity."[40] Until now they spent most of the day trying to locate household items and assess the damage, but now the family faces the reality of an uncertain future, hunger, and ultimately, survival. Would they stay on the land, working tirelessly to pull themselves out of a never-ending cycle of debt, or search for new beginnings elsewhere? They needed help to rebuild, but they could expect no such help from the Red Cross or government.[41] At the very least they hoped the debt already accumulating from the previous year's growing season might be reduced, giving them at least a minimal foothold to rebuild their lives. Wright's language is necessarily pessimistic here, drawing on historical experiences of blacks after the flood.

Richard Wright understood from his childhood years the demands of sharecropping, the necessary labor of an entire family, and the struggle to accumulate wages. Planting season normally lasted from mid-January to late

May, harvest from early August to the end of December.[42] The 1927 flood caused the most damage during March and April. Wright picks up on this by highlighting in his story that the family loses an entire planting season's labor in an instant. May asks Tom whether they will return to a contract with Burgess, the white landowner whom the family worked for before the flood and on whose land they still live. "I hate to start all over with that white man. I'd leave here if I could," Tom says to his wife. They already owe Burgess $800, not to mention losing an entire growing season because of the flood. Starting over with Burgess also meant accumulating more debt for equipment and seed, almost guaranteeing a life sentence of peonage to the land. "If we keep on like this that white man will own us body and soul."[43] The historical truth that Wright engages comes from the fears among white planters of losing black laborers to migration during the period. As Robyn Spencer argues, "Despite the planters' best efforts—or sometimes because of their efforts—Southern black agricultural laborers had always been in constant flight: moving from plantation to plantation, from state to state and, after World War I, in massive numbers from South to North. This growing labor scarcity due to out-migration of black laborers provided a context for increased determination on the part of planters to hold their laborers to the land."[44] Because the 1927 flood occurred during the Great Migration, white planters were already extremely conscious of black movement and put mechanisms into place—including the barring of labor agents from relief camps—to try to prevent the further loss of black laborers.

On cue, Burgess appears from the horizon in a horse-drawn buggy, as if he already knows the disaster might provide an opportunity for them to leave. "Well, I see you're back," Burgess says, as if somehow surprised. He feigns magnanimity in asking Tom how things are looking around the house. It was a question to which Burgess already knew the answer, since the only people who would have tools, seed, or food were probably white, those resources likely provided by the Red Cross to white survivors in need. The only thing Tom and his family owned in the world was that single cow. Tom and May are not fooled by Burgess's complete lack of interest in their plight—he chimes in almost before Tom could finish his sentence that the family still owes $800 at the store. Seeing Burgess's intention to secure the debt, Tom does the only thing he can at this moment, which is to try to negotiate a lesser amount. Burgess reminds Tom that he owes money for food and seed, and he (Burgess) has to pay for it. Wright leaves this conversation open-ended, leaving us to wonder whether Burgess does have to pay the store owner and what type of assistance he might be receiving from the Red Cross. The family would not have known these facts and could never have asked without fear of being killed; Wright writes the ambiguity into the text. What is clear, however, is Burgess's unwillingness to clear the family's debt, taken to the level of threatening Tom with information that he sent the sheriff after two of his other tenants that morning who tried to leave. "I wasn't looking for no trouble out of you Tom. . . . The rest of the families are going back."[45]

Tom knew going back into business with Burgess was a death sentence, a position meaning the family was essentially starting from scratch and with that the realization they would never achieve economic independence. A more aggressive Burgess demands that Tom get into the carriage so they can go to the store for food and supplies, supplies that would add to the debt the family carries. Wright's blues voice shines, as a pensive and thoughtful Tom weighs his options, or lack of options. Leaving might result in his being thrown in jail and separated from his family, something Tom does not want. But staying would result in a different type of jail, economic peonage for his family's future. Thoughtfully weighing his decision and family's future, Tom leans "back against the post and [looks] at the mud-filled fields." When Burgess asks one final time whether he is coming, Tom slowly climbs into the carriage with the finality of a person staring death in the face. In a sense, Wright suggests that the burden Tom shoulders at this exact moment is death, or a sort of social death where one exists but doesn't live.[46] As Burgess and Tom ride off, Sally begs her mother for molasses. May calls out to her husband to bring it back for their beloved daughter, after which she lets out a sigh, knowing that Sally is too young to comprehend the totality of what this all means, but also knowing that one day she will.[47]

A year after publishing "The Man Who Saw the Flood," Wright again broaches the racial tension of the 1927 flood in his collection of short stories called *Uncle Tom's Children.* After an introductory section, "The Ethics of Jim Crow," the five stories include "Big Boy Leaves Home," "Down by the Riverside," "Long Black Song," "Fire and Cloud," and "Bright and Morning

Star." Each story deals with some aspect of the Jim Crow South and, much as in "The Man Who Saw the Flood," the characters exert their consciousness and humanity in some form of protest or rebellion. "Down by the Riverside" is similarly situated; the characters are active rather than passive in the face of an impossible racial dilemma.[48]

"Down by the Riverside" opens with the main character, Mann, his wife, Lula, elderly mother-in-law, and young son, Peewie, trapped in their house by the flood. Wright wastes little time putting forth the "life crisis of black identity" as Lula goes into labor with no medical attention or transportation to a hospital available. Mann misses an earlier opportunity to move the family before floodwaters arrive and is now relying on his brother Bob to return with some form of transportation. "Down by the Riverside" is a story very much entangled with the complicated history of levees and the 1927 flood, as the family's safety depends on whether the local levee will hold.[49] Most of the houses in the area are already gone at the story's opening, washed away by the flood. But what also makes for a vulnerable environmental landscape in the story are the rumors circulating that black men are being forced at gunpoint into working on the levee. The family occasionally hears gunshots in the distance, causing them to wonder aloud if another black person has been killed for transgressing the racial order in some way.

In *Their Eyes Were Watching God,* Hurston also describes forced labor, positing that even in the midst of a hurricane the racial tension between blacks and whites remained largely unchanged on the "muck." In the storm's aftermath, Tea Cake and other local black men are forced under the watch of armed white men to dig graves for the dead bodies left by the storm. As a matter of racial custom and normalcy, the graves dug by the black men are separated by race. Black bodies are not to be buried with white bodies, and as many whites as possible are provided the dignity of individual wooden boxes, while all black bodies are thrown in mass graves.[50]

Hurston's emphasis on nature, like that of Wright's, defines the ways in which disasters help define the meaning of blackness and citizenship. In "Down by the Riverside," it is no easy task for Bob to secure a boat, but he finally returns with one to evacuate his pregnant sister-in-law and family. The problem emerges because Bob, unable to find an available boat anywhere, steals the boat from a notoriously racist and hostile white postman by the name of Heartfield. He sees the boat tied beside the house and, knowing Lula would die if he didn't find transportation soon, takes the risk that might doom his entire family. Mann is in complete disbelief at his brother's action, knowing full well the implications it could bring.[51] Now Mann, like Tom in "The Man Who Saw the Flood," is faced with a veritable landmine as Wright's blues voice propels the narrative forward while pressing readers to think about the vulnerability of blackness. The result is a scenario in which the family commits an assertive act to save Lula, but now must face the repercussions. Mann must make an impossible choice between his wife's certain death or that of the entire family. He could hide the boat and disavow any knowledge of his brother's act, but then would have no way to get his wife to a hospital. Or he could row the stolen boat into town and seek medical care for his wife knowing that they would both immediately be killed if authorities discover whom the boat belongs to. One way or another, the decision must be made; Lula has been in labor for four days. Finally, Mann makes the decision to row his wife to the Red Cross hospital, accompanied by their son, Peewie, and Lula's mother.[52]

The story's pace quickens as a fatigued Mann single-handedly rows the small boat against floodwaters. After rowing a few miles he sees a light shining through a window frame and takes a calculated risk to approach the house, not knowing if the inhabitants might turn violent. Maybe they would be decent enough to telephone for help and allow them a place to rest. The house is occupied by none other than Heartfield, whose family is trapped because their boat was stolen. When Heartfield recognizes the approaching boat as his own, he wastes no time firing shots at Mann and his family. To Heartfield's surprise, Mann pulls out a gun of his own and returns gunfire. Here Wright draws on a long-standing tradition of black armed self-reliance and defense in southern communities.[53] Mann kills Heartfield by shooting him in the chest in front of his family, and so must now deal with the flood, his pregnant wife, who is about to give birth, and killing the white man whose stolen boat they are riding in. By the time they reach the Red Cross hospital, which is crawling with soldiers, Lula is dead and the boat is immediately commandeered by military officials. Despondent at the loss of his wife, Mann barely hears officials tell him that his mother-in-law and young son are being sent to a local Red Cross camp and he was being sent to the levee for work. Mann is exhausted after expending a massive amount of energy rowing against the current to the hospital, but this doesn't matter to authorities at the hospital. His blackness overrides any protests he could voice about being too tired to work or the need to grieve over his wife's death. His labor is needed now, and he would go to the levee with other black men. But there is still the matter of the stolen boat and the white man he recently killed. If anyone finds out, southern racial culture demands that he be killed immediately, no judge or jury necessary. In the South, even the rumor of killing a white person or raping a white woman is enough for a black person to be killed. For the moment at least, he is given boots, a raincoat, and transportation to the levee for upward of fifteen hours hard labor.[54] Approaching the levee, Mann describes what he sees: "[There were] black lines of men weaving snake-fashion about the levee top. . . . They were carrying heavy bags on their shoulders and when they reached a certain point the bags were dumped down. Then they turned around, slowly, with bent backs, going to get more bags."[55] Wright describes the men on the levee as shadowy ghostlike figures, as if only half alive. Before the boat docks, everyone's worst fear materializes: the levee breaks and the mostly African American workers are drowned and turned into a "whirling black mass" of death and destruction.[56] For Richard Wright, similar to Du Bois, art imitated life when it came to the flood. Although the forced labor of African American men after the flood is well documented, few images in the photographic archive actually show them performing this work. Figure 4 is a rare exception, where the forced labor Wright described is given voice through the flood's visual narrative.

Wright clearly builds this part of the story around the Mounds Landing levee crevasse. It was, in fact, well documented that black men were actually working on the levee when it failed.[57] In a last-ditch effort to prevent the crevasse, black men were put to work (under the threat of violence) filling, lifting, and hauling sandbags to the levee. This was backbreaking work, as one worker held the bag open while another quickly loaded dirt into the bag using a shovel or his bare hands. Because the dampened earth was so heavy, each bag could weigh close to one hundred pounds.[58]

After the re-created Mounds Landing crevasse in Wright's story, Mann and another younger black man, Brinkley, return with soldiers to the Red

FIGURE 4. Black men performing the backbreaking work of filling and loading sandbags. Photograph by the United States Coast Guard, May 22, 1927 (place unknown). Courtesy of the National Archives and Records Administration.

Cross hospital. The two men are commanded to take a boat and rescue a stranded woman and her children who have telephoned from a house, asking the Red Cross for help. A colonel hands Mann a piece of paper with the name and address of the woman, and to his disbelief it is Heartfield's wife. They are given instructions to save the Heartfields only if they can, if not head for the hills where a Red Cross camp has been set up.[59] For the second time Mann has a way to save himself from certain death. He can easily enough persuade the younger Brinkley to call off the search en route, knowing if the Heartfield widow doesn't survive he might escape detection for the murder he committed. Wright's naturalistic writing of an active environment is very similar to Hurston's, where nonliving objects take on dangerous and humanlike elements of movement. While fighting a strong current that threatens to overturn the boat, the two men encounter a fully intact house floating down the middle of the street. Brinkley quickly turns the boat in the opposite direction as the menacing house follows close behind, as if possessed by nature. Mann holds the boat steady by clinging onto a cable wire as the house whisks by, and as they catch a full glimpse of the structure for the first time Wright describes it as a "living thing, spinning slowly with a long, indrawn, sucking noise; its doors, its windows, its porch turning to the light and then going into the darkness." Wright provides an active environmental world in which furniture, houses, and uprooted trees are all possessed by nature.[60]

Arriving at the Heartfield house, Mann pushes away thoughts of telling Brinkley the entire story so he might aid in his getaway. He also thinks of killing the widowed Heartfield and her two small children to save himself. In the end he does neither, though he is fully aware that by saving them he is sealing his own fate. He knows that both Heartfield and her son recognize him. As they disembark in the Red Cross camp, with survivors in tow, Mann has a feeling that his total body is "encased in a tight vise, in a narrow black coffin that moved with him as he moved."[61] The connection of black skin with a coffin is a powerful metaphorical and literary representation of race. Mann has several chances to save himself but consciously chooses none of them, a point of "profound passivity of the subject in the face of his own potential actual-death," literary scholar Abdul R. JanMohamed argues.[62]

The point Wright is making is about the limited options of black people during the 1927 flood. Sure enough, not long after they dock at the Red Cross camp Mann is struck over the head and taken into custody by military officials, the widowed Heartfield having accused him of stealing their boat and killing the elder Heartfield. A lynch mob of white men is formed in a matter of seconds to issue swift justice, but military officials step in to save him from certain death, if only temporarily. Mann is taken to a commander, who takes Heartfield's widow's testimony; his point of view is never considered. The commander's decision is quick and deliberate: death. Four soldiers are marching Mann to the edge of the river for an unceremonious execution. "God . . . Stop them from killin black folks!" Mann says out loud, resembling the pleas of blues singers about murder and violence. Suddenly he bolts from the grasps of soldiers toward the Mississippi River, which had provided freedom to escaping slaves, some eluding detection along its banks and others using positions as stevedores, cooks, chambermaids, and coal haulers on steamboats to aid their escape.[63] "They were going to kill him. Yes, now, he would die! He would die before he would let them kill him. 'Ahll die for they kill me! Ahll die.'"[64] Mann knew he was going to die, but he would do so on his own terms, even if that meant being killed while fleeing. It was death by resistance. He would not die being passively marched toward execution. The irony was that he never saved himself when he could have, but now he would choose the more assertive course of death in protest of the decision that others had made about his life.[65]

Richard Wright's two flood stories constitute the first published creative intellectual engagement with the historical experiences of African Americans during the 1927 flood, rooted in the sociology of black newspapers and his own intense familiarity with race and racism. Wright was not alone, however, among Mississippi-born literary writers in his fascination with the 1927 flood. Along with Tennessee Williams and Mark Twain, William Faulkner is considered among the great writers of the southern literary tradition. Born in New Albany, Mississippi, Faulkner published most of his plays, short stories, and poems in the 1920s and 1930s; his most well known works include *Absalom, Absalom!* and *The Sound and the Fury.* Faulkner's short story on the 1927 flood, "The Old Man," is part of his collection of two short stories called *Wild Palms;* the "Old Man" is a nickname of the Mississippi River as a place of ancient roots, power, and seemingly supernatural force.[66]

The story revolves mostly around the personal odyssey of a nameless convict (every figure in the story is nameless), identified only as being tall and skinny, who is sent to rescue a stranded woman with another convict, described as short and plump. After the two men are separated by the flood's force, Faulkner's tale primarily focuses on the interactions between the tall convict and nature, as well as with the woman (and unborn child) he is sent to rescue. Well before this moment, however, we can see differences between Wright's and Faulkner's views of race and nature, representing each writer's theoretical underpinnings of the flood. Race is the compelling force in Wright's exploration of the 1927 flood, whether sharecropping in "The Man Who Saw the Flood" or forced labor in "Down by the Riverside." Faulkner's narrative is more esoteric regarding the question of race. When encountered by Faulkner's main characters during the flood, African Americans and Cajuns are described as foreign, simplistic, and inferior, written in a manner representative of southern racialism during the time period. Faulkner follows Wright in his description of forced labor (white convicts sent to work on the levee) and his analysis of the Mounds Landing crevasse as a cultural image of nature's wrath and the failure of levees to protect people. Before reaching the levee for labor, convicts in Faulkner's story are intrigued by "accounts of the conscripted levee gangs, mixed blacks and whites working in double shifts against the steadily rising water; stories of men, even though they were negroes, being forced like themselves to do work for which they received no other pay than coarse food and a place in a mudfloored tent to sleep on . . . the mudsplashed white men with the inevitable shotguns, the antlike lines of negroes carrying sandbags, slipping and crawling up the steep face of the revetment to hurl their futile ammunition into the face of a flood and return for more."[67]

The notion of nonprisoners forced to work on the levee is supposed to be jarring for the convicts, but the feeling is mitigated by the idea that many of those being forced to work are African Americans. The idea of black workers being antlike posits a feeling of black subordination vis-à-vis white people and nature. Later, as the shackled convicts wait for a train to take them to the levee, they see an "inextricable jumble of beds and trunks, gas and electric stoves, radios and tables and chairs and framed pictures which a chain of negroes under the eye of an unshaven white man in muddy corduroy and hip boots carried piece by piece into the compress, at the door of which another guardsman stood with his rifle, they (the convicts) not stopping here but herded on by the two guards with their shotguns."[68] Implicitly, the white convicts believe that while they labor against their free volition under a penal system, their labor is still more valuable than black labor, and ultimately the forced labor of free black men is no less justified. "The Old Man" is a narrative of one man's personal journey brought to bear against an environmental disaster, and broader questions of race are not Faulkner's focus here. Mirroring other historical texts that limit the presence of black voices, Faulkner's analysis provides little of the contextualization of black intellectual thought regarding nature that we see in the work of Richard Wright and Zora Neale Hurston.

Hurston and Wright portray the historical antecedents of environmental (in)justice, particularly the powerful ways in which African Americans have suffered disproportionately from environmental policies and ideas we largely associate with movements from the post–Civil Rights era. The 1927 flood may not be an environmental (in)justice issue in a traditional sense, but I argue that the fundamental exploitation that serves as the root of these ideas later in the century, from housing and immobility to workplace environment, make up the intellectual framing of Zora Neale Hurston and Richard Wright's literary critique.

Historian Sylvia Hood Washington describes black people historically forced into unsustainable and dangerous living spaces as environmental "others," those spaces disciplined through environmental policies and popular opinion throughout the twentieth century. The relief stage of the flood, when white planters and National Guardsmen restricted black people's movement or forced them to live in certain spaces and not others, constitutes a historical form of environmental discipline. Certain "safe spaces" were off-limits for African Americans during the flood, including Red Cross relief camps defined as whites only, public buildings they might have shared with whites, and in most cases their own homes. White planters controlling the resources of charity defined virtually every physical space outside the surveillance of whites as undesirable for black survivors. As Washington writes, "These groups identified as 'others' were, and still are, forced to live in geographical spaces (communities) within the society that are or are becoming environmentally compromised because of their 'otherness' . . . they are the proper place for everything deemed to be undesirable (people and waste)."[69] Using the 1927 flood as a window into this "othering," Richard Wright makes the argument that blackness limited the work options, economic stability, mobility, and general quality of life for black families, themes later defined as the backbone of the environmental movement.

Situated with other written and nonwritten texts, Richard Wright's and Zora Neale Hurston's critiques of environmental disasters dispel the historical myth of black environmental illiteracy, of black bodies acted on by nature but rarely providing intellectual engagements with nature. Richard Wright's two flood stories hinge on his ability to narrate in written form the metaphorical meaning of the blues singer, providing a blueslike moment of black survival in a world where everything, including a seemingly random nature, is stacked against you. His stories represent a collective "us" similar to that of the blues singer, and the words he chooses help define the meaning of citizenship, race, and nature during the 1927 flood.

Richard Wright's political engagement with sensitive issues of race and nature mirrored not only the reality of black experiences during the flood but also messages received by black people outside the flooded region. Well before Wright's flood stories appeared in print, African Americans throughout the country were coming to many of the same conclusions about the flood as Wright. As the nation responded to this disaster with the greatest outpouring of public charity ever witnessed, African Americans struggled with the internal tension of giving money to the Red Cross, hearing that it was turning a blind eye to the forced labor and environmental discipline imposed on black bodies. At the same time, the federal government and Red Cross were incentivizing a recently war-conscious public of its patriotic duty to give, which reflected the influence of the military on the act of giving.

3 Racialized Charity and the Militarization of Flood Relief in Postwar America

In early June 1927, Neval H. Thomas, president of the Washington, D.C., chapter of the NAACP, addressed a large crowd of black Washingtonians at a local theater. He spoke at length about the 1927 flood and the responsibility of black Washingtonians to help members of the race during this disaster. Thomas also stressed the need to find a suitable method of sending charity down south that did not directly involve the American Red Cross. While the growing middle class of black Washingtonians had the potential to make a significant contribution to flood relief, Thomas remained adamant about the American Red Cross's failure to treat black flood survivors as American citizens. Thomas addressed the audience with conviction: "This great organization [the NAACP] is ever on the ramparts in defense of your civil and political rights without which we are slaves, yet it stands for aid and succor to the victims of such an unparalleled affliction, not only at the hands of nature but by those who claim a mission of mercy."[1] Thomas's words highlighted not only the exigencies of nature but also the culpability of humans during the relief process. Washingtonians should not fall into the trap of Red Cross solicitation in newspapers; to do so would victimize them along with black flood survivors in the Yazoo Delta. Instead, he told the crowd, "I am seeking out responsible Negro agencies in that state [Mississippi] to which I shall send every dollar you contribute, which will assure you that it will reach the peon for whom you give it."[2] Thomas's words hit an important mark of race and charity in the 1920s, particularly the ways in which black Americans located outside the flooded region expressed reservations about the American Red Cross, pressing into service their own forms of benevolence.

It is impossible to estimate how much of the money donated to the Red Cross came from black Americans; just as difficult would be defining the extent to which they circumvented the Red Cross as a rebuke. Both amount to finding needles in haystacks. The use of charity as a form of social control and exploitation of survivors after an environmental disaster is well documented.[3] Fears of exploitation among those providing charity, in contrast, remains largely unexplored. The 1927 flood offers hints of an obscure history of race and charity ripe for future investigation.

The Great Migration was not a "one-way ticket." Between 1915 and 1970, close to 3.5 million African Americans migrated from the rural South to urbanized spaces. Southern landscapes were not simply places of birth, but also landscapes where ancestors rested and family members continued to live. In the years and decades after migrants left for the "Promised Land," many would return to visit family; attend weddings; bury parents, grandparents, and siblings; and bring sometimes reluctant children reared in the North back to the place of their ancestral roots. It was a ritual practiced by countless black families. As much as parents would not tolerate living in constant fear of violence, death, and the shadow of sharecropping, and wanted to provide their children with better opportunities, they could not allow future generations to be unaware of previous sacrifices.[4] Former migrants and native-born northerners were connected in other ways to southern landscapes. Those intimately familiar with the South had not forgotten the lynched and mutilated bodies of family and friends hanging from trees and dragged through town as a reminder for black people to stay in their place. Black women had not forgotten being raped by white men when working as cooks and domestics in white households.[5] Black families, working as sharecroppers from sunup to sundown, had not forgotten how strong and sullen that mule could be or the sting of being cheated by unscrupulous landowners after a hard year's labor. The reality of having to constantly say "yes sir" and "yes ma'am" to adult whites and children without reciprocity never left them. Southern migrants could not forget the subtle slights of having to step off sidewalks for white people twenty or thirty years younger and the way it made their stomachs churn to have to do so.[6]

Migrants remembered the South with a conflicted identity, making it unsurprising that newly arrived northerners paid close attention to the 1927 flood, many knowing full well the dangers that surrounded blacks in the Yazoo Delta. Ida B. Wells knew as much as anyone about the southern horrors of racial violence. Born in Holly Springs, Mississippi, in 1862, her experiences in the South, like that of Richard Wright, directly informed her commitment to social justice, equality, and an unflinching crusade to end lynching. Following her parents' death from yellow fever in 1878 and a stint teaching at a rural Mississippi school, she helped lay the path millions of others would later follow to Memphis and Chicago during the Great Migration. By the 1890s she was editor of the *Free Speech* and *Headlight* newspapers in Memphis, where she began her antilynching crusade (it was in Memphis that a personal friend was killed by whites for operating a successful grocery store). After migrating to Chicago and becoming a leader in the black clubwoman movement, it should not be surprising that Wells understood what black flood survivors were up against during the 1927 flood.[7] In fact, Barnett protested Red Cross relief conditions through the Ida B. Wells Club in Chicago and, along with W. E. B. Du Bois, published detailed and lengthy criticisms of the federal government and Red Cross in the *Chicago Defender.*[8]

By late March 1927 a racial narrative was forming that would help shape the discourse in the following months. Chicagoans and Washingtonians learned about the flood through black newspapers and developed their own ideas about the disaster's racial meaning. Such messages perhaps not only influenced their decision to give money but also how they might do so. Black newspapers with wide circulation like the *Chicago Defender, Washington Bee,* and *Pittsburgh Courier,* along with smaller weeklies such as the *St. Bernard Voice* (L.A.) and *Louisiana Weekly,* covered the flood in excruciating detail. By constantly highlighting stories of mistreatment and brutality that most white newspapers ignored, articles penned by Wells and Du Bois, together with those of the editors, served two important functions. First, they provided an important counternarrative to the one posited by Herbert Hoover and the Red Cross: that black flood survivors were actually faring better after the flood than before. Second, they highlighted the Red Cross's role in conceding, if only by its deafening silence, mistreatment of blacks in relief camps.

An editorial in the *Norfolk Journal and Guide* highlighted this counternarrative, explicitly pointing out that white newspapers like the *Virginian-Pilot* and *Richmond Times-Dispatch* avoided talking about accusations of racial mistreatment. The "terrible death-dealing and devastating floods raging throughout the territory severed by the mighty Mississippi river and a dozen of its more important tributaries have exacted a tremendous toll from members of the race," the editorial began.[9] It appealed to readers for donations, yet strongly pleaded that constituents avoid donating to the American Red Cross. Instead, they suggested donating to the NAACP, fraternal organizations, fraternities and sororities, and churches, so they could be sure the money would reach poor blacks in need.[10] An editorial in the *Baltimore Afro-American* made a similar point, while also addressing the culture of calamity. The first half of the editorial condemns the sermon of a black preacher in Chicago who told his congregation that the 1927 Mississippi River Flood was a divine *Act of God* sent to punish white southerners for their evil mistreatment of black people, pointing out the consensus that blacks were suffering just as much, if not more, than whites.[11] Such framing of environmental disasters was not uncommon; even today people often look for divine meaning as a way of making sense of nature. As historian Ted Steinberg reminds us, "Floods, earthquakes, and storms as signs of God's displeasure is arguably one of the oldest ways of interpreting these events."[12] The editorial was telling for another reason, however, particularly the ways in which it makes a specific critique of race and nature. "Not only nature but the Red Cross and the Martial Law will be his enemies, and 'forced labor' will mean black labor. Blacks will be put to work helping to clear the white man's property, without wages or reward. Being poor and homeless, they will be yoked with new debts in order to get a start. . . . They will all find themselves more completely enslaved than before the flood. 'Relief' will be given to them . . . after all the whites have been taken care of."[13] We can take from this rhetoric an effort to raise money for flood relief in urban northern spaces.

By early summer, the Washington, D.C., chapter of the NAACP was holding benefit concerts attended by hundreds at the famous Howard and Lincoln Theaters.[14] Known as the "People's Theater," the Howard was a prime destination and launching pad for the careers of many black musicians and entertainers, including Duke Ellington, Louis Armstrong, Cab Calloway, Nat King Cole, and the Supremes. The Lincoln Theater was also located in the heart of black Washington and, along with the Howard, was well known as part of the "chitlin-circuit" of venues in New York City, Washington, D.C., Detroit, and Los Angeles, where black entertainers performed. Blacks in Boston also stepped forward with $1,000 raised at a midnight benefit concert at the National Theater, organized by the Boston Colored Citizens Committee. Performers such as Lew Payton's Smoky City Four, Frank Pitts' Revue (from the Palm Garden Night Club), and the Rountree Sisters, though far from enjoying national notoriety, appeared at the benefit concert in late May.[15] As historian Walter Trattner argues, the organizing of public benefit programs for welfare and relief has been around since the Civil War.[16] The 1927 flood suggests one of the first documented moments where such activities were performed by black citizens.

After raising donations from these concerts, the money still had to find its way into the hands of black flood survivors. The historical record is largely silent on this aspect of race and charity. One particular example might illustrate such a narrative. Owing to the social commitment of black churches throughout the country on a host of issues of importance, it would not be remarkable if many churches raised money during the flood relief period. Two members of a Baltimore-area church recounted their firsthand experience of taking money to Mississippi for *Baltimore Afro-American* readers. Telling a story that, by the summer of 1927, had become almost common knowledge, the men described conditions of peonage, poor health, and destitution inside and near Red Cross camps. "All of these camps are closely guarded by the militia," they informed readers. "It was necessary for us to get a pass in order to go in and get another pass in order to come out. The Red Cross explanation of this is that close guarding is necessary in order that they might keep up with those to whom relief is furnished so that there will not be overlapping and duplication."[17] Confidentially, the survivors told them how they were being kept in bondage by the perpetual threat of violence.

Responses also came from within the South as well. The Mosaic Templars and Royal Circle of Friends were benefit and aid societies created to address the many social, economic, and health needs of black southerners.

Founded in 1883 as the Mosaic Templars of Little Rock, Arkansas, by two former slaves, John Edward Bush and Chester W. Keatts, they founded the society to provide burial premiums for blacks excluded from white insurance companies. By 1927 the Templars had lodges in twenty-seven states and six overseas countries. Before it was severely weakened by the Great Depression, the Templars boasted an insurance company, a nurse training school, a loan company, and a training hospital for its members. Dr. Richard A. Williams, a Meharry-trained black physician, founded the Royal Circle of Friends twenty-six years later in Helena, Arkansas. By the 1920s the fraternity had lodges (called Circles) in several southern states as well as in Illinois and Ohio. The Royal Circle of Friends also owned and operated two hospitals and a nursing training school. Had the benefit society not moved its headquarters to Chicago in 1918, it would have suffered direct losses from the 1927 flood. Both societies raised flood-relief donations from members for flood survivors.[18]

Hearing of confirmed and unconfirmed reports of brutality during the relief period represented an opportunity for middle-class blacks to continue the reform and "uplift" the tradition of the 1910s and 1920s through organizations like the National League for the Protection of Colored Women, the National Association of Colored Women, benefit societies, and black fraternities and sororities.[19]

From the beginning of the relief stage, Wells and Du Bois were frustrated at the Red Cross's deference to the southern power structure. For black Americans in other cities to constantly hear of brutality in Red Cross relief camps on a daily basis had to make them hesitant to give money to the very institution that, for lack of action, was acquiescent to the peonage of black flood sufferers. By the 1927 flood, the Red Cross had become the single most important disaster relief organization in the country. The 1927 flood occurred decades before ordinary citizens had direct access to federal resources after an environmental disaster; the Red Cross's "mission of mercy" was the only assistance most Americans could hope for.[20] Taking the direction of its leader during the relief stage, Herbert Hoover, the American Red Cross remained reluctant to defy local customs and racial norms. Rather than put mechanisms into place that ensured the equitable treatment of black survivors, the Red Cross policy was to concede matters of race and custom to white planters and politicians in the Yazoo Delta region. On the one hand, the Red Cross lived up to its "mission of mercy" by providing food, shelter, and other resources to thousands of displaced flood victims; but, on the other hand, they were unwilling to insert themselves into vitriolic questions of race. The zeitgeist framed the ways in which they approached the color line in the Yazoo Delta. Similar to white settlement and reform workers in Progressive Era Philadelphia earlier in the century, the American Red Cross's actions were both humanitarian and discriminatory, noble and racist.[21]

The 1927 flood is part of a much longer narrative of how race, class, gender, and questions of social worth are framed through an environmental disaster. Half a century earlier, the politics of relief defined the aftermath of the Great Chicago Fire of 1871.[22] Although the origin of the fire is debatable, when the smoke finally dissipated the destruction was clear. The fire killed close to three hundred Chicagoans, and one hundred thousand residents were left homeless. The entire downtown section of Chicago was leveled and close to eighteen thousand buildings around the city burned to the ground.[23] Over $5 million poured into Chicago from across the world, and the local Chicago Relief and Aid Society took charge of donations. Prior to the American Red Cross's emergence as the national "disaster organization" in 1905, agencies like the Chicago Relief and Aid Society managed donations and allocated resources to victims after disasters. Deeply imbued with nineteenth-century ideas of social welfare, most of these small relief organizations were primarily made up of local businessmen and politicians who made decisions about worthy or unworthy sufferers. As Charles Rosenberg reminds us, the evolution of hospitals from their almshouse predecessors during the antebellum period served in part to differentiate between the deserving and undeserving sick, "those dependent because of illness rather than moral degeneracy."[24] In the aftermath of the Chicago fire, businessmen and local civic leaders defined those deserving and those undeserving of charity.[25] "Relief and Aid directors, like many nineteenth-century arbiters of charity," historian Karen Sawislak points out, "were deeply conscious of what they viewed as the potential dark side of the work of relief: that to aid 'anyone who could help themselves,' in the words of the Society director Ezra McCagg, was 'in the highest degree harmful to the person aided and to society at large.'"[26] For the Chicago Relief and Aid Society, the urban world it inhabited dictated the necessity of an independent spirit. Indiscriminate charity in the aftermath of the fire would produce a community of dependent sufferers. Charity had the potential to prevent the poor from working and might produce a population of "indigent" survivors. Benevolence was defined as stultifying and a contributing factor of poverty, crime, and urban disorder.[27]

In the interval between the 1871 Chicago Fire and the 1927 flood, the racial dimensions of charity continued to take shape. The island of Galveston, situated on the Gulf of Mexico's edge, had more than thirty-eight thousand residents when it was struck by a major hurricane in 1900. In popular culture and imagination, the 1900 Galveston Hurricane is still remembered as one of the greatest disasters in American history.[28] Winds in excess of 120 miles per hour and massive storm surges completely covered the island city with fifteen feet of water. The storm killed close to six thousand people, made more than ten thousand residents homeless, and left $30 million worth of property damage.[29] Racial animosity was infused into the recovery period as both black men and women were pressed into work under the threat of violence from whites, predating similar actions during the 1927 flood and the 1928 Lake Okeechobee hurricane. Local newspapers falsely depicted black men as looters and black women as representing an extraordinary burden on the relief dole. Black Galvestonians were expected to work on demand for any white person; those who refused were charged with "idleness" and forced into an imprisonment camp.[30] Relief supplies pouring into the city through the Red Cross and Central Relief Committee of Galveston became a window into racial difference after the storm in ways similar to the 1927 flood. In her work on religion and Progressive Era politics in Galveston between 1880 and 1920, Elizabeth Hayes Turner frames this important narrative of race and charity through the distribution of clothing sent to Galveston from around the world. "In orderly and controlled fashion the workers distributed the goods first to whites in the morning and whatever was left over to blacks in the afternoon. African Americans were reminded of what they had already been socialized into understanding . . . white people in this segregated society would always be served first. And if black women should happen to arrive ahead of whites in seeking supplies, they might be threatened with imprisonment for violating the racial order."[31]

The Galveston storm and the 1927 flood are important benchmarks for another reason. Deeply held sentiments linking the Red Cross to militarism, while common by 1927, had not yet taken shape during the Galveston hurricane. The federal government and the American Red Cross interpreted the 1927 flood as the greatest disaster of its kind. In a postwar environment, the Red Cross actively espoused military metaphors of war to portray fighting the 1927 flood as a patriotic act. Through newspapers and radio, American citizens were bombarded with images of a battle between humans and the Mississippi River that leaned on the recent transition to peace after World War I to "awaken" American citizens to their duty; the militarization of American society and charity represented a significant shift during this thirty-year period. Indeed, this shift also reflected important questions of charity and gender. Clara Barton's American Red Cross, founded in 1881, emerged out of the female-led benevolent societies and charities common during the nineteenth century.[32] Benevolence at the turn of the twentieth century, including the American Red Cross, was still considered the domain of middle-class white women. During the Galveston storm, white women used the disaster as an opportunity to prove their leadership ability and political acumen. As Turner makes clear, "The arrival of the American national Red Cross proved to city leaders that privileged white women were capable of leadership in a crisis. This association had been a catalyst for privileged Galveston women who had wanted to help in the recovery. No means had existed for their entrée into the relief system until a national agency, accustomed to putting able-bodied women into positions of leadership, had shown Galvestonians how to do it and, in addition, had provided the good name of the American National Red Cross as 'protection' for women serving in the ward relief stations."[33] By the 1920s, however, the American Red Cross increasingly began to mirror a male-dominated military that was not as open to white women; this was due in part to Clara Barton's death in 1912. But this shift is more complicated than the death of one person, even the person who founded the American Red Cross. An internal reorganization in 1905 connected the organization more firmly to the military, setting the stage for an increasing militarization of charity after World War I. Just as important was the professionalization of social work during the Progressive Era at a time when men began to enter the field in unprecedented numbers. Once the field of social work gained more stature, the Red Cross also gained more respectability in the eyes of men. Slowly men began to take over the Red Cross to such an extent that by 1927 women had largely been relegated to secretarial and nursing duties while locked out of leadership positions.[34]

Mobilizations of Nature, Mobilizations of War

The American Red Cross emerged from the International Committee of the Red Cross, which was established by the Geneva Treaty of 1864, the vision of Swiss businessman Henri Dunant and his commitment of developing individual societies among countries for the medical care and relief of wounded soldiers. During military engagements between countries, Dunant proposed that field hospitals, relief workers, medical equipment, and army medical personnel be declared neutral and that a red cross on a background of white be recognized as the emblem of relief work on battlefields.[35] However, militarization of European and Asian countries was slowly moving Red Cross societies to become more nationalistic and less neutral. Connections between Red Cross operations and military engagement became much stronger during the late nineteenth century.[36] The closer relationship between Red Cross societies and the military had significant reciprocal influences, including changes in dress patterns and operation. In Germany, Austria-Hungary, Britain, and Japan, volunteers began to dress in military-like uniforms. For example, the dress of British Red Cross personnel between the Franco-Prussian War (1870–71) and World War I changed dramatically from only a small patch on coat sleeves to boots, gloves, long button-down coats, and forage hats. Without the Red Cross insignia on the jacket, British Red Cross personnel might easily have been mistaken for soldiers, especially since they also participated in drills and field exercises, developed military formations, stood at attention, and addressed each other in military patterns of speech reflecting chains of command.[37]

Clara Barton established the first American Red Cross chapter in 1881, the purpose of which was to connect Americans during war, famine, fire, and floods, and to provide lines of communication between the public and growing federal bureaucracy. Although the American Red Cross was much slower to connect with the military, an internal reorganization in 1905 concretized its status as an auxiliary to military forces.[38] The American Red Cross also became more closely aligned with disaster relief after 1905 and dealt more with the aftermath of environmental disasters than any other society with the exception of Japan. The new charter effectively made the American Red Cross the most important disaster organization in the country by providing it with the backing of military institutions, resources, and metaphors. The Red Cross was "to act in matters of voluntary relief and in accord with the military and naval authorities as a medium of communication between the people of the United States of America and their Army and Navy."[39] When the Great San Francisco Earthquake of 1906 shook collective imaginations of how deadly the environmental world could be, the American Red Cross had already largely usurped smaller relief agencies like the Chicago Relief and Aid Society. Between 1906 and World War I, the American Red Cross assisted in more than fifty disasters and allocated approximately $6 million in disaster relief funds. Internal Red Cross funds were primarily the result of private contributions, while reorganization also provided the president of the United States power to appoint leadership.[40]

Branches of the military had surely mobilized in the past for environmental disasters, but the public had never been bombarded with such prolific images of patriotism in response to a disaster as occurred following the 1927 flood. The transition from war to peace in American society has intriguing connections with nature. In the American imagination we often like to situate historical time periods as having clear breaks. This is certainly true in how we define both military and nonmilitary engagements and the mobilization of resources and institutions during the borderland between war and peace. In our collective imagination the nation is either at war or we are at peace, but it can't be both.[41] Such framing of war and peace rarely allows for the ways in which militarism during a conflict might spill over into moments of peace. After the armistice soldiers often took a philosophical consciousness of military training into civilian life and society. Returning black soldiers made a commitment to democracy and social justice born out of a struggle for equality in segregated military ranks. Black soldiers fought fiercely for equality as soldiers and might just as easily be killed as white soldiers during the war, but upon return to American soil they could not buy a hamburger at a lunch counter in Alabama.[42] This was a particularly bitter pill for black servicemen after showing citizenship and valor during the war and enduring sacrifices other Americans were not asked to make. It was as bitter during and after World War I as it was during and after World War II, when black newspapers helped enunciate the Double "V" Campaign of victory abroad against fascism and victory at home against racism. During both world wars African American soldiers and civilians were asked to showcase their citizenship by making sacrifices while being racially mistreated in both military and civilian life. Historian Chad Williams reminds us how black soldiers became "torchbearers of democracy," serving at the vanguard of social protest movements during the twentieth century.[43]

Civilian society has a long history of using military metaphors in the portrayal of nonmilitary engagements. The eradication of certain diseases is a useful example. By the 1870s public health officials had already begun employing military metaphors in the description of health.[44] New public health language targeting the *Aedes aegypti* mosquito frequently used military metaphors in building a case for anti–yellow fever campaigns. Feeling most at home in humid and tropical landscapes like the American South, the *Aedes aegypti* transmitted via body-to-body contact the deadly and painful yellow fever that crippled bodies and cities in the nineteenth century.[45] Sometimes referred to as the Strangers Disease in New Orleans because it seemed to disproportionately afflict non-native-born inhabitants who had yet to develop immunity, yellow fever was recognized by symptoms of flulike chills, fevers, painful muscle aches, bodily bleeding, and blood vomiting that resembled black coffee grounds. Throughout much of the nineteenth century, death came quickly to those unable to recover, usually about one week.[46] *Aedes* mosquitoes preferred densely populated urban landscapes but could thrive in more rural hinterlands.[47] Public health officials feared the transportation of *Aedes* mosquitoes via train to various locales, and the insect became a rather easy target for the use of military metaphors by the early twentieth century. Mosquitoes, and hence yellow fever, "invaded" landscapes and cities, while "campaigns" were directed to slow the advancement of disease. Mosquitoes "assaulted" cities, while public officials reassured a worried public that "victory" could be won by chemical warfare.[48] In her work on the eradication of disease, historian Nancy Leys Stepan makes a more powerful connection between metaphor and disease. "There is a strong tendency in science for metaphors to become naturalized, so that they are used not as figures of speech, but are taken instead to be true descriptions of the world as it actually is. Given this tendency to reduce metaphor to reality, one is not surprised to find that military metaphors easily get connected to the idea that disease eradication itself requires military-like strategies."[49] The idea of eradicating disease could only succeed if warfare, or "brigades," was waged against a particular insect vector or disease. In his work *Mosquito Empires: Ecology and War in the Greater Caribbean, 1620–1914,* historian J. R. McNeill makes the point that those mosquitoes that carried yellow fever and malaria around the globe were a threat to worldly conquests, providing an important military advantage for those throughout the world who had developed immunity: "Although always evolving, the ecological conditions that prevailed in the Greater Caribbean after the 1640s reliably included these twin killers. Strictly speaking, they did not determine the outcomes of struggles for power, but they governed the probabilities of success and failure in military expeditions and settlement schemes. It is perhaps a rude blow to the *amour propre* of our species to think that lowly mosquitoes and mindless viruses can shape our international affairs. But they can."[50] While the *Aedes* mosquito may have represented the most visible of the disease and insect threats early in the twentieth century, many other pests also came under the cultural framework of waging war against nonhuman enemies.

Under the guise of pest control, insects were reframed not simply as unwanted nuisances but as hidden enemies of the American body politic, creating a human war against nature. Historian Edmund Russell has called this concept a "total war" against the insect world. Russell's framing of a total war hinges on the ways in which certain ideologies, strategies, and language prevalent during moments of peace might influence military engagement and how the ideologies, strategies, and language of war extended beyond conflicts into moments of peace. The result is that during the crisis of war and security of peace, "total wars" might be waged against both human and insect enemies. From an environmental perspective, Russell makes the point that "the control of nature expanded the scale of war, and war expanded the scale on which people controlled nature. More specifically, the control of nature formed one root of total war, and total war helped expand the control of nature to the scale rued by modern environmentalists."[51] Chemical warfare (sometimes even the same chemicals) could be employed in the eradication of both humans and pests. "Peaceful warfare" against insects occurred as a result of synergies between military and nonmilitary institutions at a unique moment of postwar America.[52]

The battle against insects was cast as a war for human survival. Insects were the new enemies, plotting and strategizing in unseen corners of the earth against human populations, forcing economic entomologists and the federal government to press military resources into this new fight. For entomologists it was the next "great war" against all classes of invading insects defined as alien to earth. One official for the United States Bureau of Entomology suggested that entomologists formed "a force of four hundred trained men" who courageously and relentlessly undertook campaigns against those insects threatening human populations.[53] Military metaphors of insect invasions became part of the popular imagination as well. An article published in *Harper's Weekly* less than a decade after World War I suggested that the war against insects meant nothing "less than the life or death of the human race. If man wins he will remain the dominant species on this earth. If he loses he will be wiped out by this, his most ambitious racial enemy."[54] The use of racial terminology here is telling but not uncommon. The idea of a race war was fresh in the minds of an American public on the heels of a particularly contentious pre- and postwar period when race riots erupted in East St. Louis, Illinois, and Chicago and Tulsa. Condemnations of racialized insects tapped into xenophobic perceptions of the "other," connecting a racial inferiority of insects with dominant scientific attitudes of racial inferiority toward African Americans and immigrant groups.[55] By World War II, metaphors describing racial enemies as insects had taken shape, while certain insect species introduced into American ecosystems also took on added dimensions of racial discourse. When the Japanese beetle was imported by accident to New Jersey around 1912, it was framed as an invasion of unwanted immigrants in much the same way Asian immigrants were scrutinized as they came through Angel Island. By 1960 the United States had launched an assault on the invader.[56] Even Rachel Carson made the connection in *Silent Spring* when she wrote that "mid-western states now on the fringe of the beetle's range have launched an attack worthy of the most deadly enemy instead of only a moderately destructive insect."[57] Most entomologists suggested the Japanese beetle was in no way destructive to humans or the ecosystem.

The 1927 flood also reflected notions of war versus nature and provided meaning through the discourse of charity. President Calvin Coolidge's appointment of then secretary of commerce Herbert Hoover as head of American Red Cross operations during the 1927 flood set the stage for the management of relief and Hoover's political ascent to the White House in 1928.[58] Hoover's philosophy of government had a significant influence on the 1927 flood's aftermath of charity. Born in West Branch, Iowa, he came from a Quaker and working-class background. Orphaned at the age of nine, Hoover developed his ideology of government's role from his strict religious upbringing, which promoted individualism and cooperative social responsibility. Hoover biographer Joan Wilson suggests that "it was this Quaker ideal which would be a recurring theme in his attempts to restructure the American political and economic system in the 1920s." During World War I Hoover became war manager for the United States Food Administration.[59] When the Lever Act of 1917 charged the Food Administration with organizing food production during the war, Hoover touted his Iowan roots of self-reliance when pushing citizens to grow and consume their own food products.[60] The government referred to the results as "victory gardens" and "home garden armies," predating the more well-known idea of victory gardens during World War II. As the country transitioned into a postwar economy, Hoover's politics of individualism and self-help continued to take shape during the New Era of decentralized corporatism in business and economics representative of the 1920s. Hoover believed the government should play limited roles in the lives of citizens, who should be directed in the "cooperative spirit" of assisting other Americans. The philosophy had important implications for the ways in which the Red Cross and the federal government responded to the 1927 flood under his leadership.[61] As Joan Wilson describes the prevalence of Hooverism of this era, "Government should act as a source of information, coordination, and national guidance, but there was no need for it to become a coercive force if individuals were properly educated to willingly assume social and economic responsibilities at the local and state levels through voluntary organizations."[62] Critics of Hooverism countered that private citizens could not be left solely to their own devices and that a diminishment of government intervention into the lives of citizens could ultimately lead to situations in which institutions like the Red Cross or the government might turn a blind eye to abuses of power.[63]

By the end of April, the height of the flood relief effort in the Yazoo Delta, Memphis was established as the headquarters for the Red Cross. The relief process already resembled a military operation. Secretary of War Dwight F. Davis and Secretary of the Navy Curtis D. Wilbur were in direct communication with Hoover.[64] Colonel George B. Spaulding was placed in charge of coordinating transportation connected with relief work; this included overseeing a fleet of more than 826 water and air vessels from the Army, Navy, Coast Guard, Department of Commerce, and Bureau of Lighthouses.[65] Lighthouse tenders (small vessels normally used for the operation of lighthouses), coal and oil barges, and river steamers were all pressed into service.[66] The Yazoo Delta quickly came to resemble a theater of war. Military vessels and personnel were used for a variety of emergency relief work. Cots, blankets, and tents for Red Cross camps were supplied by the War Department and sent by military convoy. Army depots from as far afield as Philadelphia and Omaha sent sandbags and tents.[67] Enlisted soldiers loaded supplies from depots and unloaded them in flooded regions. Army cooks under official order traveled to the Yazoo Delta and prepared food for thousands of survivors.[68] Army Air Corps and Navy hydroplanes carried food products and typhoid and smallpox vaccines, scouted breaches in levees, monitored river levels, and embarked on rescue missions. Pilots searched from above for marooned survivors stranded precariously in trees and on rooftops, providing intelligence for the deployment of rescue parties.[69] Navy officials ordered warships from Key West, while the Coast Guard mobilized its flotilla of large vessels, barges, motorized power boats, patrol boats, and cutters used for transporting civilians and military personnel.[70]

The Army, Navy, and Coast Guard joined the Mississippi River Commission in documenting the disaster through photographs while creating a technical armamentarium of images that brought into visual focus the meanings of war and nature. This was not the first moment the military documented a peacetime disaster, but the 1927 flood's breadth and sheer destruction demanded military engagement in ways never before imagined.[71] Military cameras created visual narratives of suffering as photographers documented

FIGURE 5. Two Navy hydroplanes are being stored on the Lower Old River. Photograph by the United States Coast Guard, May 21, 1927. Courtesy of the National Archives and Records Administration.

FIGURE 6. Navy hydroplanes preparing for rescue and surveillance work near the Yazoo Delta. Photograph by the United States Weather Bureau, May 1, 1927. Courtesy of the National Archives and Records Administration.

Red Cross relief camps, floodwaters rushing through levee breaks, trains and automobiles immobilized by floodwaters, toppled telephone poles, and flooded houses. Aerial shots from military planes captured the flood's magnitude across the landscape, and from high above images blurred the riparian lines between land and water.

The large-scale presence of the military was not lost on flood survivors, blues musicians, and Americans observing the flood from across the country. Two years after the flood, Charley Patton insinuated the role of military airplanes during the relief process in part 2 of his well-known *High Water Everywhere,* describing an environment where planes could be seen and heard circling high above the flood scene.[72] We can speculate that Patton, who may have experienced the flood firsthand, was documenting military planes bringing Red Cross supplies and transporting personnel in the Yazoo-Delta region.

Drawing on the use of technology for documenting the disaster, the Red Cross was quickly putting into place a plan for the solicitation of money from American citizens, tapping into postwar ideas of citizenship and patriotism. Hoover put his self-help and minimal government intervention theory into action. The key to inculcating the American public with a sense of patriotism and duty during a peacetime disaster was framing nature as an imminent threat to citizenship and the body politic. The 1927 flood could not simply be an environmental disaster. It had to be recast as humankind's fight for survival against nature. Floodwater was the enemy invading the Yazoo Delta's cotton-producing economy. Like pest eradication, floodwaters were defined as "other" and threatening to America. Advancing waters invaded farmers' fields and private homes as soldiers from a foreign country. The Mississippi River was suddenly reconstructed as a threat, even though, like most insects, it predated the human inhabitants by centuries.

The American Red Cross, primarily through its organ the *Red Cross Courier (RCC),* was often at the forefront of framing the disaster for an interested public. The *RCC* was more than a source of information; it also served as a means for the Red Cross to solicit money for disasters and internal funds. Metaphors of war were common in the *RCC,* and by early May it had begun framing the sides of battle for the American public. "Waters carried their onslaught farther and farther into the terrain of the helpless hundreds of thousands," one *RCC* article read. The American Red Cross was leading the nation into combat as the Red Cross flag of charity became emblematic of Americanism. It was not leading the nation alone, however. Articles described a coordinated effort between the Red Cross and the military. "There marched forward a magnificent army of succor, represented in our Southland by that 'first line' of trained, able and willing workers of the Red Cross, of the Army, of the Navy, of the Coast Guard, of the U.S. Public Health Service, coordinated into a single unit in a fight to bring men, women and children out of the slough of despond."[73] The imagery of war was relentless, if not over the top, but it served the purpose of bringing the country back into a state of military consciousness in peace times.[74] Red Cross officials like James Feiser also liberally employed such metaphors, suggesting that Red Cross soldiers formed a "battle front hundreds of miles in length with long tributary fields of action." Front lines of charity and resources must be coordinated against the Mississippi River. "Here and there the Trojan fight of the Government everywhere goes on side by side with the movement of the refugees, the establishment of camps, and the creation of food depots preparing to meet the possible needs of additional thousands should the banks crumble."[75] Feiser's interpretation of action was clear. Attacks and counterattacks, movement of people out harm's way, establishment of camps and food resources, and superior strategy could ensure victory. There could not be a truce. Victory meant subduing nature through proper "strategy" and "military maneuvering."

The Mississippi Flood of 1927 was at the epicenter of a movement of fear that revolved around disease and illness. A major concern in the immediate aftermath of disasters throughout history, but especially in the period after the discovery of germ theory, is the fear of wide-scale epidemics predicated on breakdowns in public health infrastructures. The particular imagery of stagnant floodwaters was frightening, evoking as it did images of disease and illness associated with yellow fever and malaria. The United States Public Health Service (USPHS) entered the flooded regions and immediately became involved with stemming outbreaks of disease, mostly in Arkansas, Mississippi, and Louisiana.[76] Broader messages helped frame perceptions of health and the image of disaster. "Death and Famine" was the headline of a May 7 article in the *Pittsburgh Courier* relating outbreaks of measles, mumps, whooping cough, malaria, and pellagra in fourteen Red Cross camps.[77] A July 30 headline in the *St. Bernard Voice* published in Arabi, Louisiana, read, "Steps to Prevent Disease: Residents' Health Carefully Guarded," cautioning returning residents to adhere strictly to sanitary work and requirements before entering homes and not to drink floodwater.[78] Mississippi state health officer F. L. Underwood informed an interested public that the "Mississippi Delta is threatened by a serious outbreak of pellagra, due chiefly to the lack of a sufficient milk supply."[79]

Employing an imagery of militarism and war common in the months after the 1927 flood, Red Cross medical supervisor William Redden suggested that the threat of disease and sickness in relief camps "are the gravest which the country has ever had to face in peace times." An army of health workers mobilizing to flood regions came from the American Red Cross, local public health departments, and the USPHS.[80] More than three hundred physicians, health officers, sanitary inspectors, and nurses performed public health work in Arkansas, Louisiana, Mississippi, Missouri, and Tennessee. The "battalions of nurses," as they were sometimes referred to, were primarily volunteers assigned by the Red Cross. In addition to the Red Cross and USPHS, health work in the flooded regions also included local health officials of the seven major states, the American Medical Association, medical officers from the Fourth and Seventh Corps Area Headquarters of the Army, local medical societies, and health departments of states located outside the flooded region. The American Red Cross and USPHS held tightly to their role as leaders during the entire process, spearheading a thirty-day health program consisting of massive immunizations, purification of water outlets and supplies, rapid disposal of sewage, removal of animal carcasses, oil spraying, and screening against mosquitoes.[81]

Expenditures were justified during a period of limited federal involvement by implicitly casting health as a racial issue. Commonly held early twentieth-century ideas of black bodies as inherently diseased and potentially harmful to white people undergirded the need to watch over their health.[82] At the same time, the Red Cross and USPHS took strict control over the messages of health received around the world, making a case that "sickness among the refugees has actually been less than experienced normally in the same areas."[83] Newspapers picked up this triumphalist message as an example of the unified and concerted effort between medical practitioners and federal agencies. Casting notions of medical paternalism aside for a moment, this dominant narrative has served to minimize the racial dimensions of charity and obscure a more accurate rendering of deaths from the flood. The reality for black people in the Yazoo Delta and other parts of the Deep South was a lifetime outside official health surveillance—from the cradle to grave—making it unlikely that this limited exposure to a few public health officers significantly elevated black health.[84]

Clearly, metaphors of military skirmishes were entrenched in the way the disaster was framed to the American public. It was equally the case that appeals for money were cast around militarism. The 1927 flood was explained as the single greatest peacetime disaster in history, and victory on the battlefield necessitated coordination of relief efforts.[85] Public information was crucial for constructing relief and key to Hoover's solicitation plan. By the 1920s radio technology was a powerful mechanism for communicating with the public at large and delivering important social service programming.[86] Radio served two important functions during the flood: it served as a warning system for people in the flood's path and provided information to citizens outside the flooded regions. A *New York Times* article crystallized the importance for readers while also connecting ideas to a broader military metaphor. "Among the first relief units arriving in the stricken country were radio outfits of the United States Army. These with the aid of airplanes performed a notable service directing rescue work."[87] The radio station WABC in New York also opened airwaves to the Red Cross. Beginning Saturday, April 30, and extending for three straight days, WABC suspended regular broadcasting to air relief programming. Donations totaling in the thousands poured into the station, prompting other radio stations to air flood relief appeals. Actors and public figures appealed to citizens in ways that helped elevate the profile of the disaster for people who might normally be uninterested. By 1927 Will Rogers had become a political radio commentator in addition to being famous as a real-life cowboy and movie star. People sent money to the Red Cross after listening to Will Rogers and other celebrities on the radio and being persuaded by their voices to contribute.[88]

Herbert Hoover used radio both to solicit money and to connect with Americans in ways that would serve him well during the 1928 presidential election. His national stature rose significantly during the relief effort. Americans constantly read about his actions in the flooded regions and heard his voice on the radio. In late April, Hoover addressed the nation from Memphis over the NBC radio network, finding an opportunity to personally manipulate metaphors of war. "In every home behind the battle line," Hoover suggested, "there is apprehension and anxiety."[89] Hoover posited engineers as also forming an important front line of defense. "It is a great battle which the engineers are directing. They have already held important levees against the water enemy." Americans must have pride in their fellow citizens and be ready to take part in the battle by bearing charity's burden.

Hoover also made appeals through short "instructive" films produced in abundance during World War I. Targeting both soldiers and civilians, the military and the USPHS manufactured short films and posters on almost every public health threat imaginable, from cancer and diabetes to the proper way of brushing teeth. Hoover's flood relief activities were captured in at least four silent short films. Black-and-white still footage was donated from Pathé News, Paramount News, Fox Films, and other news agencies constructing Hoover as the great humanitarian. One short film showed Hoover and Secretary of War Dwight Davis touring an undisclosed flooded area by boat. A series of silent captions told the story for viewers: "The levees sagged and snapped and the unharnessed waters of the raging Mississippi poured over the land far and wide wreaking distress, misery and death from Illinois to the Delta. A Noah's Ark of 1927." Another short film from August 1928 was called *Master of Emergencies*, one of the many nicknames Hoover was given during the 1927 flood. This film was more biographical in nature, using earlier Hoover footage from his secretary of commerce days along with the 1927 flood to demonstrate his managerial skills. The narrative was of a person capable of leading the nation through the greatest peacetime disaster, where the Mississippi River "went on its greatest rampage" and levees "melted like sugar." Messages conveyed in these films had more than a hint of paternalistic racism that mirrored Red Cross publications, popular images, and paintings—all of which were designed to elevate Hoover's stature in the public's imagination. One particular line in a Hoover short film read, "Old auntie meets them too," with a statuesque Hoover standing in the middle of a Red Cross relief camp surrounded by poor African Americans. It clearly evoked an image of Hoover as the sole savior of African Americans in the flooded region.[90]

President Calvin Coolidge also used radio to send messages to the American public. By early May, Coolidge issued a proclamation asking the public to donate a minimum of $10 million, quite a significant and lofty goal in 1927. "The situation in the Mississippi Valley has developed into a grave crisis affecting a wide area in several states," he wrote in an appeal through the *RCC*. "There are now more than 200,000 flood refugees who have been driven from their homes. This number is being increased daily as fresh breaks in the levees inundate the country on either side of the river." Coolidge continued, "These refugees are being fed, sheltered and clothed by the American Red Cross, acting as the agent for the American people. The burden of their care will continue for many more weeks." He concluded the appeal by concretizing the American Red Cross's singular role. "For the purpose of coordination and effectiveness in the administration of the relief fund, I recommend that all contributions be forwarded to the nearest local Red Cross Chapter, or to the American National Red Cross headquarters offices at Washington, St. Louis, or San Francisco."[91] Coolidge's proclamation was immediately picked up by newspapers across the country and translated into the popular war-and-nature metaphor.

A barrage of images and appeals laid the groundwork for the American Red Cross's national and international fund-raising project. Between April and August 1927, newspapers provided round-the-clock coverage as money came in from all over the world.[92] Haiti sent $500, and Hawaii promised to send money even though it was also raising funds for the devastating magnitude 7.6 earthquake that struck Kita Tango, Japan, on March 7, 1927, killing over fifteen hundred people and destroying ten thousand houses. Almost immediately, American communities and cities set goals of how much money they wanted to raise. A May 1 *New York Times* article told readers that "there has been no disaster of the kind that called more urgently for aid in the form of money contributions. No limit can be set at this time to the relief fund. Twice and even three times the minimum of $5,000,000 may be needed. Every city and town must be asked to increase its original quota. When little far-off Guam cables $940 to the Red Cross it is time for every American community to wake up to the calamity of the Mississippi Flood of 1927."[93]

In fulsomely patriotic language, the article suggested to readers that "their suffering is your suffering" and by not acting they were forsaking citizenship and duty. Using jarring terms like "wake up," the article attempted to shock Americans out of complacency by portraying the 1927 flood as a national problem. But the *New York Times* did more than appeal to a sense of patriotism. It also warned that "the army of sufferers may be swelled by many thousands. The pressing duty is to help generously in the work of relief."[94] The message was clear, American citizens had a responsibility to the flood sufferers and a responsibility to the region.

Finally, volunteers and citizens took to the streets, canvassing neighborhoods from door-to-door asking for donations. Private organizations took donations from employees and members. Children put together lemonade stands on corners. One afternoon in Brockton, Massachusetts, the high school band marched through neighborhoods asking for money. Average Americans sent what they could, five cents, ten cents, or one dollar. One couple from Shawnee, Oklahoma, sent one dollar to the local Red Cross with a letter titled "Mississippians." The letter said, "My husband and I are sending our last dollar to go for benefit of the Mississippi flood suffer[ers] and a prayer that it may help some one." Churches took up two separate collections, one for the church and the second for the Red Cross. Appeals were read in the 432 Roman Catholic churches of New York asking for donations to be taken up the next Sunday. A letter from Cardinal Hayes of New York appealed to both American nationalism and Catholicism, suggesting that many of the flood sufferers in Louisiana and Mississippi were staunch Catholics.[95] Theater houses put on plays, performances, and benefit concerts, with the proceeds forwarded to the Red Cross, while the Motion Picture Theater Owners of America Association made arrangements for Red Cross volunteers holding cans to walk up and down aisles taking money while producers donated proceeds from ticket sales.[96] The latter moment predated and reminds us of the well-known "walking mothers" and celebrity balls of the March of Dimes connected with polio research in the 1930s and 1940s.[97] The 1927 flood and March of Dimes showed the influence and power that concerts and celebrities might wield over an interested public, shaping awareness, charity, and protest around environmental disasters and public health.

Charity represented a significant mechanism for introducing all Americans to the 1927 flood and the importance of giving. As natives and former migrants in other cities paid close attention to the 1927 flood through word of mouth, family, newspapers, and the process of charity, the 1927 flood was also transformed into an impetus for migration out of the flooded region.

4 Where Sixteen Railroads Meet the Sea

Migration and the Making of Houston's Frenchtown

The 1927 flood occurred during the height of the Great Migration, highlighting important ways the environment significantly shapes patterns of movement. Environmental displacement is an anxious and uneasy movement; there is often no choice but to migrate out of certain vulnerable landscapes. But mobility is also akin to freedom, and the decision to migrate after the 1927 flood represented powerful acts of individual and group expression. Most scholarship to date has yet to fully grapple with the crucial role of environmentalism in shaping movement, in particular how floods, hurricanes, tornadoes, the proliferation of boll weevils, and other environmental events add an additional layer to the ways in which lynching, violence, political intimidation, the exploitative system of sharecropping, and economic poverty historically influence migration patterns. The 1927 flood reminds us to acknowledge the environment's role in migration narratives.

The well-documented movement of Katrina survivors from New Orleans to Houston was preceded by the similarly documented yet long-forgotten movement after the 1927 flood. Self-described Creoles of color, mostly from Southwest Louisiana, moved to Houston after the disaster, adding to the development of a unique ethnic enclave in the middle of the city called Frenchtown. Louisiana Creoles of color are tied historically to slavery and *gens de couleur libre* (free people of color) in the American South and Caribbean; they are mixed with French, Spanish, German, and Indian blood.[1] While these differences of lineage are certainly important for how we think about the history of identity politics, for the purpose of this chapter I use the term "Creoles of color" primarily because this is how Frenchtown migrants historically described themselves. My argument is that many of the same factors shaping broader migration and immigration patterns, including kinship networks, trajectories of movement, and movement between border states, are part of how Frenchtown developed after the 1927 flood.

The Frenchtown neighborhood was originally settled by Creole of color migrants in the early 1900s, and it continued to serve as the foundation for successive waves of migrants to the city, mostly from Southwestern Louisiana. Houston was not the only destination; migrants also formed Creole of color settlements throughout Texas, including Beaumont (Pear Orchard), which was just over the Louisiana line, Port Arthur, Anahuac, Liberty, McNair, Ames, Raywood, and Barrett Station. These migrant communities paled in comparison to Houston's Frenchtown, which, by the 1927 flood, was a neighborhood with a ten-block radius bounded by Collingsworth Street, Russell Street, Liberty Road, and Jensen Drive. The neighborhood was called Frenchtown because migrants from Louisiana sometimes referred to one another as "Frenchmen," and though still very much a rural outlier inside a growing energy capital, by the early 1920s the neighborhood was taking shape as a unique social and cultural space rooted in Louisiana culture.[2] The 1927 flood sent waves of migrants into this neighborhood, making part of Frenchtown's legacy a historical remembrance of why so many decided to say goodbye to Louisiana and hello to Texas. I am not suggesting this was a large-scale migration out of Louisiana into Texas following the 1927 flood. Because so many people were in flux in the southern states at this time for many social, cultural, and economic reasons, tracking down the migration pattern after a single flood is impossible.

As Robyn Spencer and John Barry have argued, there was a strong sentiment among some African Americans that the flood was the last straw. Having grown tired of being mistreated in the years before the flood and, finally, in Red Cross relief camps during the crisis period, it seems clear that many blacks and Creoles of color internalized the flood as an opportunity or reason to make a change.[3] Letters received by Walter White of the NAACP suggested to him that some black flood survivors "would rather be drowned in the flood than be forced to go back to the plantation from which they had come."[4] Journalists and other witnesses suggested that many thousands were escaping the relief camps and leaving the region. It seems clear that emigration out of the region did occur after the flood, though many questions remain unanswered. Where did they migrate? Did they leave temporarily and come back, or leave and never return? If they still owed sharecropping wages, returning to those areas even years later would have been a risky proposition. Did they migrate to Memphis and perhaps on to Chicago and other areas? How did they migrate, individually and collectively, some with money and others without money, food, and other resources? These questions are difficult to answer, but it is also what makes the Frenchtown migration narrative so intriguing and provocative. The migration of Creoles of color to Frenchtown following the disaster represents a microhistory, and in many ways perhaps, a micromigration. Whether the migration from Louisiana to Texas was a movement of thousands or just a trickle, oral history, census records, and newspapers suggest an important narrative that extends the influence of the disaster well beyond the floodwater's reach. What Frenchtown reveals, however brief and limited in scope, is a window into the ways in which the 1927 flood represents broader narratives of migration.

The Rising Energy Capital and the Making of Frenchtown

Houston, approximately fifty miles from the Gulf of Mexico, seemed like a city at the bottom of the world when it was founded in 1836. Early on, the city and its hinterlands resembled the cotton- and timber-producing regions of the Yazoo Delta, Louisiana, and other parts of Texas; by the early twentieth century, Houston was shifting from a dependency on cotton and farming into becoming one of the country's most important energy capitals. This transformation from a largely agrarian lifestyle to energy production also significantly shaped what would later be known as the Gulf Coast region.[5] Historian Joseph Pratt also connects this transformation of a cotton-producing region into an oil capital with important developments of transportation networks linking Houston to the broader world. The construction of roads and navigable waterways connected Houston with interior regions of Texas and other states, while boosterism around railroads not only connected Houston to a marketplace of ideas and goods but also became part of the city's identity. "By 1860, Houston was the starting point or terminus for some 80 percent of the approximately 500 miles of track that had been laid in Texas," Pratt points out, "and its rails reached out up to 90 miles into the hinterland in several directions."[6] During the post–Civil War years, when the Southern Pacific Railroad completed lines in Houston, the city developed ties to interior Texas and states in the North, South, and Midwest. Railroads were not only big business but a big employer as well.

By 1900 Houston had a population of forty-five thousand residents, with growth spurred on by the expansion of the railroad business. The largest boon to the region came on January 10, 1901, however, when the Spindletop oil gusher near Beaumont, Texas, ushered in a new era of financial and economic transformation.[7] Soon thereafter, other oil gushers were discovered closer to Houston, and Houston quickly changed into a boomtown and energy-producing capital. The region's oil was largely useless until it was refined, meaning that the oil economy also had to produce oil refineries that changed raw oil into crude ready for shipment across the country.[8] By the 1910s oil refineries such as the Gulf Oil Company, Standard Oil Company, and the Texas Company were supplanting cotton-related industries in Houston and its outskirts toward the Gulf of Mexico and the Louisiana border, proving the extent to which energy and oil were taking control of the region. In the decades after the Houston Ship Channel opened in 1914, numerous oil refineries lined the channel on both sides, completing both the economic and aesthetic shift in the city's new image. The development of Houston as an energy capital and transportation hub made it a city of vast opportunities. Oil refineries and other oil-related industries, the Houston Ship Channel, railroads, and the still-viable cotton-producing industry of the city's past made Houston a potentially rich environment for migrants and others in search of better economic opportunities.[9] By 1930 refineries employed close to nineteen thousand workers between Houston and the Louisiana border, some fifty miles away. As described by Pratt, "The giant industrial plants that refined crude oil became a primary source of industrial jobs and a powerful engine of growth for the upper Texas and Louisiana coasts, with the Houston Ship Channel gradually emerging as the center of this vast refining region."[10]

By 1927, Houston was already considered a mecca for migrants from Louisiana, a place where "16 Railroads Met the Sea."[11] The term became popular as an illustration of migration on the Southern Pacific Railroad, which linked Louisiana and Arkansas to Texas. Houston's railroads did not just connect an expanding marketplace of goods and products related to oil industries; they also connected people and condensed space, influencing migration patterns. Travel patterns during the Great Migration were often influenced by railway lines and routes. The well-known Illinois Central Railroad connected Alabama and Mississippi to Chicago, while the eastern Seaboard Air Line and Atlantic Coast Line Railroads connected Florida, Georgia, Virginia, South Carolina, and North Carolina to Washington, D.C., Philadelphia, New York, and other cities in the Northeast. Heading west, the Union Pacific Railroad connected Texas with California and Nevada.[12] The Southern Pacific's rise tied Louisiana and the interior of Texas to Houston and the growing oil region on the city's outskirts.

The growth of the railroad industry in Houston was important for additional reasons. It highlighted the importance of both intraregional movement patterns and the largely underrecognized trajectories of movement during the Great Migration. The shorter cross-border movement of Creoles of color would fit into the broader narrative of intraregional movement to Texas from Louisiana during this period. Migration patterns were not always long distance. As historian Earl Lewis makes clear in his discussion of migration to Norfolk, Virginia, during World War II, the ship-building industry attracted skilled and unskilled laborers from the Deep South and surrounding countryside. New York, Philadelphia, and Chicago were the choice destinations for many during the Great Migration, but for many others, the land of opportunity was in southern urban cities.[13]

Southern and western cities became destinations for rural southerners looking for better social and cultural opportunities as well. In our historical preoccupation with certain trajectories of movement from the South to the North, we have largely minimized other movement patterns from the South to other parts of the South, and to a lesser extent, the South to the West.[14] Southern cities like Houston, Tulsa, and Jackson, Mississippi, experienced tremendous increases in population between 1910 and 1930. As historian Bernadette Pruitt reminds us, "While most southern cities witnessed significant population losses among blacks compared to northern urban centers, Houston experienced a second and more dramatic migration surge."

Houston's black population increased 40 percent between 1910 and 1920 and experienced an increase of close to fifteen thousand black residents in the decade after World War I.[15] More recently, Los Angeles and Richmond, California, as well as Las Vegas, have received much-needed attention from migration scholars. By the 1930s and 1940s the growing desert city of Las Vegas attracted migrants from Mississippi and Alabama in search of jobs and opportunities from gaming industries.[16] Important movement patterns from Texas and Florida to California are still almost completely left out of migration narratives. These patterns force us to rethink the traditional lens through which we understand displacement and movement associated with the 1927 flood.

"Louisiana, 1927"

It was Alzina's turn to rise early this particular morning and make coffee for her father before he went off to work. While Alzina was in the kitchen making coffee, her younger sister Mabel looked out the window to see what had become a familiar sight during the spring of 1927. Water was accumulating in the distance and inching closer to the Prejean household.[17] Alzina was one of at least eight children born to Victorien (Victor) and Aurelia (Agnes) Prejean in Scott, Louisiana, in Lafayette Parish, about 125 miles east of the Texas border. Like many other people in Lafayette Parish, the Prejeans were farmers, growing a diverse mix of sugarcane, vegetables, cotton, and corn; they sold what they needed in the local marketplace to provide for the family. Alzina and her siblings were surrounded by a large network of family, as both sets of grandparents lived in nearby Carencro, Louisiana, and numerous aunts and uncles also lived in Scott. By 1927 the Prejeans had constructed important social networks and community ties that would become part of their survival in Louisiana and relocation in Houston.[18]

Victor Prejean saw the menacing floodwaters coming toward his house and immediately went outside to place a stick in the ground as a way of marking not only how fast the water was coming but also the flood's depth. The water Mabel saw forming in the distance early that morning was turning into a real threat, as the stick her father used to mark water levels in the distance was, by the late morning, inching closer and closer to the house. The family immediately began securing farm animals by moving them to higher ground and gathering as many personal belongings as they could before the backwaters forced them to leave. Like so many others that doubted the flood's severity, once they realized how serious the situation was the Prejeans had to act quickly to save themselves. Victor decided the family was no longer safe, so they left by horse and buggy to seek refuge with nearby relatives in Louisiana whose homes were not flooded. The Prejeans were fortunate to have family members they could stay with during the flood; their mixed Creole ancestry would have dictated placement in one of the "colored" relief camps springing up in Louisiana.[19]

Southwestern Louisiana was particularly hard hit by the 1927 flood, largely because of levee breaks along the Atchafalaya River. The Atchafalaya originates near Simmesport, Louisiana, where the Old River Structure connects the Mississippi and Red Rivers through a seven-mile stretch of canalized river. It represents the main distributary of the Mississippi and Red Rivers, meaning it flows away from rather than into a main stem. Situated west of the Mississippi River, it takes a southeasterly path roughly parallel to the Mississippi River before emptying into the Gulf near Morgan City, Louisiana. The Atchafalaya is a short river, only 140 miles from origin to completion, and compared to the Mississippi it takes a much more direct course to the sea, which is one reason it experienced such pressure during the 1927 flood, as floodwaters sought quick paths to the Gulf. Backwater levees along the Atchafalaya had significantly weakened by late April in North Central Louisiana, but a huge crevasse near Bayou des Glaises intersected with another crevasse farther south near Melville to send over a million cubic feet of floodwater into Southwest Louisiana in a path two hundred miles long and roughly fifty miles wide. These are the floodwaters that reached where the Prejeans lived.[20] As the Mounds Landing crevasse sent tidal waves of floodwaters across the Yazoo Mississippi Delta, breaks along the Atchafalaya River pushed floodwaters onto landscapes in Southwestern Louisiana. Figure 7 shows a levee crevasse near Melville, Louisiana, in late May that caused rip currents of between twelve and fifteen miles per hour on the Atchafalaya River. At first glance, it is difficult to tell the land side versus the river side of the levee, but sandbags are always stacked on the side facing the river. In the figure, you can clearly see bags stacked along the levee opposite where the cows are grazing. In the distance you can also see the tops of houses covered with backwater.

FIGURE 7. A crevasse near Melville, Louisiana. Photograph by the United States Coast Guard, May 20, 1927. Courtesy of the National Archives and Records Administration.

Weeks after being displaced, the Prejeans returned home to find knee-high water still remaining and high water marks near the ceiling.[21] Dead farm animals floated outside the house. Though they had tried to save as many animals as they could, the speed with which the flood rose forced them to leave before most of the animals could safely be secured, leaving them to fend for themselves against the flood.[22] This was not uncommon; receding backwaters left tons of mud and dead animals throughout Arkansas and Mississippi, effectively blurring the lines between land and water. In Southwest Louisiana, marine life was temporarily transformed as thousands of crawfish were deposited on the landscape. There were so many crawfish that people could not avoid stepping on them in public and cars squashed them driving down the road. As in Mississippi and Arkansas, Louisiana residents guarded against inopportune and dangerous encounters with water moccasins, rattlesnakes, alligators, and other dangerous animals.[23]

One example in particular highlights the importance of understanding the vulnerability embedded within the landscape and how people tried to make sense of changes within their physical environment. Margaret Landry Attaway was just seven years old during the 1927 flood, and her family lived in Lafayette, Louisiana.[24] When the levee near Morganza sent floodwaters through the areas of Parks, Cecelia, and Breaux Bridge, the Red Cross immediately set up a relief camp near Breaux Bridge. The Attaways, like the Prejeans, were Creoles of color, and Attaway's father did not want to enter a relief camp. He decided the family would ride the flood out at home and sent word for other family members nearby to join them. Resembling the Okies traveling west after the Dust Bowl, Attaway's aunts, uncles, and cousins arrived in covered and uncovered wagons with all their possessions.[25] The family made do as best they could by spreading mattresses from wall to wall on the second floor.[26] It would be three long months before Attaway's extended family felt safe enough to return to their homes; this was roughly the same time that most other flood victims were displaced. Margaret Attaway's favorite aunt, Tanta Melie, returned home and found that floodwaters had reached all the way to the attic, but she was thankful that her house was spared. She also found something that haunted the entire family, though, and would be told to successive generations as family lore. A full-grown horse was sprawled in the living room—dead. For years the family speculated how a full grown horse weighing well over a ton could fit through Tanta Melie's narrow front doorway. They wondered whether the beast was alive when it entered the house or already dead, its body taken over completely by floodwaters. The thought of a live horse flailing around in her living room made Tanta Melie uncomfortable, but so too did the idea of death pervading her living space. Most of the family agreed—if only as a way of taking some solace—that the horse was probably dead before floodwaters pushed it against the house, contorting its body and breaking bones as its body squeezed through the front door. Of course the immediate concern was how they were going to remove the dead animal from the house. It was far too heavy to lift and navigate through a small doorway, so they had no choice but to butcher the horse piece by piece, a process made unbearable by the foul smell of mud and the decomposing carcass. Making matters worse, blood inevitably spilled onto the living room floor as the horse was being cut up. Decades later, Attaway recalled that her mother was so disturbed by the incident she didn't allow her to visit Tanta Melie's house for nearly a year.[27]

For the Prejeans, the loss of the upcoming crop was the most devastating and heartrending aspect of the flood. Years later, Mable Prejean Guillory recalled there would have been a bumper crop that year, meaning they were expecting an extraordinarily abundant harvest season.[28] Instead the family faced a life-changing decision: whether to stay in Louisiana and rebuild their lives with an eye toward the next farming season or begin a life elsewhere. An informal social network was already in place in Texas, which helped them make the decision to leave Louisiana.

Like so many other migrants, the Prejeans moved in piecemeal fashion. They tried other places before finally settling in Houston's Frenchtown. It was common during the Great Migration for individuals or families to migrate in stages to Chicago or New York. Some could not afford to migrate to a destination in one trip, while others were not exactly sure where they wanted to settle.[29] In the early fall of 1927, the Prejeans decided to settle in Jefferson County, Texas, near Beaumont, ninety miles east of Houston. Beaumont was a border town just across the Texas-Louisiana line, and the Prejeans did not arbitrarily choose it; rather, they tapped into a network of migrants who had already treaded a path there in the 1920s.[30] Victor Prejean hesitated to give up farming, which he had done his entire life; however, he was unlike poor sharecroppers who were rarely able to gain any type of economic foothold with farming. Farming was not immediately an option for him, though, largely because the family needed quick money to survive after the move, forcing him to find work at a local refinery connected to the region's growing oil economy.

Prejean resisted doing anything outside of farming, and he shared with other migrants the painful realization that factory work presented its own sets of parameters and limitations in the "Promised Land."[31] Not only was the work tedious and long, but the color of his skin prevented him from applying for and entering higher-paying positions. Because the family was so large and money so limited, Victor and Agnes were concerned that they would not survive long under the circumstances of their new life in Beaumont. They were bartering the relative security and economic stability of farming in Louisiana for the equally long hours and low pay of the factory clock in Beaumont. Gone also was the advantage of consuming vegetables grown on their own land for their survival.

The early days in Texas were a struggle for the Prejeans, and they stayed in Beaumont only a year before moving again, this time to Brazoria County, closer to the growing railroad and energy capital of Houston.[32] Unlike Jefferson County, which was nearer to the Louisiana border and firmly in the oil-producing corridor, Brazoria County was still mostly farmland, though it lay in Houston's expanding hinterlands. The money the family saved in Jefferson County allowed them to move back into the familiarity of farming in Brazoria County, although things were not exactly the same as they were in Louisiana. Victor and Agnes had been landowners in Louisiana, but in Texas tried their hand at sharecropping for a white property owner named Pickman. Their experience of sharecropping was common in the South, beginning the growing season indebted to a landowner for the house in which they lived and the seed and tools obtained on credit from a local store.[33] For close to two years the family stayed in Brazoria County, working as sharecroppers, each year doing just well enough to get by. In a painfully ironic twist, during their second year the Prejeans again faced hardship at the hands of an environmental disaster when a hundred-mile-per-hour hurricane swept through Brazoria County, tearing off roofs and forcing the family into an underground storm shelter. In the wake of this latest disaster the family poised itself to move a third and final time. This would be the shortest move of all, just across the county line into Harris County and the city everyone was talking about.[34]

Even before the entire family moved to Houston, Victor Prejean found work at a meatpacking house on Jensen Drive in the heart of Frenchtown. Over the next two decades he held jobs at packing houses, oil companies, and the Houston Ship Channel, and like so many other workers in the 1930s, he found himself out of work during the Great Depression. Victor Prejean, who had a light complexion and could often pass for white, rarely disclosed his Creole identity outside Frenchtown, instead allowing potential employers to make their own assumptions about his racial makeup. It is unclear what he might have said when asked his race, but it is clear he occasionally lost jobs in Houston when employers found out he was a "Negro"—the custom of southern racial dynamics recognized only white or nonwhite. By 1930 Victor and Agnes had built a small house at 3208 Delia Street in the heart of Frenchtown to accommodate their family of eight, which included fifteen-year-old Mabel, fourteen-year-old Sarah, eleven-year-old Inez, nine-year-old

Olivia, seven-year-old Effie, and the youngest child and only surviving boy, five-year-old Wallace. One child, Nelson, had died of pneumonia before the 1927 flood and the family's move to Texas. The oldest child, Alzina, did not move with the family to Texas but instead remained in Louisiana.[35]

At last the Prejeans were settled in Houston and Frenchtown. They had become part of a movement to Texas. Though this movement is not well documented historically as part of the 1927 flood's lore, it is a part of the rich texture of Frenchtown understood largely through oral culture and memory. In many ways the Prejeans were representative of other 1927 migration narratives from Louisiana to Frenchtown. Sisters Lena and Sarah Mouton arrived in Frenchtown well before the Prejeans; their entire family rode on the Southern Pacific Railroad to Houston.[36] The extended family included relatives who worked as sharecroppers in Lafayette and, following the familiar story, the 1927 flood destroyed all their crops for the coming season. They had contemplated migrating to Frenchtown well before this, but the disaster and losing their crops was the last straw. As difficult a decision as it was to leave, the Moutons also saw the flood as an opportunity to begin life anew. Unlike the Prejeans, the Moutons didn't migrate piecemeal to Frenchtown. The father secured a job at a local meatpacking house. Lena was around twenty years old and married when she arrived in Frenchtown; the 1930 census shows her husband, Maurice, and two children, Junius (age two) and Aria (age nine). They lived in a small-frame house with Lena's sister Eva and Eva's husband, Joseph, at 3212 Rose Street. Eva and Joseph had also migrated from Louisiana, although it is not clear exactly when; they had three children of their own, including Henry (age two), Beatrice (age three), and Mary (age eight).[37] The living quarters were cramped. Census records clearly show a strong pattern of migration from Louisiana to Houston by 1930.[38] Decades after their own migration to Frenchtown, Lena and Sarah recalled in an interview that many other families from Southwest Louisiana, particularly the areas surrounding St. Martinsville, Lafayette, and Le Beau, migrated and resettled in Frenchtown after the flood.[39]

"Goodbye, Louisiana, I'm Going to Texas"

Louisiana migrants and native Houstonians alike found work as bricklayers, mechanics, plumbers, and carpenters, as well as within the growing energy sector and railroad industries. The Houston Ship Channel, Gulf Oil Company, Cotton Compress Oil Company, Houston Packing Company, Englewood Rail Yard, and Southern Pacific Railroad employed large numbers of laborers, as did local hotels, grocery stores, glass factories, garages, hospitals, gas companies, and barrel factories. Frenchtown residents also benefited from opportunities very close to their own community, including a local lard plant on Quitman Avenue, the Cotton Compress Oil Company on Whitney Street, and a paper factory on Clinton Drive.[40]

Like other migrants, Creoles of color found jobs through word of mouth and kinship networks connecting Louisiana to Texas. They often called each other "cousin" (pronounced "couzan"), and stories about migration to Houston became part of their broader cultural and ethnic identity. A popular story among Creoles of color comparing Louisiana to Houston says, "dear couzan, this is heaven over here, we only work half a day," suggesting the nine-to-five workday of energy industries was preferable to the dawn-to-dusk hours farming sometimes required.

Scholars have described at great length the importance of kinship networks in shaping Great Migration patterns and trajectories of movement throughout the country. People learned of job opportunities, housing, and how to enroll children into school and secure health services through a web of information that included black newspapers carried south by black train porters, informal networks of kin and fictive kin, and organizations like the National Urban League, which was emerging as an important resource for migrants in urban spaces.[41] Many migrants already had a temporary place to stay in the apartments or homes of people who had preceded them north, or, in the case of Houston, west.[42]

Frenchtown was quickly becoming a bustling and energetic community by the late 1920s. Residents were entrepreneurial and did not always rely on oil-related sectors for opportunities; they created rich spaces of community cohesiveness and support by the early 1930s that contributed significantly to the neighborhood's vitality. As a result, there were very few reasons Frenchtown residents had to travel outside the community: residents operated grocery stores, laundry services, and bakeries. Jerry Sanders owned a dry cleaner's on Brewster Street. Chevelier's grocery store was also on Brewster Street, and Angelina Duckless Landry and her husband, Raynard, operated a grocery store between Jewel and Delia. Jensen Drive was considered the hub of Frenchtown's business district; residents referred to it as "Downtown Jensen" for its centrality and the accessibility of everything from grocery to hardware stores.[43] Census records suggest that by 1930 Frenchtown had a population of roughly five hundred residents, making the ten-block-wide community densely populated. The fluctuating population rooted in migration and the cultural mingling of Louisiana and Texas identities gave the neighborhood a unique feeling. It is possible that population was larger, as not all residents may have been counted by census takers. Visitors frequently commented on how different the community felt from other neighborhoods in Houston, for reasons ranging from the smell of Louisiana home cooking and the sound of zydeco to the array of colors of people speaking a patois of French and English.[44]

The area where Frenchtown began to take shape was mostly uninhabitable marshland in the 1910s and 1920s, but early residents made use of the landscape through farming and buying small plots of land to build modest houses. Community residents developed a sense of cohesion not only through the ways in which they welcomed migrants from Louisiana but also in how they helped each other build houses. By the early 1920s, small well-built houses dotted the neighborhood. But it was the process of community building itself that was really important. Neighbors came together on weekends and after work to lend their specialized skills. One person might be well equipped to deal with physical dimensions, another with construction or maintenance; perhaps someone else might handle the sawing and shaping of lumber. Houses were simple yet sturdy; most were constructed out of boxcar lumber, scrap metal, and anything else residents could get their hands on.[45] They secured materials from a Southern Pacific rail yard located just outside of Frenchtown, assisted by friends and contacts outside the community. Between 1923 and 1934, Ben Stubberville, an African American man who lived with his family on the outskirts of Frenchtown, had a contract with the Southern Pacific to clear and discard scrap wood and metal from the junkyard. John Gordon, a longtime resident of Frenchtown and among its earliest settlers, recalled that Stubberville was perhaps initially hired by the Southern Pacific to recruit laborers in Louisiana for railway work in Houston following the 1927 flood, after which he was given a contract to sell lumber for his own profit. His ability and willingness to provide residents of Frenchtown with needed supplies at cheaper rates was critically important to the community's development. After Stubberville died in 1934, Mose Trahan, a Frenchtown resident, secured the contract and continued to provide boxcar lumber and scrap metal for the community into the 1930s and 1940s.[46]

The mixed ancestry of Creoles of color resulted in a full spectrum of skin complexions, ranging from those indistinguishable from white to others who were much darker. While some Creoles of color identified with the social and cultural experiences of African Americans in Louisiana and Houston, others chose instead to identify with the European lineage of their Creole ancestry. Many understood themselves as a distinct ethnic group of mixed ancestry that was neither black nor white, but uniquely Creole.[47] Nonetheless, the surge in population and increasing segregation of neighborhoods in Houston by the early twentieth century would essentially lump all "blacks" in the same areas. As one scholar has noted: "By the end of the nineteenth century the centers of black population were southwest of downtown in the Fourth Ward, especially along San Felipe Street, southeast of downtown in the Third Ward, and in the Fifth Ward, northeast of the business district. Although none of these areas were totally segregated, in the early twentieth century the largely black parts of the city were becoming increasingly black, and by the 1930s white families in these areas were rare."[48] Between 1920 and 1930 the black population of Houston increased from roughly 34,000 to 63,000, many having arrived from "rural areas in Texas and Louisiana . . . to attend high school or to get a job."[49] By 1930 Houston had a total population of approximately 293,000 residents. In comparison to other cities like Chicago or New York, Houston still maintained a small-town feel because of its low population density and ties to outlying areas in Texas and Louisiana that many residents retained.

The relationship between Creoles of color and African Americans in Texas was complicated, reflecting how blackness and whiteness was constructed in urban spaces throughout the country. There was no such thing as a monolithic "black community" in urban spaces anymore than there was a single-minded "white community"; group identities and class consciousness represented important markers of constructed difference on a number of physical and geographical levels. Migrants arriving in New York, Chicago,

Cleveland, Houston, and other cities experienced exclusion from native-born residents who viewed newcomers as taking jobs, opportunities, and housing they believed rightfully belonged to them. Migrants might also face discrimination on the basis of economic status, skin complexion, ethnicity, and religion. Not only were newcomers arriving from the South and border states, but in some places, including New York and Boston, waves of Caribbean immigrants complicated ideas of blackness. Historian Irma Watkins Owens suggests that similarities of complexion between African Americans and Caribbean immigrants sometimes provided only an illusion of communality in Harlem during the Great Migration. Misconceptions and unfamiliarity between African Americans and Caribbean immigrants did result in tension between the groups, though they were both struggling to survive in harsh urban landscapes.[50]

Questions of racial difference and preference also began to emerge in Houston by the 1920s and 1930s. Texas-born blacks found it much more difficult to secure some of the energy-sector jobs than blacks born in Louisiana, whom employers seemed to prefer. "Unlike most Texas African Americans who had been historically shut out of the skilled crafts," historian Bernadette Pruitt notes, "a significant number of Louisiana blacks worked as skilled craftsmen."[51] Not only did some industries prefer what they considered to be hardworking African Americans and Creoles of color who once worked among the harsh sugarcane of Louisiana, but resentment by blacks toward Creoles of color was also the result of the latter being able to obtain higher wages by employers who assumed they were white.

Creoles of color operated on a middle ground between the rigid black/white racial structure of Houston. While Mexican immigrants occasionally fell under the umbrella of whiteness when it suited political expediency, Creoles of color were never considered white if their Creole background was discovered. First-generation migrants into Frenchtown spoke a patois, mixing French and English, which was jarring to individuals hearing it for the first time. Second- and third-generation Frenchtown residents mostly spoke English and understood only certain sentences and words of Creole patois; this process resembled first- and second-wave generational differences among Caribbean and eastern European immigrants in the United States.[52] Sometimes older Frenchtown residents who didn't teach their children patois spoke French around adults when they didn't want children listening to their conversations. Victor and Agnes Prejean, on the other hand, taught their children to speak both English and the French patois, a process that contributed to how they were treated as children growing up in Houston. Mable and Inez attended segregated schools in Houston, including Crawford Elementary School near Jensen Drive and Wheatley High School. Not white enough to be accepted by white children outside their community and not black enough for black children, Mable and Inez found school a particularly harsh environment.[53]

But different speech patterns and appearance were not the only factors that made Creoles of color different. The overwhelming majority of Creoles of color in Louisiana practiced Catholicism, while most African Americans in Louisiana and Texas were either Baptist or African Methodist Episcopal. By 1930, out of a population of approximately eleven million African Americans in the country, only about two hundred thousand identified with the Catholic faith.[54] Religion was an important part of the Great Migration's origin; at the same time, denominational differences were powerful determiners of inclusion or exclusion in cities across the country. The migration movement itself was cast in religious terms by early leaders, and not unlike the Exodusters of the 1870s, leaders framed it in biblical terms as an exodus to the Promised Land. Through word of mouth and Robert Abbot's "Great Northern Drive" printed in the *Chicago Defender,* the Great Migration was understood by some migrants as a movement directed by the hand of God.[55]

Not only did individuals and families migrate, entire neighborhoods and institutions uprooted as well, a process Allan Ballard reminds us of when describing church members migrating from South Carolina to Philadelphia and reconstituting home churches in their new urban landscape, sometimes even keeping the same or similar name. Migrating church communities were easily recognizable through strong southern traditions, worship styles, and membership with deep roots in South Carolina. Once churches were established in Philadelphia, they not only served the spiritual and emotional needs of members but also continued to form a physical space of introduction into urban life for waves of successive migrants into the city.[56] But denominational differences and styles of worship were also among the many ways recently arrived migrants and native-born groups manufactured differences between themselves and others. New migrants into cities found they could face exclusion based on whether they were Baptist, Catholic, African Methodist Episcopal, Colored Methodist Episcopal, or Primitive Baptist.[57]

Religion was a defining feature of Creoles of color in Frenchtown. Whatever interactions they had with other groups during the week, when Sunday arrived they practiced Catholicism. The problem they encountered in Houston was the dearth of Catholic churches available for them to worship in. St. Nicholas Catholic Church, founded in 1903, was still the only black Catholic church in the city when the Prejeans and others began arriving, but it was four miles away. Some families took the local streetcar the distance every Sunday, while others walked both ways on mostly unpaved and muddy streets. Creoles of color were barred from most white Catholic churches because of their ethnicity and were segregated in Mexican Catholic churches. Although Our Lady of Guadalupe Catholic Church was within walking distance from Frenchtown on Navigation Drive, Creoles of color were relegated to the back pews during church services and took communion and confessed to priests on a segregated basis. They were essentially silent participants with no voting power within the church and had very little interaction with other parishioners outside the church.[58]

Victor and Agnes Prejean were among the migrants and longtime residents who supported the construction of a Catholic church in Frenchtown to serve the spiritual and other needs of the community. By late 1927 community residents were holding planning meetings; raising money by selling gumbo, boudain, and pralines; and holding zydeco dances. They also reached out to the Baltimore-based Josephite Priests, a branch of the Catholic Church that staffed and provided resources for churches throughout the country for additional funding.[59] Original plans were to build the church on Delia Street near the heart of Frenchtown, but when a piece of land was donated on nearby Sumpter Street it became the perfect place for the new church. Construction took place between April 1928 and June 1929, and community residents themselves took up the work of building the church, as they did their homes. On June 9, 1929, close to two hundred people were in attendance at the dedication ceremony and first mass at Our Mother of Mercy Catholic Church. The simple wooden structure was originally a mission of

St. Nicholas Catholic Church, but the next year Our Mother of Mercy was officially recognized as a parish of the Catholic Church.[60]

Not only did Our Mother of Mercy represent the legacy of Frenchtown, but it was also uniquely tied to the 1927 flood.[61] Our Mother of Mercy quickly became one of the backbones of Frenchtown as waves of migrants continued to come from Louisiana. Victor and Agnes Prejean were among the original founders and most vocal leaders during the church's early years, and in May 1931 two of their children, Inez and Olivia, were among the first class to take First Communion at Our Mother of Mercy. For the Prejeans and others the church provided more than spiritual guidance and resistance to the outside world of racism. A charter school was started in the early 1930s staffed by Sisters of the Holy Family, an order of African American nuns founded by Henriette Delille in New Orleans.[62]

Southern migrants were influenced by their introduction into their new urban landscapes, but they also infused their new surroundings with the culture and traditions of the "Old Country." Everything from traditional foodways to styles of worship bore the imprint of migrants. In Houston and other cities, working-class political activism was taking shape by the 1930s, largely through the efforts of southern migrants.[63] Black communities in Cleveland and Pittsburgh took on highly transparent political identities stemming from the migrants arriving from Alabama and Mississippi. Newcomers also developed social migration clubs in cities to strengthen ties to home places and make connections with each other in new environments. When migrants established North Carolina and South Carolina clubs in Washington, D.C., or the Monroe Social Club in Los Angeles, they served the purpose of fellowship as well as a place to formulate protest activities.[64] These clubs served as a fund-raising and social outreach arm for church activities, provided well-established networks for newly arriving migrants, and became a platform for migrants from the South to socialize and retain their unique southern culture.[65] The process was similar for Creoles of color migrating to Texas.[66] Cooking was an important part of this migration narrative: boudin (sausage casing stuffed with rice, pork, seasonings, and liver), a fish stew called coubeyonne, and various forms of shrimp gumbo all made their way from Louisiana to Texas. Migrants also introduced a breakfast dish called "cush cush" made from boiling and crumbled cornmeal mixed with a natural sweetener.[67]

Louisiana-based zydeco music, like the blues, also traveled from Louisiana to Texas. As recently as the 1950s and 1960s, the pronunciation and spelling of *zydeco* varied widely. Alternatively pronounced and spelled *zordico, zodico, zologo, zarico,* and *zottico,* the music was popularly referred to during the early years of migration to Houston as French *la las*. The transition from *la las* to the common pronunciation of the word *zydeco* is unclear. The word *zydeco* is thought to originate from the French *Les haricots sont pas salés,* a Creole of color folk expression meaning "the beans are not salted." There are many interpretations of this phrase, but usually it represents a commemoration of the hard times and struggle of farmers making a subsistence living on the land. The French pronunciation of *les haricots* is roughly translated into English as some form of "le zarico" or "lez arico." The *les* pronunciation takes on the sound of the letter *z* when integrated with the word *haricot,* where the *h* and *t* become silent.[68] *Zydeco* became the universal term for the music; for some, *la las* represents its Louisiana roots, while *zydeco* defines the more urbanized rhythm and blues experiences of Louisianians in Texas.[69] Whether called *la las* or *zydeco,* the music has strong roots in the American blues, incorporating Louisiana accordion and rubboard music with the rhythm and blues of Mississippi, Louisiana, and Texas. Zydeco is a fast-paced music rich with bilingual lyrics and complex rhythms; the variety of instruments, including the button or piano accordion, rubboard (called the *frottoir*), drums, bass, guitar, and violin, all form part of the musical texture that helps define the music's uniqueness. In many ways, Zydeco represents the pressures of migration.[70]

Zydeco and la las formed an important social and political outlet for Frenchtown residents beginning in the 1920s, taking on meaning as the soundtrack of important community events and social gatherings that connected migrants from Louisiana. The North and South Carolina clubs in other cities took the form of la las in Houston for Frenchtown migrants; people often visited friends and neighbors for socializing, dancing, eating, and listening to music. Thus, la las represented not only the music of Louisiana but an important act of community building in Houston. During the early years of Frenchtown most la las were held in someone's home, and though houses were small these events might bring out the entire community. Except on special occasions, la las were normally held on weekends, and local musicians and bands, many originally from Louisiana, often stopped by to play.[71]

By the 1950s, Frenchtown was also known for zydeco clubs, which attracted people from all over Houston. The clubs included the Continental on Des Chaumes Street, Matinee on Lyons Avenue, El Dorado, Whispering Pines, Creole Knights Social Club, and Paradise Club; all were located within two miles of Frenchtown.[72] Frenchtown had become the proving ground for zydeco musicians and bands in Houston; only after appearing at one of the la las or social clubs in the community would they be stamped as authentic. This was true for everyone, including Clifton Chenier, the undisputed king of zydeco and by far the most popular and influential of any zydeco musician.[73] Chenier represented to zydeco what Bessie Smith and Charley Patton were to the blues. Born in 1925 near Opelousas, Louisiana, by the 1940s and 1950s Chenier was known throughout the world and performed regularly in Frenchtown. Chenier modernized zydeco by infusing newer forms of instrumentation with blues and Louisiana washboards; during the height of his popularity in the 1950s and 1960s, he was performing not just in Louisiana and Texas but also overseas, taking the music that began in Louisiana as la las to ports around the globe.

In the midst of this cultural and physical migration, other seeds of change were being planted on the national level. In chapter 5 we shift our attention to the ways in which the 1927 flood set the stage for local and federal politics between 1928 and 1933. Because the flood had significantly shaken many people's belief that the configuration of flood control could adequately protect the Yazoo Delta plantation economy, southern politicians and engineers renewed their demands for a more comprehensive flood control plan. In 1928 Congress passed the newest Flood Control Act, which highlighted the need for upgrading levees. Under the jurisdiction of the United States Army Corps of Engineers and the War Department, the nation would undertake this important work, using mostly black laborers. The federal government funneled money into the region for levee construction, though the Corps of Engineers, like the Red Cross, stayed clear of local racial politics. The result was that local contractors and politicians seized control over federal resources and put into place a system of debt peonage that stripped black workers and families of livable wages.

5 Every Day Seems Like Murder Here

The Mississippi Flood Control Project in New Deal–Era America

> Images of what I had seen in Mississippi—the grim little river towns, rain-soaked levees, suspicious white faces, poverty-beaten Negroes—stayed fresh in my mind for a long time.
>
> —Roy Wilkins in his autobiography, *Standing Fast*

In early January 1933, Roy Wilkins and George Schuyler emerged in front of a packed house at the historic Abyssinian Baptist Church in New York City's Harlem. The NAACP was holding its annual celebration gala and the crowd waited in eager anticipation for what the two men had to say about their recent trip south, when they had posed as laborers investigating charges of debt peonage and violence in Mississippi Delta levee camps. A native Missourian, Roy Wilkins had been editor of the black-owned *Kansas City Call* newspaper before his appointment as assistant secretary of the NAACP in 1931.[1] George Schuyler was a New Yorker and known in black circles as a conservative poet and freelance writer. A month earlier, in December 1932, on the heels of a pending federal investigation of levee camps, the two men volunteered for the extremely dangerous mission. Schuyler was familiar with the South's social and cultural terrain but midwesterner Roy Wilkins had little experience with the region.[2] Wilkins later recalled in his autobiography, *Standing Fast,* that he had only been to the Deep South once in his life and was perhaps a bit naive about the risk he was taking. In the chapter "Up in Harlem, Down in the Delta," he recalled the danger of disclosing their identity even to black levee camp workers who might betray their trust. The entire task would prove more daunting for Wilkins, whose northern accent and upper-middle-class demeanor always threatened to blow his cover.[3]

After placing a tight lid on the project, Wilkins and Schuyler traveled from New York City to Memphis and the home of black millionaire Robert R. Church, who directed the men to Beale Street for work pants, boots, and bags for their mission; Wilkins and Schuyler wanted to transform their physical appearance and demeanor into that of southern laborers. With fifty dollars apiece and aliases for safety, Roy Wilkins changed his name to Roy Jones and Schuyler to George Smith. The two men then boarded the Yazoo and Mississippi Valley Railroad from Memphis en route to the Delta.[4] Reluctantly they decided to split up to cover more territory even though they were much safer together. Wilkins rode the train to Greenville, Mississippi, where he bid farewell to his partner, who traveled another ninety miles to Vicksburg. Both men were alone now, and as Wilkins would later recall, he felt like "a spy deep within enemy lines."[5]

Hoping to secure work, Wilkins found a vacancy at a local boarding house on the outskirts of a Greenville levee camp. It was an unusually cold and blustery December night in the Delta and the landlady who rented the room watched the suspicious stranger closely. It was hard to fool those black southerners who had seen so much, and he felt uncomfortable from the looks of curiosity. When he stuck his hands over a stove in the front room, the landlady noticed his smooth and uncalloused hands and made a point of commenting so the other men could hear that he didn't look like a workingman. Wilkins had to respond swiftly and assertively, explaining his hands and northern accent by telling the woman he had been an elevator operator in St. Louis before losing his job during the Depression.[6] Although his assertive response temporarily satisfied the landlady, he had to explain his behavior again the next morning. Temperatures had dipped below freezing overnight and in an unconscious act he naively asked the landlady where he could get some heat before work. She told him a bucket of coal could be purchased for twenty-five cents but immediately followed with the admonishment that the workingmen she knew didn't need such luxuries as heat in the morning. They simply got up, put on their work clothes or overalls without complaint, and went to work. Wilkins realized, "[My] greenness was showing through dangerously, and I warned myself to be more careful."[7]

Wilkins and Schuyler spent a total of three weeks undercover in several levee camps, gathering valuable information at boardinghouses, in informal gatherings, and after work when workers were more relaxed and willing to talk. Most men Wilkins encountered worked from six in the morning until six at night, many using levee work as supplemental labor to farming and sharecropping. The long hours, irregularity of pay, and an unfair commissary system were among the most common sources of frustration for workers.[8] In a levee camp near Lake Providence, Louisiana, Schuyler observed that men working twelve- to sixteen-hour days were obligated to pay commissary fees for the use of water and the food that cooks prepared. In Mississippi camps near Tallulah, Mounds Bayou, and Delta Point, as well as in Eyebrow, Deer Park, Duckport, and Waterproof in Arkansas, most black men received between one dollar and two dollars per day, about a dollar and a half less than what white workers, who were in the minority, were being paid. [9] From the perspective of Wilkins and Schuyler, it seemed very difficult for levee workers to get out of debt and make "livable wages" through a system specifically designed to push black workers to work as much as possible for as little pay as possible.

Soon after returning to New York, Wilkins published an article called "Mississippi River Slavery1933" in the NAACP's *Crisis* magazine; in it he highlighted much of what he witnessed in the South.[10] "While there is complaint from workers on all the forms of exploitation, the greatest wail is against the irregular pay day system," Wilkins wrote. "The men grumble over the small pay, long hours, cursing, beating, food, tents, commissary fleecing, but they reserve their greatest bitterness for the contractor who won't pay you even that little you got coming."[11] Pay periods were deliberately drawn out two or three months so workers could accumulate debt in the commissary system. "The longer the pay days are withheld, the more food and clothes the men buy at the camp Commissary at the high prices in vogue there. There is the money lending business which all foremen carry on at twenty five cents interest on the dollar. Then there are those other deductions: a lump sum, three or four dollars a week for commissary, whether one uses that amount or not; fifty cents for drinking water; fifty for the cook (single men pay this); fifty or seventy five cents tent rent."[12] Under this system laborers might work upward of three months and receive only a dollar or two for payment after deductions. To Wilkins the hypocrisy was how this system of peonage occurred "under the supervision of the U.S. Army Corps of Engineers, in mockery of the American flags that flew on staffs erected in the camps. It was a system of peonage organized by the federal government and paid for with American tax dollars."[13]

The colossal failure of levees during the 1927 flood led directly to public demands for a national flood control policy in the Mississippi Valley as well as plans for redesigning the Mississippi River.[14] Illinois representative Frank Reid chaired hearings before the House Committee on Flood Control for a new flood control plan. The hearings began in November 1927 and lasted until February 1928, with hundreds of experts presenting a broad array of critiques and plans for improving Mississippi River flood control and navigation. Chief among the issues debated was whether the "levees only" policy should be protected or disbanded. Some suggested a series of cutoffs, reservoirs, reforestation, alternate channels, and spillways, in addition to elevating and strengthening existing levees. In May, Congress quickly passed the Jones-Reid Bill, alternately known as the 1928 Flood Control Act. At the time it was passed some called it the "greatest piece of legislation ever enacted by Congress," with a price tag of approximately $325 million.[15]

Corps officials nicknamed it Project Flood, and although part of the plan included building levees higher and wider in the Lower Mississippi Valley, the most symbolic change was a shattering of the "levees only" policy that had previously ruled. Project Flood forever changed the idea of flood control in the Mississippi Valley by including a series of cutoffs, spillways, reservoirs, and floodways, all serving the purpose of lessening the impact of future floods. Priority over flood control and funding also shifted primarily from local ownership to the federal government, meaning that in the Yazoo Delta at least, local levee boards were no longer burdened with the task of levee construction and funding. The federal government now took on this burden, and as one scholar has suggested, it "set a precedent for the New Deal, by requiring the federal government to actively intervene in local and regional economic development."[16] The NAACP renamed this process of levee building by the federal government and Army Corps of Engineers the

Mississippi Flood Control Project (MFCP), symbolizing not only a long history of levee construction in the Yazoo Delta but also what this new federal presence in the region meant for black people's lives.[17]

The MFCP has largely been excluded from historical narratives of race and environmental history. Levee camps were microcosms of daily survival in the Yazoo Delta, a landscape where "everyday seems like murder." When bluesman Charley Patton sings this line in "Down the Dirt Road Blues," he is articulating the power of survival and wants to imply much more than the actual threat of death black people faced daily from lynching and murder. "Murder" is an evocation of the social limitations and constraints of social death that Richard Wright reminds us of through historical fiction: a lifetime spent struggling for citizenship and humanity in the midst of economic and physical oppression.[18]

As a reminder, the blues is more than simply an art form—it is also a medium of helping people both bear witness and cope emotionally and intellectually with the experiences of blackness in America. The importance of blues in representing black historical realities is clear in the way it provides valuable cultural perspectives otherwise unavailable to historians. Recorded-era blues of the 1920s and 1930s commented on events that were more universal to black experiences. Blues singers and novelists framed commentaries of the 1927 flood from accounts from survivors, black newspapers, and secondhand stories. These sources informed and created a deep sociology of knowledge around the disaster. The MFCP was another such moment for country blues singers.

Both survivors' and secondhand stories of violence and peonage circulated around the country, and the NAACP generated national interest by engaging in a letter-writing campaign to Congress, publishing articles in black newspapers, and bombarding members and nonmembers alike with information about debt peonage, all of which served to heighten black Americans' awareness of life inside levee camps. But as we witness from the 1927 flood, art also serves in part as the soundtrack of an event or movement. We could not fully understand, for example, how black people in Red Cross relief camps were forced at gunpoint to load sandbags on levees in 1927 without Lonnie Johnson's "Broken Levee Blues." Nor can we comprehend the double environmental burden of race without Richard Wright's blues voice and his descriptions of the ways black people suffered the pains of second-class citizenship at the moment of a destructive environmental event. Levee camp songs help explain to the world what many knew to be true and what others knew little about, in some cases foreshadowing and other times backing up the protests from levee camp workers themselves and the NAACP.

Our historical preoccupation with the political and engineering history of levees and debates at the turn of the twentieth century over "levees only" policies tells only half the story of flood control. Absent from this master narrative are the triangular struggles of power between the federal government, local levee contractors, and the thousands of black workers trying to squeeze out an existence inside federally funded levee camps by 1933. This chapter focuses on the ways in which the NAACP's commitment to ending the debt peonage described by Roy Wilkins and George Schuyler in the 1930s traces its roots back to the 1927 flood.[19] Flood control must therefore have a dual meaning revolving around not only the long-standing engineering debates by the Army Corps of Engineers but also the control of black bodies who built levees; the process itself transformed into an important contestation over civil rights between 1928 and 1933. As the Mississippi River and Yazoo Delta teetered on the brink of destruction from an environmentally harsh "levees only" policy during the 1927 flood and afterward, so too did black bodies whose labor was considered expendable in service to the nation and environment. Both black labor and the environment were pushed to the verge of destruction; both land and people were left vulnerable by policies whose goal was to extract as much as possible from them while leaving nothing to fall back on.[20]

Two particularly insidious forms of subordination in the post–Civil War South included the debt peonage associated with sharecropping and the convict-lease system. Convict-labor systems "operated not merely as a corrupt and unjust penal system," labor historian Alex Lichtenstein suggests, but also as "a system of labor recruitment, control, and exploitation particularly suited to the political economy of a post-emancipation society."[21] Though convict-lease systems were officially abolished by 1908, work camps and debt peonage continued to exist during the twentieth century in almost every industry imaginable, including sharecropping, domestic servitude, highway building, railroad work, lumber and mill industries, and levee camps.[22]

In the years following the 1927 flood the condition of southern black laborers remained poor; the Roaring Twenties were not so roaring for African Americans, as depressed cotton prices and peonage kept most in abject poverty. As the 1920s turned into the Depression era, T. Arnold Hill of the National Urban League commented that at no time in the seventy years since the end of slavery had the "economic and social outlook seemed so discouraging" for African Americans.[23] By 1927 levee camps had developed well-deserved reputations for violence and the expendability of black labor. William Hemphill was a northern-born white levee inspector working in an isolated camp near Friars Point, Mississippi, in 1905. Framing his experiences as something of a sojourn by a foreigner into exotic and wild lands, he occasionally published articles in a northern newspaper on life inside a Yazoo Delta levee camp, explaining everything from the technical dimensions of levees to violence directed at black workers. Demonstrating his own bias and ideas of race, at one point he writes, "If one of the white foremen shoots a couple of niggers on the works, and it by no means is an unheard of or infrequent thing, the work is not stopped. They are buried at night and that's all there is to it."[24] The violence experienced by black levee workers was a microcosm of life under the ruling thumb of Jim Crow.

The struggle to earn a living wage and escape poverty was formidable for levee camp workers. Levee work was often a source of seasonal supplemental wages rather than a primary source of income. For example, black farmers and sharecroppers would use intervals between planting and harvesting to work in other industries. Planting season normally lasted from mid-January to late May of each year, while harvest season extended from August to the end of December.[25] For two or three months many black sharecroppers hoped to provide additional income for their families through seasonal levee work, a reality recognized by Roy Wilkins when he visited the Yazoo Delta. "Poverty kept these country black people in a state of abject peonage," he observed. "The shortage of cash drove them to work on the levees in the off season between planting and harvest."[26] As historian William Jones reminds us, levee camps were not alone in drawing black farmers away from fields in the hope of securing additional wages. A similar process occurred when black farmers entered the lumber industry in Louisiana, North Carolina, and Mississippi.[27]

Black levee camp workers were likely to be defined as pathological and criminal rather than wage earners struggling to secure livable wages. Sociologist Howard Odum, who coined the term "Black Ulysses" in the 1920s, codified popular imaginations and myths of work camps as spaces of a contemptuous black pathology rooted in a culture of wandering laborers.[28] Odum typified contemporary academic notions of scientific racism, arguing that black workers were inherently oversexualized, violent, and morally bankrupt wanderers across the southern landscape who maintained little or no connection to family.[29] Scholars have rightly refuted Odum's characterizations of black laborers and work camps by arguing that they were in fact not "wanderers," but local men who, like the workers described by Roy Wilkins, strategically worked in such industries to supplement their incomes and help support their families. Supposed characteristics of pathological African American working-class culture were also commercialized through "race records" in the 1930s.[30] William Jones describes the personal bias exhibited by folklorists John and Alan Lomax during their meeting and recording of bluesman Huddie Ledbetter. Clearly they held certain ideas of the "natural" pathology of African American men and what was "authentic" for their audiences. "Ledbetter preferred to perform in a suit and bow tie," Jones notes, "but the Lomaxes convinced him to don overalls and a bandanna that more closely fit their image of a rural worker . . . underscoring Odum's contention that African American manhood was personified by the southern working-class outlaw."[31]

The task of describing daily life inside levee camps under the MFCP is difficult for many reasons. Records detailing the experiences of African American levee camp workers are scattered and uneven, and workers themselves left few footprints. The few recorded interviews of levee workers in the 1920s and 1930s and investigative reports produced by the American Federation of Labor in December 1931, along with two reports by the NAACP within a three-month span in late 1932, provide only glimpses into the experiences of levee camp workers.[32] Country blues singers of the 1930s also provided an important explanatory framework for understanding African American survival inside the camps.

Robert Brown was born on July 15, 1910, in Walnut Ridge, Arkansas. Following the path laid by other Mississippi and Arkansas blues singers who migrated to Chicago and other urban recording centers, by 1932 he was recording with Blue Bird Records under the pseudonym Washboard Sam. He recorded "Levee Camp Moan" in 1941 or 1942, giving voice to the recent battle over wages on the MFCP and long history of levee construction. "I worked in a levee camp just about a month ago. We slept just like dogs eat beans both night and day; but I never did know just when we were due our pay. They had two shifts on day and the same two shifts at night."[33] The uncertainty of pay was the blues hook, or "life crisis" of black identity for levee workers.

Levee camp workers arose early for work, usually around three in the morning, preparing for the day's hard labor. Some might immediately harness and feed mules, which would work alongside them, while others repaired broken wheelbarrows and carts used to carry materials. Most worked from the dark of morning until the dark of night, pulling twelve-hour shifts with few breaks.[34] By 1933 the MFCP maintained a workforce of between twenty-five thousand and thirty-thousand workers in the Yazoo Delta alone; the overwhelming majority were African American men.[35] The federal government had decided on a system of awarding contracts for levee construction in the region to local businessmen or planters—many of whom used the levee contracts as supplemental to their own primary source of accumulating wealth—with the anticipation of stimulating the local economy. For example, John L. McWilliams contracted a government camp near New Orleans. B. H. Flynn operated a camp near Alexandria, Louisiana. J. W. Noble maintained a camp near Natchez, Mississippi. Levee construction companies and corporations also found a niche in the federal government's long-term commitment to levee construction. The company of Morrow and Harris operated camps near Yazoo City, while the Memphis-based Southern Pine and Land Company operated camps in both Tennessee and Mississippi.[36] Some camp operators were so notoriously violent that workers avoided them at all costs. R. T. Clark in Natchez, Mississippi, was known as the "Terror of the River" because of how murderous and violent foremen were toward black workers. The Lowrence brothers operated several camps in Arkansas and Mississippi in the 1920s and were widely considered to be among the most violent and oppressive operators to work for. The experience of working for the Lowrence brothers was best summed up by a black levee worker who explained in an interview that he would work for the Lowrence brothers when he was dead.[37]

Camp operators were responsible for a specific stretch of levee within a levee district, and depending on the levee district's size there might be numerous operators working side by side. For example, the Memphis levee district alone maintained more than seventy contractors while the Vicksburg district had close to fifty. The size of levee camps also varied significantly, ranging from fifteen-worker outfits to larger camps with a workforce of more than two hundred. There were both residential and nonresidential camps, depending on location and the desire of camp operators. Camps in more isolated areas were more likely to be residential, particularly if dense swamp and marshlands made access difficult.[38] Dangerously overcrowded residential housing largely came in the form of semipermanent tents resembling miniature cities in the swamp. The structures lacked adequate ventilation, screens, floors, and sometimes windows; there was little concern for the transmission of disease in camp housing by camp operators or local public health officials. Tents were so poorly constructed that one levee camp worker described the process of having to dig ditches and throw dirt against the structures to keep from being flooded when it rained, the process itself forming cisterns of water that might become breeding grounds for mosquitoes carrying malaria and yellow fever.[39] Camps operating closer to populated areas like the one Roy Wilkins visited might be nonresidential, meaning workers either lived at home and traveled to the work camp on a daily basis or found temporary lodging at boarding houses.

Levee building was especially backbreaking and dangerous work in the decades before the 1940s and the widespread use of caterpillar tractors. The building and extension of levees entailed clearing thick canebrakes, swamps, and forested lansdscapes, as well as digging and hauling large amounts of dirt. Levee engineering varied from place to place but typically included a batture, barrow pit, berm, crown, and banquette.[40] A batture is a mile of forested landscape situated between the river and levee, ideally forming a first line of defense against the encroachment of flood waters. The barrow (or borrow) pit is a place from which workers remove large amounts of dirt for the actual lifting (meaning elevating) of levees. Barrow pits might be fifteen or sixteen feet deep, spanning an area three hundred feet wide while gradually sloping up to level ground, serving the dual purpose of providing materials for the construction of levees and a second line of defense as floodwaters would have to fill the barrow pit before reaching the levee.[41] The barrow pit was the site of a yeoman's effort where teams of workers hauled thousands of cubic feet of dirt per day from pit to levee. Workers on the front end called "lumpers" filled mule-drawn carts with dirt, tree roots, pulled stumps, and other debris accumulated in the process of clearing land. "Drivers" navigated mule-drawn carts with loaded materials to the levee where "dumpers" unloaded the debris onto the levee specifically to elevate its grade, sometimes navigating dangerously narrow planks of wood with wheelbarrows fifteen feet high.[42] The berm is a stretch of level ground on the levee and might be thirty to forty feet wide. Depending on a community's tax base, some levees might also be topped with a crown six to eight feet wide, and a final buttress called a banquette. Raising levees took considerable time since materials had to settle for long periods. Workers might elevate a levee three or four feet before moving to another stretch, allowing this initial stretch to coalesce for months before returning to begin the process of elevation again.[43] There are few images of levee workers on the MFCP in the photographic archive. Figures 8 and 9, showing wheelbarrow work during the 1927 flood, give us a brief glimpse into the dangerous nature of working on levees. Wheelbarrows filled with dirt became heavier for workers as the day wore on, exacerbated by having to walk those high and narrow planks of wood.

Machinery used in levee building, including caterpillar tractors, scrapers, and stump pullers, was dangerous, and it is likely that accidents occurred at a much higher rate than the historical record reveals. There are only scarce references in the historical literature of camp workers suffering injury from stump pullers or other machinery. One worker named Johnny Young suffered a broken arm while using a stump puller in the Sternberg levee camp. After the injury he reportedly received only six dollars after working for fifteen days at the rate of one dollar and twenty-five cents per day for a twelve-hour day. Garland Maxwell, another worker in the Sternberg camp, reportedly received no compensation for wages earned after injuring his foot using drilling equipment.[44] While workplace accidents and injuries have historically led to changes in the law and increased public awareness of working-class identity,

FIGURE 8. Black men in Arkansas carting loads of dirt to fortify the levee during the flood. Photograph by the Illinois Central Railroad, May 16, 1927. Courtesy of the National Archives and Records Administration.

FIGURE 9. Workers shown from behind in a typical environment in which they were forced to labor. Photograph by the Illinois Central Railroad, May 16, 1927. Courtesy of the National Archives and Records Administration.

levee camp workers had little recourse.[45] Racism largely excluded black workers from the more skilled and better-paying jobs that included dragline operators, machinists, spotters, mechanics, and drivers, positions that paid from five to eight dollars per day. Black workers, on the other hand, were trapped in the mundane drudge work of levee building. They might spend upward of twelve hours per day bending over a shovel, lifting dirt and placing such strain on their backs that by the end of a shift many could barely stand up.

The harsh nature of levee work was exacerbated by the common practice of debt peonage on the MFCP. Gene Campbell, who most likely was born in East Texas (the exact place and date are unknown), was a country blues singer representing the Texas blues tradition, which included Blind Lemon Jefferson and Texas Alexander. His 1930 "Levee Camp Man Blues" emphasizes the withholding of wages that Washboard Sam also talks about, but unlike most blues songs describing levee camps Campbell places a specific focus on the commissary system. It represents one of the few songs in the blues repertoire on levee camps that explicitly talks about the commissary and what it meant for black workers. "These contractors are getting so slack; they pay you half of your money and hold the other half back. A levee camp man ain't got but two legs you know; but he puts in the same hours that a mule do on four."[46]

Workers derisively nicknamed the camp stores that exploited laborers "robissaries." As Wilkins and Schuyler explained, workers paid commissary fees or incurred credit for numerous items and services, including food, sleeping cots, blankets, water, and ice.[47] Some camps required workers to pay for living quarters and the dining hall even if they didn't live in the camp, while others deducted commissary fees of three to five dollars even if workers never used the store. In ways that closely resembled the lien practices of sharecropping, commissaries offered what were called "drags," or extensions of credit automatically deducted from wages but difficult for workers to manage.[48] Contractors could charge workers whatever they wanted for commissary items and miscellaneous products, knowing that every cent lost by black laborers was profit for them. In the more isolated camps workers might have little choice but to use the commissary and be exposed to the price gouging that often occurred. At the Powers Construction Camp near Lake Village, Arkansas, a twelve-pound sack of flour that cost sixty cents in the commissary was thirty cents in local stores. A fifteen-cent pound of salt pork cost no more than six cents at surrounding stores. Condensed milk was twenty cents in the commissary, well over the eight cents people outside the camp were paying.[49] The NAACP argued that such unscrupulous practices were widespread on the MFCP and put black levee camp workers in a morass of wage labor and exploitation.

Herbert Hoover rode his popularity as "relief manager" during the 1927 flood to a victory over Democrat Alfred Smith in the 1928 presidential election, though he remained unpopular among African Americans.[50] When the stock market crash of 1929 sent the country into the Great Depression, Hoover's popularity plummeted among most Americans, setting the stage for the ascendance of Franklin Delano Roosevelt of New York to the White House in 1932.[51] Roosevelt was given the difficult task of bringing the country out of the depression and making a "New Deal" for America. Still, historians have long suggested the New Deal was perhaps a "raw deal" or "no deal" for African Americans as early as the First Hundred Days, a "halfway revolution," in the words of William Leuchtenberg.[52] The NAACP did not firmly commit to exposing MFCP debt peonage until late 1932, at a time when Hoover's presidency was clearly vulnerable and months before the New Deal was put into place. When the federal government began putting mechanisms of the New Deal into place, the NAACP was already positioned to demand changes on behalf of black levee camp workers.

The 1927 flood provided an important continuum for the ways in which the NAACP demanded that the federal government protect African Americans. As word spread of mistreatment in Red Cross relief camps, the NAACP immediately pushed for Herbert Hoover, then secretary of commerce, and President Calvin Coolidge to take the lead and provide protection for displaced black flood survivors. Word of mistreatment in Red Cross camps was most unwelcome news for Herbert Hoover, who was looking to capitalize on his new status as relief manager during the flood. Complaints from the NAACP and black newspapers were becoming a nuisance. Due in no small measure to the NAACP, Hoover reluctantly agreed to authorize a special civilian commission in late May 1927 to look into the allegations of mistreatment and peonage inside Red Cross relief camps.

Almost immediately, the NAACP questioned the appointment of a civilian rather than federal committee. Most within the organization took the civilian committee as a smoke screen to pacify the most vocal black voices regarding Red Cross camps. Who would head the civilian committee and constitute its members? Would they have the necessary protection to conduct the investigation and be unyielding in vocalizing what they found? What authority would a civilian committee have to bring significant changes if not backed by the threat of federal legislation or power? These were the most pressing questions the NAACP presented to Herbert Hoover regarding a civilian committee. For the NAACP, their fears were realized when Hoover announced the appointment of Robert Russa Moton to head what was called the "Colored Advisory Commission." A disciple of Booker T. Washington, Moton had taken over as head of the Tuskegee Institute after Washington's death in 1915. Hoover was very familiar with Moton and Tuskegee through past endowment campaigns by the school. Like Washington before him, Moton's conservative approach to race relations made him more agreeable to many whites. Moton was given authority to choose the sixteen-member commission: those named included J. S. Clark, president of Southern University in Louisiana, Claude Barnett of the Associated Negro Press, L. M. McCoy, president of Rust College in Mississippi, Eugene Kinckle Jones of the National Urban League, the YMCA's Eva Bowles, Albon Holsey, National Business League secretary, and three members of Moton's staff at Tuskegee. While the political and racial sensibilities of the committee varied from person to person, it was telling that Moton did not choose a single committee-member with ties to Washington's rival NAACP, a point that infuriated W. E. B. Du Bois, Ida B. Wells, Walter White, and others.[53]

The "Colored Advisory Commission" released two reports on conditions of peonage inside Red Cross relief camps, the first submitted to Herbert Hoover and James Fieser of the Red Cross on June 14, 1927. The sixteen commission members broke into small groups and visited Red Cross camps for ten days, mostly in the Yazoo Delta. Logistically, the investigation was difficult because rarely were committee members allowed to talk to black survivors without local white supervision, necessarily calling into question the ability of survivors to be completely truthful about their experiences without fear of white violence.[54] Although commission findings suggested that many camps were public health threats and African Americans were subjugated to daily forms of brutality—including forced labor, restriction of movement, and the rape of black women by National Guardsmen—the first submitted report provided little criticism of Herbert Hoover or the Red Cross. As expected by the NAACP, the first report brought about little in the form of change.

The second report, submitted in early July, was more candid on unsanitary conditions, brutality at the hands of National Guardsmen, and the slavery-like conditions of some camps, but like the first report was also largely swept under the rug by the Red Cross. The second report also reported that some black survivors preferred residing in swamps, woods, abandoned buildings, and living with neighbors (and strangers) rather than subjecting themselves to Red Cross relief camps.[55]

Criticisms of the civilian commission came immediately. Ella R. Hutson, president of the San Diego branch of the Negro Women's Council, wrote letters to both Herbert Hoover and James Feiser about relief camps. "I note in the request of the Race Welfare Committee and the Baptist Minister's Alliance that the government make an investigation of the inhuman treatment of the men, women and children of the Negro race. . . . I further note that in compliance with that request a Negro committee has been appointed. Now do you mean that they are to be considered part of the Federal Government, and if you do not mean that, then by appointing these Negro men, you meant to pass the buck to them and relieve the responsibility from the white man's shoulders."[56] Hutson is making a not-so-subtle distinction of power between a civilian and federal committee, along with pointing out the proper responsibility of the federal government to protect the lives of African Americans. "I can see no other reason," she later writes, "why you should not have carried out the request made of you, unless you were afraid of incurring the disfavor of the Mississippi and Arkansas hoodlums and making yourself unpopular with those blood thirsty savages. Well does every thinking man and woman know that a Negro committee appointed in the South has its hands tied and cannot make an investigation and ascertain the real facts of all the unfairness as practiced by the Red Cross there in the South and the outrageous treatment of Negroes in those southern localities, as the Federal Government could through you, if you were not afraid of criticism from the uncivilized South."[57]

W. E. B. Du Bois uses equally assertive language when writing in the NAACP's *Crisis* magazine that "we have grave suspicions that the colored committee recently appointed by Mr. Hoover to investigate flood conditions and peonage in the Mississippi Valley will be sorely tempted to whitewash the whole situation, to pat Mr. Hoover loudly on the back, and to make no real effort to investigate the desperate and evil conditions of that section of our country. Slavery still exists in the Mississippi Valley and this Committee knows it." Du Bois went on to say that not standing up for black people at this important moment of advancement would be unforgivable.[58] He saw in this moment not only the possibility of correcting injustices after an environmental disaster but also an opportunity to bring the particular experiences of black flood sufferers in the Yazoo Delta into a much broader discourse on race. For Du Bois the 1927 flood was a snapshot of the discrimination and racism African Americans throughout the United States faced and a defining moment of race and citizenship on a national level.

The impotence of the 1927 civilian committee would weigh heavily on the minds of NAACP officials as they insisted the federal government investigate the treatment of black laborers on the MFCP in the summer of 1932. President Herbert Hoover responded to the NAACP in much the same way he had five years earlier as secretary of commerce, by putting distance between African Americans and the federal government. For the second time, Hoover appointed a civilian committee headed by Robert Moton in October 1932, this time to investigate levee camps under federal jurisdiction.[59] NAACP leaders were dismayed at this second civilian committee, defining the president's action as yet another example of his refusal to take the experiences of black people seriously enough to mobilize the federal government. Civilian committees could serve an important function in society, but NAACP leaders rightly believed that only the federal government had the power to prevent further abuses of black flood survivors and laborers on the MFCP. Remembering the failure of the 1927 civilian committee to bring significant changes, it came as little surprise, and perhaps even something of a relief, that the second Moton-led civilian committee never materialized.[60]

The 1927 flood also foreshadowed a delicate balance between race and federalism.[61] Politicians and planters in the Yazoo Delta were far from a self-contained society resistant to outside or federal assistance. Southern politicians and planters were not necessarily opposed to outside resources, as long as they maintained control over how those resources were being used.[62] There is little difference, for example, between how local planters controlled Red Cross resources during the 1927 flood and how slowly money trickled down to black farmers and laborers under New Deal alphabet programs, including the Agricultural Adjustment Act, the Works Project Administration, the National Recovery Administration, and the Federal Emergency Relief Administration.

The NAACP focused much of its attention on what it considered to be inherent hypocrisy within the MFCP contractor system, including the widespread practices of withholding wages and supporting exploitative commissaries. The MFCP was funded by the federal government under the jurisdiction of the United States Department of War, an argument the NAACP used for demanding the protection of black workers. NAACP leaders made the case that since levees were built with federal dollars, the federal government had a responsibility to protect those performing work in service to the entire nation. Part of the 1928 Flood Control Act's intent was that a well-designed system of flood control would benefit everyone in the country. While the local contractor system might not have been inherently flawed, it nonetheless stimulated seeds of exploitation and mistreatment because of its reliance on localism. From the federal government's perspective, the local contractor system encouraged local entrepreneurship by giving local interests a stake in levee construction. But the system was tilted in favor of contractors and not workers in ways that resulted in a vastly decentralized and unequal distribution of resources. Local contractors were largely responsible for their own stretch of levee construction and were free to conduct daily operations according to their own rules. Corps engineers were primarily interested in maintaining technical specifications of levee construction, rarely concerning themselves with questions of racial justice.

Roy Wilkins wanted to address the lack of clarity about whose responsibility it was to protect black workers against mistreatment. For their part, corps engineers maintained their own racial ideas of black inferiority, expressed in full when pressed by the NAACP to take a stronger stance on ending exploitation in levee camps.[63] Charles G. Holle, first lieutenant for the Corps of Engineers, submitted a report to the Mississippi River Commission in early 1933 arguing black inferiority as the basis for mistreatment. The report described

African American workers as mentally undeveloped and childlike.[64] The long intervals between pay periods and the withholding of wages were argued away as normal and necessary for the welfare of black workers who could not be trusted to take care of themselves without white supervision. If paid on a regular basis, Holle argued, workers would lose all their money gambling and in other frivolous pursuits. With strong undertones of paternalism, the corps defended the withholding of wages as in the best interests of black workers.[65] Holle's report admitted that an epidemic of overcharging in commissaries was common throughout the MFCP, but again provided justification by placing blame on the genetic deficiency of workers. It was inevitable, Holle reported, that largely uneducated and illiterate workers would be overcharged. The report concluded with the recommendation that making inquiries into overcharging was a waste of time.[66]

For many white southerners, the intent of divorcing black levee camp workers from wages needed little explanation. For Holle and others, the zeitgeist provided protection and justification for the corps' inaction. Though it has been at the forefront of the country's most important and far-reaching land and water construction projects, the Army Corps of Engineers has had very little to say about issues of race, class, and labor. Like the American Red Cross, throughout its history the corps has maintained a decidedly neutral stance on the race question, not wanting to insert itself into "local customs" of the South. Historical accounts of the corps also disclose little about the racial dynamics of construction projects, focusing primarily on the technical, political, and land impact of this work. But in the 1930s, the NAACP enjoined the corps to consider race and labor, forcing it to acknowledge ties to the federal government and the responsibility it had to protect not only citizens from environmental dangers but also citizen laborers who worked on the unrewarding, sometimes dangerous projects under its command. The NAACP's role in pushing the Army Corps of Engineers to take some responsibility for the violence and discrimination occurring under its watch is a requiem of the importance for making visible long-standing narratives of race and environmentalism in the historical record.

Roy Wilkins and Walter White faced the quandary of how best to confront the problematic contract system, and particularly whether dealing with an uninterested Army Corps of Engineers was better than dealing with local contractors like the Lowrence brothers or R. T. Clark. The corps, because of its connection to the federal government, was clearly the lesser of two evils. Early on, Wilkins and White pushed for an end to the local contractor system and for levee construction to fall completely under the Army Corps of Engineers. This might seem contradictory to what Roy Wilkins says in his autobiography, in which he forthrightly criticizes the debt peonage that occurred under corps leadership.[67] The important point for Wilkins and the NAACP, however, was the corps' connection to the federal government, meaning it represented an entity that was supposed to protect the rights of all citizens. Wilkins and White considered that ending injustices through mechanisms of the federal government would prove more practical and realistic than trying to address debt peonage solely through a southern political culture resistant to changes in race relations. Ultimately, the MFCP was never transferred to the Corps of Engineers, but the NAACP held fast to its commitment of using the federal government as a vehicle for change in New Deal America.

Coming of the New Deal

Building on experiences developed through the 1927 flood a half decade before, NAACP leaders attacked the contractor system by pushing for a federal investigation and hearing on debt peonage. By the fall of 1932, the NAACP had demanded attention from the War Department. On August 22, the NAACP sent a copy of an undercover report conducted the previous summer by a member named Helen Boardman, to Herbert Hoover, Secretary of War Andrew Hurley, Attorney General William DeWitt Mitchell, and to twenty-five United States senators; the report was accompanied by an explicit request to correct the conditions in federal levee camps. Boardman's report preceded the follow-up investigation by Wilkins and Schuyler by a few months.[68] A graduate of Grinnell College in 1913 and the New York School of Social Work in 1914, Boardman held positions at the Psychological Research Worker Bureau of Educational Experiments, the Michigan Children's Aid Society, and the Institute of Social and Religious Research. She also maintained ties to the American Red Cross, working in disaster relief after a 1925 tornado near Murphysboro, Illinois, a South Florida hurricane in 1926, and the 1927 flood. Boardman also worked for the NAACP, investigating the lynching of a Little Rock, Arkansas, man in 1927, and peonage conditions of black southerners during the 1927 flood.[69] Although still dangerous if found out she worked for the NAACP, as a white woman Boardman could move freely in the Yazoo Delta region, gathering information with little fear of loitering laws. Her credentials with the American Red Cross sometimes put local whites at ease in her presence.

The NAACP often relied on undercover investigations, sometimes conducted by white members of the organization. The fair-skinned assistant secretary Walter White occasionally went undercover himself, passing as a white man. According to historian David Levering Lewis, "Because Walter White looked so white, his services to the NAACP were invaluable, but they also placed him in situations of awful danger. Aboard a train leaving a Deep South lynching bee, the assistant secretary was once challenged by a suspicious white passenger who boasted that he could always spot a 'yaller nigger' by the absence of half moons on the fingernails. White's half moons saved him."[70] In the fall of 1919, the same year as the Chicago Race Riot, sharecroppers in Phillips County, Arkansas, had the "gall to hire a maverick white Arkansas lawyer to help organize and incorporate a farmer's protective association in order to compel landlords to open their books on prices and profits of supplies and cotton revenues," Lewis writes. "The normal practice in that part of Arkansas, Du Bois explained to the [New York] *World's* readers, was for a farmer to sell to the planter and wait a full year to be told 'how much his crop was worth, and what is the balance due' for the supplies bought on credit from the company store. It was slavery by another name, but to dispute such an arrangement was 'in Arkansas custom, to dispute white supremacy.'"[71] During a remarkable seven-day stint of violence, close to two hundred people were killed, including five whites. Over a thousand black men were rounded up and arrested in Phillips County, some quickly sentenced to death by November in a southern kangaroo court and others sentenced to upward of twenty-five years in jail. Walter White's undercover work as a white reporter in Phillips County and subsequent publishing of his account in *The Nation* provided a firsthand glimpse of the "surreal barbarity" against black sharecroppers in what would become known as *Moore v. Dempsey* (1923), the Supreme Court decision freeing six of twelve black sharecroppers sentenced to death (the other six were later freed) for their role in Phillips County.[72] Like so many others in his position, White's ability to pass as white could bring him face to face with extreme racial violence, but could just as easily result in his own harrowing escape from the same barbarity that he was investigating.

Boardman traveled from New York to the Yazoo Delta in August 1932 with the intention of investigating camps from New Orleans to Memphis. Because of previous attempts to investigate levee camp conditions, most notably by the American Federation of Labor in 1931, Boardman, like Roy Wilkins and George Schuyler, sometimes encountered a dense wall of silence from blacks and whites. Nonetheless she was able to interview ex-levee camp workers, editors, organized labor representatives, and welfare workers, as well as interview and personally observe twenty-two levee camps. Boardman interviewed black and white levee camp workers, white contractors and foremen, and other people with inside knowledge of the camps. "Friends" of the NAACP were also placed undercover in some of the camps to corroborate information. These men were mostly, but not always, black. The NAACP wanted to paint as clear a picture as possible of worker conditions on the MFCP.[73]

Hoover deferred the report to the War Department and the office of Major General Lytle Brown, who immediately responded in an antagonistic tone, describing the low (or no) wages the government was paying as "customary" in the region.[74] Following a harshly worded response from Walter White citing Brown's contempt, Secretary of War Hurley wrote White directly: "I regret that General Brown did not assure you a thorough, unbiased and fair investigation of your complaints, I will do so now."[75]

This was just the beginning of a cat-and-mouse game between the NAACP and the War Department. Lytle Brown wrote to White asking him to furnish the name and address of his investigator to make arrangements for an inquiry session conducted by the War Department. White refused the request, thinking it imprudent to disclose the identity of the investigator until the hearing. Brown contacted White again, informing him that a hearing would take place in Vicksburg, Mississippi, presided over by the president of the Mississippi River Commission. Brown states contemptuously in his letter, "Should you desire the testimony of your investigator to be taken, I will transmit his name and address, with the desire, to the President [of the] Mississippi River Commission, and he will make all arrangements for the testimony. If you do not desire that the testimony of your investigator be taken, or if you are indifferent in the matter, kindly consider my request for the necessary information as cancelled."[76] Brown's letter assumes the investigator was male, and probably black, but the larger concern for the NAACP was location. Walter White and Roy Wilkins were adamant that the hearing take place in Washington, D.C., or New York City. Vicksburg or any other place south of the Mason-Dixon line was far too dangerous for the NAACP.[77]

After a brief back and forth, the War Department reluctantly agreed to hold an initial hearing in Washington on September 22, 1932, at the Office of Chief Engineers in the Munitions Building led by Assistant Chief of Engineers George B. Pillsbury. The press was not allowed in the hearing—a stunt the NAACP countered by having a prepared statement ready to distribute to reporters waiting in the wings. There were only five people present at the hearing that morning: Walter White, Helen Boardman, George Pillsbury, an unknown Army captain, and a stenographer.[78] The inquiry session was a contentious affair as Pillsbury immediately seized on the NAACP strategy of omitting names and some background information to protect workers, suggesting the report was general and lacked specificity.[79] At one point Pillsbury asked why laborers not receiving money owed to them did not seek recourse in the law, blatantly ignoring what levee camp workers and most other African Americans already knew to be true: as second-class citizens there was little recourse for them in the law.[80]

By late September the NAACP had persuaded New York Senator Robert F. Wagner to introduce a resolution in the 72nd Congress calling for a senatorial investigation of levee camps backed by the president; the NAACP preferred this to the earlier prospect of a civilian committee appointed by Hoover. Wagner, who represented New York State in the Senate from 1927 to 1949, was best known for his support of Social Security legislation and labor. The National Labor Relations Act of 1935, also known as the Wagner Act, restated the right of workers to collective bargaining, and through the newly created National Labor Relations Board, strengthened workers' ability to organize independent unions through certified elections.[81] Determined not to let the treatment of levee workers be swept under the rug, the NAACP mobilized local branches in a massive letter-writing campaign to senators supporting the Wagner resolution. In particular, they concentrated heavily on "no reply" senators or those straddling the fence in their support of Wagner. The NAACP also enlisted the support of African American newspaper editors, civic organizations, and church leaders throughout the country, impressing on them the importance of the fight. Walter White personally asked newspaper editors to write articles detailing the MFCP and to urge readers themselves to write letters to their senators.

From Los Angeles to Kansas City, local NAACP chapters held rallies in branch offices and churches to raise both awareness and money so the organization could continue fighting for levee workers.[82] The NAACP compared the nationwide battle at hand, including the mobilization of local branches and letter-writing campaign, to the recent blocking of John J. Parker to the Supreme Court in 1930. After Herbert Hoover nominated Parker for the Supreme Court on March 21, 1930, the NAACP (and American Federation of Labor) lobbied fiercely against the appointment of the North Carolina judge, citing racist statements he made while running for governor of North Carolina in 1920. Black political enfranchisement, the judge noted at the time, was "a source of evil and danger to both races."[83] As historian David Levering Lewis describes the moment, "NAACP branches were mobilized and mass meetings held across the country with greater resolve than at any time since the Birth of a Nation campaign."[84] The battle to defeat Parker lasted six weeks and marked the first rejection of a nominee to the Supreme Court in thirty years.[85]

As the administrations changed and the First Hundred Days of the New Deal got under way, the NAACP began to focus on what it believed was the limited way in which levee work was defined. Levee work was largely nonunion labor and, in the lexicon of the federal government, long defined as "emergency," somehow making it different from other civil engineering projects. "River work," as it was sometimes called, differed from the construction of buildings, bridges, and tunnels because of this emergency tag.[86] In light of unionized efforts in other industries restricting workers to eight-hour days and the "prevailing rate of wages" on government contracts, the NAACP pushed for inclusion of the MFCP with other civil engineering projects.[87] Roy St. Lewis, assistant attorney general for the Department of Justice, responded to NAACP charges of eight-hour-law violations by arguing that those limitations did not apply to persons engaged in the construction or repair of levees. F. L. Payne of the War Department made a similar argument regarding "prevailing rate of wages," suggesting "the law enacted by Congress providing for the payment of prevailing rates of wages by contractors under contracts with the Federal Government is specifically limited, under its terms, to contracts for the construction of buildings. The law is not applicable to the construction of levees, revetments and other work generally included in the flood control project."[88] Prevailing rate of wages was part of the controversial Davis-Bacon Act passed by Congress in 1931; it required contractors receiving money from the federal government to pay workers on a scale customary in the region. The exclusion of nonunionized and black laborers from the parameters of the act reflected the discriminatory intent to pay those groups even less than what was customary in the region.[89]

The NAACP went so far as to take the issue of "prevailing rate of wage" up with experts in the House of Representatives Committee on Labor. Of concern was the potential wages lost by black levee workers on the MFCP in 1932. In a report provided by Roy Ellis of the Committee on Labor, black workers were losing millions of dollars on the MFCP. The report focused on just three areas, Memphis, Vicksburg, and New Orleans, where black workers received $1.25 per day for upwards of fourteen hours of labor versus the standard $2.00 per eight-hour day on other government-financed contracts. As discussed earlier in this chapter, however, it was exceedingly difficult for many black workers to receive the minimum of $1.25 on the MFCP. Ellis employed a simple formula of using a minimum percentage of workers on the payrolls with the government standard of a ten-hour day, estimating a loss of approximately $1,412,225 in these three areas alone.[90] For the NAACP, "The lives, the welfare of the entire group is at stake. For if this fight is won, a decisive blow will have been struck for better working conditions and opportunity and decent wages for colored workers throughout the country."[91] If over a million dollars was lost in 1932 for just three areas, the monetary loss on the entire project was so significant as to make this battle the single most important fight for African Americans in the country, with ramifications not just of the present, but also for the future economic status of black workers.[92]

Roy Wilkins and George Schuyler conducted their undercover investigation amid these ongoing conversations, hoping their firsthand testimony would help lead to a senatorial investigation. After months of filibustering and delay, the senate passed a resolution on February 22, 1933, to initiate a special committee of three senators, headed by Robert Wagner, to investigate the MFCP. Republican senator Gerald Nye of North Dakota and Democratic senator Hubert Stephens from Mississippi were the other members. The exploitation of levee camp workers under the United States flag would now have a national audience. On April 15, 1933, the headline in the *Chicago Defender* read, "Open Levee Slave Probe: Wagner to Head Quiz in South."[93]

After focusing on saving the financial system and banks during the First Hundred Days, New Dealers looked for ways to stimulate the economy through employment and industry. Industry would be an important tool for national recovery, and the construction of levees was an important part of this process. Section 7(a) of the National Industrial Recovery Act (NRA), signed by Roosevelt on June 16, stipulated that industry codes should maintain limits on hours worked in a day and standards for minimum wages.[94] The NAACP highlighted Section 7(a) by lobbying the National Recovery Administration to include levee workers as part of industry codes to elevate wages, reduce hours, and improve conditions of workers. In July 1933 some $37 million was allotted by the Public Works Administration for flood control work in the lower Mississippi Valley, effectively bringing river work under the public works regulations of the National Industrial Recovery Act.[95] This was not a clear-cut victory for the NAACP, however. The reality for most black laborers under the NRA was far more complicated. The NRA symbol of the blue eagle was, in the words of the African American newspaper *Norfolk Journal and Guide,* a "predatory bird instead of a feathered messenger."[96] Some in the African American press renamed it the "Negro Removal Act," but having the MFCP included under New Deal protection was nonetheless considered a victory for the NAACP and the future wage-earning potential of black levee workers.[97]

The NAACP's work between 1927 and the New Deal helped bring about significant changes in the protection of black levee camp workers. As necessary as the senatorial hearings on camp conditions were, just as important was the national attention workers received from the NAACP's campaign to end widespread abuses on the MFCP. "We didn't turn Mississippi into

Canaan, of course," Roy Wilkins would later say in his autobiography, but its work in the years after the 1927 flood and well into the New Deal helped lay the foundation for workers' rights battles of the 1930s and the 1940s. The wages of some levee workers went up, even if only moderately in the range of ten to thirty cents per hour, and work hours were limited to thirty a week by the Public Works Administration.[98] Without question, debt peonage continued to occur in levee camps after the 1930s. New Deal legislation primarily focused on the prevailing rate of wages and eight-hour days but did little to address other problems on the MFCP, particularly the continuing violence, the commissary system, and various mechanisms for withholding wages.[99] Although the NAACP moved on to other questions of labor and civil rights, it continued to monitor levee camp workers in the region by sending representatives to camps and receiving notices from workers and friends through 1934 and beyond. Some reports were positive, but more common were reports of brutality, violence, and exploitation; these were promptly forwarded to the War Department.[100] Abusive levee camp operators were sometimes reprimanded by the War Department. "War Department Fires Brutal Levee Camp Boss: Used Lash to Punish Worker" was the headline of a February 3, 1934, article in the *Chicago Defender.* The work of ensuring that black levee camp workers were treated fairly extended well beyond the initial Mississippi Flood Control Project.

Historians have given scant attention to the meaning of race, labor, and environmental history, and as Richard White puts it, "One of the great shortcomings—intellectual and political—of modern environmentalism is its failure to grasp how human beings have historically known nature through work."[101] Black levee camp workers had little say in decisions made in the levee-building process, and were rarely given the tag "river man," a term used to describe a local person with particular knowledge of the river. African Americans understood the meaning of levees primarily through labor and a historical struggle to accumulate wages under an exploitative system.

For a brief moment between the 1927 flood and the early stages of the New Deal, black levee workers emerged from their longtime invisibility into a national conversation about race. Much of this conversation was a direct result of the 1927 flood and the need for a more detailed and comprehensive flood control plan to protect the Yazoo Mississippi Delta. The 1927 flood also provided momentum for the NAACP entering the New Deal period, as conditions of peonage were still fresh in the minds of African Americans. The 1927 flood demanded attention from the federal government to better protect citizens, and the NAACP seized on this transformative moment in the nation's flood control history to push for equality and better treatment for the people who actually built the levees.

CONCLUSION

When the Levee Breaks

The 1927 flood was an important moment in the long history of disaster relief and federalism. One of the main questions that arises from the history of the 1927 flood, and in fact the history of all environmental disasters, is where one can look for help in times of distress. Who is responsible for the alleviation of suffering after a disaster in the form of relief? It may be true that early in the American Republic concessions were made to provide disaster relief for victims of environmental disasters, but true to form, the meaning of relief was already a contested and divisive exercise in civic engagement. From the late eighteenth century onward, the federal government occasionally provided relief to specific individuals and communities after environmental disasters, though relief came in the form of specific and localized bills for the relief of individuals, not a systematic or infrastructural commitment by the federal government to all disaster victims. In other words, the federal government essentially conducted itself as a court of law, making case-by-case determinations of the worthiness or unworthiness of citizens for disaster relief.[1] A devastating 1827 fire in Alexandria, Virginia, has sometimes been credited as the beginning of federal relief, though legal scholar Michele Landis counters this idea by suggesting that "direct payments from the federal treasury to relieve 'sufferers' actually began nearly 40 years earlier, in 1790. These payments began as a series of private bills for the relief of individuals, and gave way by 1822 to general relief bills benefiting a defined class of claimants. By the time of the 1827 Alexandria fire, Congress had already granted 27 separate claims for relief, encompassing thousands of claimants and millions of dollars, for relief following events such as the Whiskey Rebellion, the slave insurrection on St. Domingo, and various fires, floods, and storms."[2] Recipients of disaster relief had to demonstrate more than incalculable loss from a specific disaster. They also had to prove that they were in no way culpable for their own suffering. "Concerns among members of Congress about the equitable application of these precedents contributed to the construction of narratives that distinguished among events and petitioners—certain events were compensated while others were ignored. Successful appeals told of events in a particular narrative form: sudden, unforeseeable events for which the claimant was blameless."[3] From the earliest moments of disaster relief in the United States, access to federal relief was a direct result of claimants' ability to prove with little doubt they were worthy sufferers. For most claimants, this meant showing that a disaster, through no fault of their own, resulted in a loss of economic and class status within their communities. It also meant that most blacks and the "ordinary poor" had little chance of petitioning the federal government for individual relief bills because of citizenship status or the inability to prove a loss of class status.[4]

The piecemeal fashion of federal disaster relief in the United States extended well into the twentieth century. Hurricanes, tornadoes, and floods were largely considered local problems to be dealt with by local governments and private citizens.[5] So too were other disasters considered by some to be more economic and "nonnatural," such as the Great Depression. Before World War II, the federal response to environmental disasters came mostly in the form of rehabilitating public buildings, bridges, roads, and other physical structures. The American Red Cross, not the federal government, was largely tasked with the responsibility of helping people rebuild their lives. As Ted Steinberg reminds us, "It is not often realized that no permanent means of government disaster assistance existed in this country until very recently. . . . Even as late as 1969, no formalized means existed to help individual citizens in the wake of catastrophes. The reigning relief ethos was nicely summed up by George Hastings of the Office of Emergency Preparedness, then charged with executing all federal relief efforts, when he remarked in a moment of bravado, 'We deal with things and not with people.'"[6]

A reluctant federal commitment to private citizens slowly began to take shape in the decade after World War II. In 1953 President Harry Truman made concessions for the newly formed Small Business Administration to make loans available to disaster victims, but it was clear from the beginning that this was a loan program rather than charity.[7] This early attempt at providing systematic federal relief to citizens was diluted by extensive applications, insurmountable bureaucratic red tape, and Small Business Administration loan officers who made decisions as to who was worthy or unworthy to receive loans.

Ultimately it was a spate of deadly environmental disasters between March 1964 and August 1969 that set the stage for a consistent federal presence in disaster relief. A major tsunami struck the California coast, floods hit the Pacific Northwest, and tornadoes swept through parts of the American heartland; and then came Hurricane Betsy in 1965 and Hurricane Camille in 1969. During this period some eight hundred Americans were killed in different parts of the country, prompting Senator Birch Bayh (D-Indiana) to introduce legislation that resulted in the Disaster Relief Act of 1969 and the beginning of a more concrete federal presence in the lives of disaster victims. The act cleared the way for the federal government to provide temporary housing for displaced victims, food stipends, and help with the clearing of private property for American citizens.[8]

Nonetheless, the increasing role of federalism in the twentieth century tells only half the story. The importance of different kinds of texts and ways of knowing about the historical past, specifically the 1927 flood, is a major underlying theme of this book. Although the Red Cross stepped into a position of disaster relief early in the century, its conspicuous absence on affairs of race made their presence contestable for many African Americans. In the Depression-era decade of the 1930s, the Red Cross continued to be a symbol of racialized charity by an organization with ties to the federal government. I have made the case in this book that African Americans circumvented the Red Cross during the 1927 flood. By the 1930s African Americans in the Yazoo Delta were already very cognizant of the ways in which the Red Cross and charity could be a source of racial pain.[9] The employment of charity as a controlling mechanism that resulted in racial discrimination and humiliation was already a familiar experience for black people when Depression-era

Red Cross stores were put into operation by the federal government. Poor blacks received leftover rations from whites and were often turned away empty-handed and hungry. In some areas of the Yazoo Delta blacks had to bring a note signed by a white person to receive supplies from the Red Cross store, a stinging reminder of similar practices of charity during the 1927 flood. When blues musicians including Walter Roland, Lucille Bogan, Walter Davis, Sonny Scott, Sonny Terry, Huddie Ledbetter, and others recorded variations of the "Red Cross Store" between the 1930s and 1950s, they were explaining not only what it was like to be black during the Depression but also a framework for how we can think about a much longer narrative of race and charity.

Lucille Bogan recorded one of the first versions of the Red Cross blues with her "Red Cross Man" in July 1933. Born in Mississippi around 1897, Bogan first recorded with Okeh records in 1923 and continued making records at least through the mid-1930s. Accompanied on piano by bluesman Walter Roland, who also recorded versions of the Red Cross blues, Bogan frames her explanatory narrative around Depression-era poverty and exploitation. "If anybody don't believe, I got a Red Cross man, go out in my backyard, look at my Red Cross can. Red Cross gives my man, three days a week, sack of Red Cross flour, hunk of old white meat. Now you've got to go, you can't go to no Hill, you got to go to the Red Cross store."[10] Bogan tells a story of how blacks were last to receive government rations and the ways in which the process of relief itself was used as a form of racial surveillance. Guido Van Rijn suggests in his work on Depression-era blues that when Bogan, who spent a large portion of her childhood in Birmingham, refers to Hill, she is perhaps describing an Alabama store owned by James B. Hill and Nelson P. Hill associated with the Piggly Wiggly food chain.[11]

Walter Roland's version of the Red Cross blues, also recorded in 1933, is among the most well-known of all recordings on the Depression era. Born around 1903, "Red Cross Blues" was Roland's first popular recording and was set against the Depression-era backdrop of food relief. "You know them Red Cross folks said they sure don't treat you mean; don't want to give you nuthin but two or three cans of beans. But you know the government are takin in charge now, says they gonna treat everybody right; says they give em two cans of beans now and one little can of tripe."[12]

Ultimately the 1927 flood served as a precursor to the welfare politics of the Great Depression, particularly the ways in which resources were controlled during the 1927 flood and New Deal. In his sweeping study of the Yazoo Delta, historian James Cobb argues that white planters made a habit of monopolizing Agricultural Adjustment Act payments during the Depression. "Although planters made good use of New Deal relief agencies when it served their purpose to do so, with the government paying thirty cents an hour for rural work relief and landlords offering farm labor only seventy-five cents for a fourteen-hour day, local whites did their best to get relief programs suspended at harvest time. In the mid-1930s a black newspaper reported that all WPA projects in the Delta had been suspended in order to provide 'cotton pickers for distressed plantation owners after planters complained that federal projects used workers ordinarily available for picking cotton.'"[13] The relationship between the 1927 flood and the New Deal can be seen through the lens of charity, race, and the long history of disaster relief.

Charity was also central to the aftermath of Hurricane Katrina, particularly the increased use of faith-based organizations and alternatives to the Red Cross. Framed by the media as a shift in charitable norms and diminishing faith in a revered organization, post-Katrina discussions of charity actually bore a remarkable continuity to the ways in which African Americans during the 1927 flood placed their imprint on the disaster through the process of giving from afar.[14]

From the 1900 Galveston Hurricane through Hurricane Katrina, almost every disaster in twentieth-century America has been infused with some form of racial discourse. In the aftermath of Hurricane Katrina, comparisons between the 1927 flood and that storm were common; appropriate in some ways and missing the mark on others. After Katrina, the country once again searched for ways to interpret the disaster through various forms of popular culture. The popular 1970s rock group Led Zeppelin recorded a song called "When the Levee Breaks" in 1971: it was popular then but took on a more exalted status as commentary in the days and months after Katrina. The irony, of course, is that "When the Levee Breaks" was originally recorded by Kansas Joe and Memphis Minnie in 1928 as commentary on the 1927 flood. Lizzie Douglas was born June 3, 1897, in Algiers, Louisiana, where she lived before moving with her family to Walls, Mississippi, just south of Memphis, when she was seven or eight years old. After receiving a guitar for her birthday, Douglas became a hit at local parties playing for family and friends throughout the countryside. Her early love of music and blues prompted Douglas to leave Mississippi for Memphis and the Beale Street scene, where she adopted the stage name Memphis Minnie in the late 1910s and began touring with the Ringling Brothers Circus during World War I. By the 1920s she was, along with husband Joe McCoy, among the first artists to record for Columbia Records. Born around 1905 near Raymond, Mississippi, Joe McCoy was also drawn to Beale Street as a blues guitarist in the 1920s: he met Lizzie Douglas there. During the 1927 flood they were still living in Memphis when stories of displacement started arising from the Yazoo Delta.[15] They recorded "When the Levee Breaks" in June 1929—a powerful critique of vulnerability and the failure of technology. "If it keeps on raining, levee's going to break; and the water gonna come and have no place to stay. Oh, crying won't help you, praying won't do no good; when the levee breaks, mama, you got to move."[16] Broken levees might be interpreted as the direct cause of homelessness, displacement, and pain in the song, but the Mississippi River's invisibility in the lyrics also suggests the importance of human-created suffering, a cultural portal through which we might understand black thought around race and the environmental world.

The popularity of Led Zeppelin's version provides an important platform for a discussion of blues and history. Prior to Katrina most Americans knew very little about the 1927 flood, the "levees only" policy, the debt peonage experienced by poor African Americans, or the wealth of blues songs recorded about this single event. During the process of listening to Led Zeppelin's version, far too many people fail to understand its origination in the blues vernacular and epistemology of black culture. Ultimately, Kansas Joe and Memphis Minnie's "When the Levee Breaks" is a powerful remembrance and continuum between two disasters in two different centuries, as relevant to one particular time period as the next. Hurricane Katrina, like the 1927 flood, can be understood through the political and collective interpretative framework of the blues. "The picture of twenty thousand slowly dying African Americans chanting 'we want help' outside of New Orleans's Convention Center," scholar Clyde Woods argues, "was a blues moment."[17] In New Orleans, stranded and marooned residents inside the

Superdome and on city bridges highlighted the lack of planning and evacuation needed for a city with a vulnerable landscape and long history of hurricanes. It was, however, the images of dead bodies floating facedown in floodwaters and abandoned on the side of the road that provided the most visually powerful sign of neglect and racial pain: the blues. Perhaps nothing better symbolizes a breakdown of societal mechanisms and structural inequality than the inability or unwillingness of a nation to protect its own citizens in need.[18]

"Refugees" and the Legacy of Frenchtown

In the days after Hurricane Katrina, news outlets, reporters, and citizens made a practice of referring to Gulf Coast residents as "refugees." For good reason, black leaders decried the use of the word after Katrina as a derogatory indictment of black citizenship in America. "Did the flood wash away our citizenship too?" the Reverend Al Sharpton quipped in an interview for Spike Lee's documentary. Broadly defined as a person seeking refuge or protection during some form of war or political unrest during which citizenship status is untenable, descriptions of Katrina victims as refugees drew the ire of black intellectuals as indicative of a people without a country or going through a state of civic unrest in the country where they currently hold citizenship status. Interestingly, this is a somewhat common term of past environmental disasters, not solely emblematic of Katrina. The term was routinely used by W .E. B. Du Bois, Ida B. Wells, the NAACP, and black newspapers such as the *Chicago Defender* during the 1927 flood when describing homelessness caused by the flood or the mistreatment of black people in Red Cross relief camps. Prior to Katrina the term was also commonly used by scholars writing about past environmental disasters; a colloquial, if perfunctory, way of describing individuals displaced and made homeless by a disaster.

Regardless of how the term was used in the past and in what context, the term took on a specific racial connotation during Katrina. Perhaps common as a description of both black and white survivors of an environmental disaster in the past, using the term after an environmental disaster is now unthinkable. Katrina shaped not only how we think about resiliency and vulnerable populations, but also how it shaped the discourse of citizenship and the uncritical approach behind the ways in which we frame calamitous events and the people who suffer from them. Nonetheless, nuggets of truth might still be found in the word. Perhaps what the vitriolic discourse behind the word "refugee" kept hidden from view was the experiential truth for black people during the 1927 flood and Katrina, that they were treated not only as second-class citizens, but at times as if they were strangers, and indeed "refugees," in their own land.

A lasting legacy of Katrina will surely also be the meaning of displacement for thousands of New Orleans residents temporarily and permanently relocated to Houston and other cities in ways that forced the redistribution and allocation of resources from education and housing to health care. Seventy-eight years after Creoles of color migrated from Southwest Louisiana to Houston following the 1927 flood, the neighborhood of Frenchtown once again helped shape the meaning of migration and displacement following an environmental disaster. Frank Broussard's family was one of the original families that migrated to Frenchtown from Louisiana in the 1920s. Still living in Frenchtown with his family on the land owned by his ancestors, Mr. Broussard opened the doors of his home to displaced victims of Hurricane Katrina in 2005, taking in several family members from Louisiana and Mississippi. In a 2005 *Houston Chronicle* article titled "A Friend in Texas," Mr. Broussard described part of Frenchtown's Katrina legacy: "That's the way we lived around here . . . not only did we help the French people, but we also welcomed everyone into our house and community. That's part of the Creole heritage."[19] I make the point in this book that environmental disasters are an important part of migration narratives, and the migration to Houston after the 1927 flood set the stage for later migration and displacement patterns after Katrina.

Frenchtown maintains a tenuous presence within the city of Houston. The neighborhood is almost invisible within the Houston landscape, and few residents connect its legacy back to the 1927 flood. In 1991 the Frenchtown Community Association was established for the sole purpose of documenting and restoring Frenchtown's rich historical legacy and advocating for increased resources and protection from the city. Following years of lobbying state and federal agencies, in 2009 the Frenchtown Community Association and Harris County Historical Commission successfully gained recognition for Frenchtown as a Texas historical neighborhood. In addition to this recognition, two historical markers were placed in the community. One marker describes the influence of zydeco on the history and culture of Texas brought to the state by Louisiana migrants. "In the 1920s, Creole families from Louisiana, known as 'Creoles of Color' migrated to Houston, establishing the neighborhood known as Frenchtown. In addition to their culture and language, they also brought their music to Houston. Zydeco, a fusion of traditional Creole music and other styles, became an important form of expression for the families that settled in Frenchtown . . . musicians blended the music, also known as La-La, with jazz and blues to form the distinctive sound known as zydeco."[20] A second marker commemorates the 1927 flood's history in the making of Frenchtown. "A distinct ethnic cultural group, 'Creoles of Color' developed in Louisiana in the 18th and 19th centuries with roots in French, Spanish, African and Native American cultures. They spoke standard or Creole French and practiced Catholicism. Free persons before the Civil War, they lost their special status with the onset of Jim Crow laws, and many turned to sharecropping to survive but suffered further with declining agricultural prices and drought. Escaping the devastating 1927 Mississippi River Flood, many fled west via highways and rail lines. In Houston, they took jobs in industries related to oil construction and railroads. They established a tight-knit culturally unique community called Frenchtown." These markers serve as a permanent reminder of the connection between Louisiana, Texas, and the 1927 flood.

Located in the shadow of downtown Houston, Frenchtown has endured neglect from the city and resisted both attempts to permanently displace residents and the construction of a major freeway cutting a path through the community's boundaries. The neighborhood is small, almost the same size it was when migrants arrived in the 1920s. Frenchtown streets are narrow, in most places only wide enough for one car to pass at a time, a reminder of pioneering residents who traveled mostly by horse or foot during the neighborhood's early years. Many of the houses that were built in the 1920s and 1930s remain part of the neighborhood, strong enough to withstand Houston's harsh climate and occasional hurricane. Most houses are simple one-story dwellings with two or three bedrooms, resembling the shotgun houses that once marked southern landscapes in cotton-growing areas of Texas, Louisiana, and Mississippi.

Today, Frenchtown exists at the intersection of multiple historical narratives, situated in a textured if mostly forgotten past while bracing itself for an uncertain future. The fate of Frenchtown has been the fate of other neighborhoods in urban America: second- and third-generation descendants of original pioneers opting to live in the suburbs after World War II or making the decision to leave the main city altogether.[21] Although zydeco is mostly silent in Frenchtown today, the history of Louisiana and the 1927 flood is still fresh in the minds of the few residents that remain with ties to original pioneers.

The 1927 flood was a defining moment in American history. Like a snapshot of the past, the disaster provided a window into race and citizenship, particularly how African Americans defined their citizenship in relation to others. Some expressed a desire to leave the place of their birth, find alternative charitable outlets that would ensure that black victims received resources, or experienced frustration at being mistreated and coerced into labor. Blues musicians and literary giants used the disaster to explain the experiences of race in the 1920s and 1930s through creative art, while the NAACP applied the experiences of the flood to demand livable wages for black levee camp workers during the New Deal. These separate, but integrated, communities are all tied back to the 1927 flood through a flood diaspora of race and race consciousness. The 1927 flood remains a historical reminder of the nation's complicated narrative of race and environmentalism, a narrative that becomes most visible during a catastrophic event. African Americans in the flooded region and across the country understood the 1927 flood as both an environmental crisis and a crisis of race in an era decades before the modern civil rights movement.

NOTES

Introduction

1. Robyn Spencer, "Contested Terrain: The Mississippi Flood of 1927 and the Struggle to Control Black Labor," *Journal of Negro History* 79 (Spring 1994); John Barry, *Rising Tide: The Great Mississippi Flood of 1927 and How It Changed America* (New York: Simon and Schuster, 1997).

2. Mikko Saikku, *This Delta, This Land: An Environmental History of the Yazoo Mississippi Delta* (Athens: University of Georgia Press, 2005).

3. Barry, *Rising Tide*, 21–32; Pete Daniel, *Deep'n As it Come* (New York: Oxford University Press, 1977), 3–17; Lyle Saxon, *Father Mississippi* (New York: Century, 1927).

4. Saikku, *This Delta, This Land.*

5. David Cohn, *Where I Was Born and Raised* (South Bend, Ind.: University of Notre Dame Press, 1935), 1–4.

6. Ari Kelman, *A River and Its City: The Nature of Landscape in New Orleans* (Berkeley: University of California Press, 2003); Keith Wailoo, *Dying in the City of the Blues: Sickle Cell Anemia and the Politics of Race and Health* (Chapel Hill: University of North Carolina Press, 2001), 19–20.

7. James C. Cobb, *The Most Southern Place on Earth: The Mississippi Delta and the Roots of Regional Identity* (New York: Oxford University Press, 1992), 1; Robert L. Brandfon, *Cotton Kingdom for the New South: A History of the Yazoo Mississippi Delta from Reconstruction to the Twentieth Century* (Cambridge, Mass.: Harvard University Press, 1967), 24–29; Robert W. Harrison, *Alluvial Empire: A Study of State and Local*

Efforts toward Land Development in the Alluvial Valley of the Lower Mississippi River (Little Rock, Ark.: Pioneer, 1961), 5, 20.

8. Cobb, *Most Southern Place on Earth,* 1–2, 335.

9. Ibid.; Mart Stewart, *"What Nature Suffers to Groe": Life, Labor, and Landscape on the Georgia Coast, 1680–1920* (Athens: University of Georgia Press, 1996); Cohn, *Where I Was Born and Raised,* 43.

10. Cobb, *Most Southern Place on Earth,* 153, 183, 231, 324.

11. Saikku, *This Delta, This Land,* 137.

12. Kelman, *River and Its City,* 87–119, 161–71; Donald W. Davis, "Historical Perspective on Crevasses, Levees, and the Mississippi River," in *Transforming New Orleans and Its Environs: Centuries of Change,* ed. Craig Colten (Pittsburgh: University of Pittsburgh Press, 2000), 92–100.

13. Craig E. Colten, *An Unnatural Metropolis: Wresting New Orleans from Nature* (Baton Rouge: Louisiana State University Press, 2005), 19–32.

14. Ted Steinberg, *Acts of God: The Unnatural History of "Natural" Disaster in America* (New York: Oxford University Press, 2000).

15. Colten, *Unnatural Metropolis,* 19–32.

16. Davis, "Historical Perspective." Louisiana, Mississippi, Alabama, and Missouri were among the states who applied for this act.

17. Davis, "Historical Perspective," 96–100; Charles Royster, *The Destructive War: William Tecumseh Sherman, Stonewall Jackson, and the Americans* (New York: Random House, 1991); David Potter, *The Impending Crisis: America before the Civil War, 1848–1861* (New York: Harper and Row, 1976).

18. Barry, *Rising Tide,* 45–53, 88, 100; Colten, *Unnatural Metropolis,* 19–32; Todd Shallat, *Structures in the Stream: Water, Science, and the Rise of the U.S. Army Corps of Engineers* (Austin: University of Texas Press, 1994).

19. Edward Larson, *Sex, Race, and Science: Eugenics in the Deep South* (Baltimore: The Johns Hopkins University Press, 1996).

20. Marc Reisner, *Cadillac Desert: The American West and Its Disappearing Water* (New York: Penguin, 1993).

21. Samuel P. Hays, *Conservation and the Gospel of Efficiency: The Progressive Conservation Movement, 1890–1920* (Pittsburgh: University of Pittsburgh Press, 1999), 2.

22. Hays, *Conservation,* 3.

23. Ibid., 91.

24. Cobb, *Most Southern Place on Earth,* 79; Davis, "Historical Perspective," 92–93; Kelman, *River and Its City,* 161–71; Barry, *Rising Tide,* 88, 100; Colten, *Unnatural Metropolis.*

25. Barry, *Rising Tide,* 13–32; Gay M. Gomez, "Perspective, Power, and Priorities: New Orleans and the Mississippi River Flood of 1927," in *Transforming New Orleans*

and Its Environs: Centuries of Change, ed. Craig Colten (Pittsburgh: University of Pittsburgh Press, 2000); Kelman, *River and Its City*, 157–97.

26. Barry, *Rising Tide*, 14.

27. Ibid., 14–15

28. Saikku, *This Delta, This Land*, 27–28.

29. Barry, *Rising Tide*, 1–14; quotation cited from Barry on Henry Waring Ball.

30. Barry, *Rising Tide*, 173–209; Daniel, *Deep'n as it Come*, 3–12; Saxon, *Father Mississippi*, 279–90; "Mississippi Valley Flood Disaster of 1927: Official Report of Relief Operations" (Washington, D.C.: American Red Cross Printing, 1927).

31. Daniel, *Deep'n as it Come*, 88–91.

32. Khalil Gibran Muhammad, *The Condemnation of Blackness: Race, Crime, and the Making of Modern Urban America* (Cambridge, Mass.: Harvard University Press, 2010), 157.

33. John Dollard, *Caste and Class in a Southern Town* (New York: Doubleday Anchor, 1937), 2.

34. *The Blues Brothers*, released June 20, 1980, Universal Studios.

35. John Lee Hooker, *The Country Blues of John Lee Hooker*.

36. *Living with Music: Ralph Ellison's Jazz Writings*, ed. Robert O'Meally (New York: Modern Library, 2001), 15–34.

37. Hasan Kwame Jeffries, *Bloody Lowndes: Civil Rights and Black Power in Alabama's Black Belt* (New York: New York University Press, 2009).

38. Earl Lewis, "To Turn as on a Pivot: Writing African Americans into a History of Overlapping Diasporas," *The American Historical Review* 100, no. 3 (June 1995).

39. Ibid., 775.

40. Spencer, "Contested Terrain"; Barry, *Rising Tide*.

41. Theodore Rosengarten, *All God's Dangers: The Life of Nate Shaw* (New York: Avon, 1975); Robin D. G. Kelley, *Hammer and Hoe: Alabama Communists during the Great Depression* (Chapel Hill: University of North Carolina Press, 1990).

42. Rosengarten, *All God's Dangers*.

43. Leroi Jones, *Blues People: The Negro Experience in White America and the Music That Developed from It* (New York: Morrow Quill, 1963), 67.

44. Clyde Woods, *Development Arrested: The Blues and Plantation Power in the Mississippi Delta* (New York: Verso, 1998), 109, 111; Daphne Harrison, *Blues Pearls: Blues Queens of the 1920s* (New Brunswick, N.J.: Rutgers University Press, 1990), 56–57.

45. Eileen Southern, *The Music of Black Americans: A History* (New York: W. W. Norton, 1997).

46. Davarian L. Baldwin, *Chicago's New Negroes: Modernity, the Great Migration, and Black Urban Life* (Chapel Hill: University of North Carolina Press, 2007), 172–73.

47. Houston Baker, *Blues, Ideology, and Afro-American Literature: A Vernacular Theory* (Chicago: University of Chicago Press, 1984); David Levering Lewis, *When Harlem Was in Vogue* (New York: Alfred A. Knopf, 1981).

48. Baker, *Blues, Ideology, and Afro-American Literature,* 196–97.

49. Howard W. Odum and Guy B. Johnson, *The Negro and His Songs* (Chapel Hill: University of North Carolina Press, 1925); Howard Odum, *Negro Workaday Songs* (Chapel Hill: University of North Carolina Press, 1926).

50. Texas Alexander, "Levee Camp Moan Blues."

51. Woods, *Development Arrested,* 81–87.

52. Fred J. Hays, *Goin' Back to Sweet Memphis: Conversations with the Blues* (Athens: University of Georgia Press, 2001).

53. There is a rich literature on this idea of a blues voice and interrelations between the blues and novels with a black blues life. I draw extensively on Farah Jasmine Griffin, *"Who Set You Flowin'?": The African-American Migration Narrative* (New York: Oxford University Press, 1995); Cheryl A. Wall, *Worrying the Line: Black Women Writers, Lineage, and Literary Tradition* (Chapel Hill: University of North Carolina Press, 2005); and Baker, *Blues, Ideology, and Afro-American Literature.*

54. Griffin, *"Who Set You Flowin'?,"* 32–33.

55. Steinberg, *Acts of God.*

56. Chad Louis Williams, *Torchbearers of Democracy: African American Soldiers in the World War I Era* (Chapel Hill: University of North Carolina Press, 2010).

57. Steinberg, *Acts of God;* Eric Klinenberg, *Heat Wave: A Social Autopsy of Disaster in Chicago* (Chicago: University of Chicago Press, 2003).

58. Richard White, *The Organic Machine: The Remaking of the Columbia River* (New York: Hill and Wang, 1995).

1. Down the Line

1. James D. Anderson, *The Education of Blacks in the South, 1860–1935* (Chapel Hill: University of North Carolina Press, 1988).

2. Paul Farmer, *AIDS and Accusation: Haiti and the Geography of Blame* (Berkeley: University of California Press, 1993).

3. Wall, *Worrying the Line,* 17.

4. Angela Y. Davis, *Blues Legacies and Black Feminism: Gertrude "Ma" Rainey, Bessie Smith, and Billie Holiday* (New York: Vintage Books, 1998); David Evans, "High Water Everywhere: Blues and Gospel Commentary on the 1927 Mississippi River Flood," in *Nobody Knows Where the Blues Come From,* ed. Robert Springer (Oxford: University of Mississippi Press, 2006).

5. James Giesen, *Boll Weevil Blues: Cotton, Myth, and Power in the American South* (Chicago: University of Chicago Press, 2011).

6. Dianne Glave, *Rooted in the Earth: Reclaiming the African American Environmental Heritage* (New York: Lawrence Hill, 2010); Kimberly Smith, *African American Environmental Thought: Foundations* (Lawrence: University of Kansas Press, 2007).

7. James Grossman, *Land of Hope: Chicago, Black Southerners, and the Great Migration* (Chicago: University of Chicago Press, 1989), 29; Giesen, *Boll Weevil Blues.*

8. Langdon Winner, *The Whale and the Reactor: A Search for Limits in an Age of High Technology* (Chicago: University of Chicago Press, 1986).

9. Davis, *Blues Legacies and Black Feminism,* 91.

10. Ibid.

11. Chris Albertson, *Bessie* (New York: Stein and Day, 1972), 127.

12. Ibid., 127–28. Emphasis added.

13. Davis, *Blues Legacies and Black Feminism,* 108–10; Albertson, *Bessie,* 127–28.

14. Davis, *Blues Legacies and Black Feminism.*

15. Bessie Smith, "Backwater Blues."

16. Barry, *Rising Tide,* 201.

17. Ibid., 202.

18. Fred Chaney, "A Refugee's Story," manuscript, Mississippi Department of Archives and History, Jackson, Miss.

19. Ibid.

20. Barry, *Rising Tide,* 196–206, 240; Daniel, *Deep'n as it Come*; Saxon, *Father Mississippi.*

21. Barry, *Rising Tide,* 196–206, 240; Daniel, *Deep'n as it Come.*

22. Daniel, *Deep'n as it Come*; William Alexander Percy, *Lanterns on the Levee: Recollections of a Planter's Son* (New York: Alfred A. Knopf, 1941).

23. Evans, "High Water Everywhere."

24. Alice Pearson, "Greenville Levee Blues."

25. Percy, *Lanterns on the Levee,* 257–70; Barry, *Rising Tide.*

26. Percy, *Lanterns on the Levee,* 258.

27. Ibid., 258–69.

28. Lonnie Johnson, "Broken Levee Blues."

29. The notice was reprinted in the *Chicago Defender,* June 4 and 11, 1927; see also Spencer, "Contested Terrain," 170–81.

30. Percy, *Lanterns on the Levee,* 265–68.

31. *Chicago Defender,* June 16, 1927; *Vicksburg Evening Post,* May 6, 1927; Walter White, "The Flood, the Red Cross, and the National Guard," *Crisis* 35 (January, February, and March 1928). See also Barry, *Rising Tide,* 314–17, 319–32.

32. Spencer, "Contested Terrain," 175–76.

33. *Chicago Defender,* July 16, 1927; Official Report of the Mississippi National Guard, 12–16, Box 3880, File 0562, NAACP Papers, Library of Congress, Washington, D.C.

34. *Jackson Daily News,* April 30, 1927; *Daily Clarion Ledger,* May 7, 1927; Spencer, "Contested Terrain," 170–81; Nell Irvin Painter, *Exodusters: Black Migration to Kansas After Reconstruction* (New York: Alfred A. Knopf, 1976).

35. Saidiya V. Hartman, *Scenes of Subjection, Terror, Slavery, and Self-Making in Nineteenth-Century America* (New York: Oxford University Press, 1997), 148.

36. See Lawrence Levine, *Black Culture and Black Consciousness: Afro-American Folk Thought from Slavery to Freedom* (New York: Oxford University Press, 1997); Hartman, *Scenes of Subjection.* For a legal history of abolitionism and travel during slavery, see Edlie Wong, *Neither Fugitive nor Free: Atlantic Slavery, Freedom Suits, and the Legal Culture of Travel* (New York: New York University Press, 2009).

37. "Flood Region Now Has New Menace: Lack of Sufficient Milk Has Caused Outbreak of Pellagra," *Louisiana Weekly,* August 6, 1927.

38. Alan Kraut, *Goldberger's War: The Life and Work of a Public Health Crusader* (New York: Hill and Wang, 2003).

39. Kraut, *Goldberger's War;* Harry M. Marks, "Epidemiologists Explain Pellagra: Gender, Race, and Political Economy in the Work of Edgar Sydenstricker," *Journal of the History of Medicine* 58 (January 2003); Daphne Roe, *A Plague of Corn: The Social History of Pellagra* (Ithaca: Cornell University Press, 1973); Elizabeth Etheridge, *The Butterfly Caste: A Social History of Pellagra in the South* (Westport: Greenwood, 1972).

40. "Flood Region," *Louisiana Weekly.*

41. For a general study of health and segregation in the South, see Edward Beardsley, *History of Neglect: Health Care for Blacks and Mill Workers in the Twentieth-Century South* (Knoxville: University of Tennessee Press, 1987), 121–57; Keith Wailoo, *Dying in the City of the Blues: Sickle Cell Anemia and the Politics of Race and Health* (Chapel Hill: University of North Carolina Press, 2000).

42. Vanessa Northington Gamble, *Making a Place for Ourselves: The Black Hospital Reform Movement, 1920–1945* (New York: Oxford University Press, 1994), 142; Thomas Ward, *Black Physicians in the Jim Crow South* (Fayetteville: University of Arkansas Press, 2003); Beardsley, *History of Neglect.*

43. Beardsley, *History of Neglect.*

44. Spencer, "Contested Terrain," 176.

45. Anonymous letter, *Chicago Defender,* June 16, 1927.

46. Spencer, "Contested Terrain," 170–76.

47. Ibid.; Richard Price, *Maroon Societies: Rebel Slave Communities in the Americas* (New York: Anchor, 1973); *Vicksburg Evening Post*, May 24, 1927.

48. Fred J. Hay, *Goin' Back to Sweet Memphis: Conversations with the Blues* (Athens: University of Georgia Press, 2001), 5–9; Stephen Calt and Gayle Wardlow, *King of the Delta Blues: The Life and Music of Charlie Patton* (Newton, N.J.: Rock Chapel, 1988).

49. Charley Patton, "High Water Blues."

50. George Carter, "Rising River Blues."

51. Winner, *Whale and the Reactor*, 19.

52. Kelman, *River and Its City*, 4.

53. John Martin Hammond, *Winter Journeys in the South* (Philadelphia: J. B. Lippincott, 1916), 115–17; T. L. Nichols, *Forty Years of American Life* (London: Longmans and Green, 1874), 132; Kelman, *River and its City*, 158, 161–72.

54. Hammond, *Winter Journeys in the South*, 115–17.

55. David Cohn, *Where I Was Born and Raised* (Notre Dame: University of Notre Dame Press, 1935), 43.

56. Arthur O'Keefe Papers, New Orleans Public Library, Louisiana Room; Kelman, *River and Its City*, 161–71.

57. "Safety Assured in New Orleans: Merchants and Residents Concerned over False Reports about City," *New Orleans Times-Picayune*, May 4, 1927.

58. Kelman, *River and Its City*, 161.

59. Ibid., 174.

60. Arthur O'Keefe Papers; Kelman, *River and Its City*, 171–96.

61. "Red Cross Appeal," *New York Times*, April 30, 1927; *Memphis Commercial Appeal*, April 20, 1927; "Cut Levee is Order of Governor," *Plaquemines Protector*, April 30, 1927; Kelman, *River and Its City*, 171–96.

62. Arthur O'Keefe Papers; Kelman, *River and Its City*, 178–80.

63. Kelman, *River and Its City*, 179.

64. Ibid., 182.

65. Ibid., 171–96; *New Orleans Evening*, April 29, 1927; *St. Bernard Voice*, April 30, 1927.

66. Kelman, *River and Its City*.

67. Ibid., 171–96; "Cut Levee," *Plaquemines Protector*; "Government Financial Aid Assured Flood Zone Farmers," *Christian Science Monitor*, May 4, 1927; "Reparations Body Decides Methods to Handle Claims," *Plaquemines Protector*, May 14, 1927; "Prompt Action Needed," *Plaquemines Protector*, June 25, 1927.

68. Mamie Till-Mobley, *Death of Innocence: The Story of the Hate Crime that Changed America* (New York: Ballantine, 2004).

69. Mattie Delaney, "Tallahatchie River Blues."

70. See Jacqueline Jones, *Labor of Love, Labor of Sorrow: Black Women, Work, and the Family from Slavery to the Present* (New York: Basic Books, 1985), 80–94.

71. Sippie Wallace, "The Flood Blues." Sippie Wallace died in 1986 in Detroit, Michigan.

72. John McPhee, *The Control of Nature* (New York: Farrar, Straus and Giroux, 1989), 41–42; Barry, *Rising Tide,* 173–209, 238–58.

73. Rosemary Howe Scioneaux, interview by Michel F. Schexnayder, Louisiana State Archives and History, Baton Rouge.

74. Ibid.

75. Ibid.

76. Bessie Smith, "Homeless Blues."

77. Griffin, *"Who Set You Flowin'?"*

78. Bessie Smith, "Homeless Blues."

79. Griffin, *"Who Set You Flowin'?"*

2. Burning Waters Rise

1. David Levering Lewis, *The Portable Harlem Renaissance Reader* (New York: Penguin, 1995), 100–105.

2. Ibid.

3. There is a rich literature on this idea of a blues voice and interrelations between the blues and novels with a black blues life. I draw extensively on Griffin, *"Who Set You Flowin'?"*; Wall, *Worrying the Line*; and Baker, *Blues, Ideology, and Afro-American Literature.*

4. Paul Outka, *Race and Nature from Transcendentalism to the Harlem Renaissance* (New York: Palgrave Macmillan, 2008), 173–74.

5. Ibid. 172.

6. Henry Louis Gates Jr., *Figures in Black: Words, Signs, and the "Racial Self"* (New York: Oxford University Press, 1987).

7. See Kimberly Ruffin, *Black on Earth: African American Ecoliterary Traditions* (Athens: University of Georgia Press, 2010).

8. Sylvia Hood Washington, *Packing Them In: An Archaeology of Environmental Racism in Chicago, 1865–1954* (New York: Lexington, 2004), 22.

9. William Cronon, *Uncommon Ground: Rethinking the Human Place in Nature* (New York: W. W. Norton, 1996).

10. On discussions of wilderness, see Roderick Nash, *Wilderness and the American Mind* (New Haven: Yale University Press, 1967); Cronon, *Uncommon Ground.*

11. Nash, *Wilderness and the American Mind.*

12. William Cronon, "The Trouble with Wilderness; or, Getting Back to the Wrong Nature," in *Uncommon Ground: Rethinking the Human Place in Nature,* ed. William Cronon (New York: W. W. Norton, 1996), 79–80.

13. Ibid.

14. Ibid., 79.

15. Leslie Schwalm, *A Hard Fight for We: Women's Transition from Slavery to Freedom in South Carolina* (Urbana: University of Illinois Press, 1997); Peter Wood, *Black Majority: Negroes in Colonial South Carolina from 1670 through the Stono Rebellion* (New York: W. W. Norton, 1996); Judith Carney, *Black Rice: The African Origins of Rice Cultivation in the Americas* (Cambridge, Mass.: Harvard University Press, 2002).

16. On the consumerism of leisure, see Jennifer Price, *Flight Maps: Adventures with Nature in Modern America* (New York: Basic Books, 1999).

17. William Tuttle, *Race Riot: Chicago in the Red Summer of 1919* (Urbana: University of Illinois Press, 1996).

18. Jo Ann Robinson, *The Montgomery Bus Boycott and the Women Who Started It: The Memoir of Jo Ann Gibson Robinson* (Knoxville: University of Tennessee Press, 1987).

19. Smith, *African American Environmental Thought,* 3.

20. Ibid., 11.

21. Alain Locke, ed., *The New Negro: Voices of the Harlem Renaissance* (New York: Simon and Schuster, 1992).

22. Lawrence Buell, *Writing for an Endangered World: Literature, Culture, and Environment in the U.S. and Beyond* (Cambridge, Mass.: Belknap Press, 2003).

23. Donald Worster, *Dust Bowl: The Southern Plains in the 1930s* (New York: Oxford University Press, 1979), 54.

24. Constance Webb, *Richard Wright: A Biography* (New York: Putnam Press, 1968); Keneth Kinnamon, *The Emergence of Richard Wright: A Study in Literature and Society* (Urbana: University of Illinois Press, 1972); Michel Fabre, *The Unfinished Quest of Richard Wright* (Urbana: University of Illinois Press, 1993).

25. Webb, *Richard Wright;* Kinnamon, *Emergence of Richard Wright.*

26. Lewis, *Portable Harlem Renaissance Reader.*

27. Abdul R. JanMohamed, *The Death-Bound-Subject: Richard Wright's Archaeology of Death* (Durham, N.C.: Duke University Press, 2005); Kinnamon, *Emergence of Richard Wright.*

28. Zora Neale Hurston, review of Uncle Tom's Children in "Stories of Conflict," *Saturday Review of Literature* 17, April 2, 1938.

29. Countee Cullen, review of Uncle Tom's Children, *African,* April 1938.

30. Ralph Ellison, review of Uncle Tom's Children in "Recent Negro Fiction," *New Masses,* August 5, 1941.

31. Richard Wright, "The Ethics of Jim Crow," in *Uncle Tom's Children* (New York: Harper and Row, 1938).

32. Richard Wright, "The Man Who Saw the Flood," *New Masses* 24 (August 24, 1937): 110. *New Masses* was a left-wing organ begun in 1926 by former writers and contributors of the *Liberator.* Over the years, contributors to the *New Masses* included Richard Wright, Ralph Ellison, Langston Hughes, Max Eastman, and Carl Sandburg. The journal stopped publication in 1948.

33. Wright, "Man Who Saw the Flood."

34. JanMohamed, *Death-Bound-Subject.*

35. Wright, "Man Who Saw the Flood," 112.

36. Outka, *Race and Nature;* Buell, *Writing for an Endangered World.*

37. Zora Neale Hurston, *Their Eyes Were Watching God* (New York: HarperCollins Books, 1937); Cheryl A. Wall, *Women of the Harlem Renaissance* (Bloomington: Indiana University Press, 1995), 139–41, 189–94; Valerie Boyd, *Wrapped in Rainbows: The Life of Zora Neale Hurston* (New York: Scribner's, 2003), see chapter entitled "A Glance from God." On Hurston's use of anthropology, see also *Dust Tracks on a Road* (Philadelphia: J. B. Lippincott, 1942) and *Mules and Men* (Philadelphia: J. B. Lippincott, 1935).

38. Wall, *Women of the Harlem Renaissance,* 193.

39. Hurston, *Their Eyes Were Watching God,* 151–52.

40. Baker, *Blues, Ideology, and Afro-American Literature.*

41. Wright, "Man Who Saw the Flood."

42. See Jones, *Labor of Love,* 80–94.

43. Wright, "Man Who Saw the Flood."

44. Spencer, "Contested Terrain," 171.

45. Wright, "Man Who Saw the Flood."

46. Ibid.; Orlando Patterson, *Slavery and Social Death: A Comparative Study* (Cambridge, Mass.: Harvard University Press, 1982).

47. Wright, "Man Who Saw the Flood."

48. Wright, *Uncle Tom's Children.*

49. Ibid.

50. Hurston, *Their Eyes Were Watching God.*

51. Wright, *Uncle Tom's Children.*

52. Ibid.

53. Charles M. Payne, *I've Got the Light of Freedom: The Organizing Tradition and the Mississippi Freedom Struggle* (Berkeley: University of California Press, 1995).

54. Wright, *Uncle Tom's Children,* 74–80.

55. Ibid., 81–82.

56. Ibid.

57. Barry, *Rising Tide.*

58. Ibid., 196–206; *Jackson Clarion-Ledger,* April 24, 1927; *Memphis Commercial Appeal,* April 22, 1927; "Troops in Flood Area to Imprison Farm Hands; Herd Refugees Like Cattle," *Chicago Defender,* May 7, 1927; Percy, *Lanterns on the Levee,* 249–70.

59. Wright, *Uncle Tom's Children.*

60. Ibid., 88–89.

61. Ibid., 95; JanMohamed, *Death-Bound-Subject,* 53.

62. JanMohamed, *Death-Bound-Subject,* 53–56.

63. Thomas C. Buchanan, *Black Life on the Mississippi: Slaves, Free Blacks, and the Western Steamboat World* (Chapel Hill: University of North Carolina Press, 2004).

64. Wright, *Uncle Tom's Children,* 102.

65. JanMohamed, *Death-Bound-Subject,* 56.

66. William Faulkner, "Old Man (The Wild Palms)," in *The Faulkner Reader: Selections from the Works of William Faulkner* (New York: Random House Press, 1953).

67. Ibid., 357.

68. Ibid., 361.

69. Washington, *Packing Them In,* 22–44.

3. Racialized Charity and the Militarization of Flood Relief in Postwar America

1. "Neval H. Thomas Pleads for Flood Sufferers," *Norfolk Journal and Guide,* June 11, 1927.

2. Ibid.

3. Carl Smith, *Urban Disorder and the Shape of Belief: The Great Chicago Fire, the Haymarket Bomb, and the Model Town of Pullman* (Chicago: University of Chicago Press, 1996); Spencer, "Contested Terrain"; Barry, *Rising Tide.*

4. Joe William Trotter, *Black Milwaukee: The Making of an Industrial Proletariat, 1915–45* (Urbana: University of Illinois Press, 1985); Earl Lewis, *In Their Own Interests: Race, Class, and Power in Twentieth-Century Norfolk, Virginia* (Berkeley: University of California Press, 1991); James Grossman, *Land of Hope: Chicago, Black Southerners, and the Great Migration* (Chicago: University of Chicago Press, 1989); Claude Brown, *Manchild in the Promised Land* (New York: Touchstone Press, 1965).

5. Leon Litwack, *Trouble in Mind: Black Southerners in the Age of Jim Crow* (New York: Vintage Press, 1999).

6. See Jones, *Labor of Love*; Litwack, *Trouble in Mind.*

7. Letter from Ella Hutson to James Feiser, July 20, 1927, Herbert Hoover Presidential Library, West Branch, Iowa; Mia Bay, *To Tell the Truth Freely: The Life of Ida B. Wells* (New York: Hill and Wang), 3–6.

8. Bay, *To Tell the Truth Freely.*

9. *Norfolk Journal and Guide,* Saturday, May 7, 1927; Barry, *Rising Tide.*

10. *Norfolk Journal and Guide,* Saturday, May 7, 1927.

11. "Flood Not God's Way to Punish Dixie Whites," *Baltimore Afro-American,* May 21, 1927.

12. Steinberg, *Acts of God,* xxi.

13. "Flood Not God's Way," *Baltimore Afro-American.*

14. *Norfolk Journal and Guide,* June 11, 1927.

15. "Boston Adds $1,000 to Flood Fund," *Pittsburgh Courier,* May 28, 1927.

16. See Walter Trattner, *From Poor Law to Welfare State: A History of Social Welfare in America* (New York: Free Press, 1998).

17. "Flood Relief Tests America Says Hawkins," *Baltimore Afro-American,* May 14, 1927.

18. *Norfolk Journal and Guide,* Saturday May 7, 1927; A. E. Bush and P. L. Dorman, *History of the Mosaic Templars of America* (originally published by authors in 1924 and long out of print, the University of Arkansas began reprinting this book in 2008). G. P. Hamilton, *Beacon Lights of the Race* (New York: E. H. Clarke, 1911).

19. Deborah Gray White, *Too Heavy a Load: Black Women in Defense of Themselves, 1894–1994* (New York: W. W. Norton, 1999); Evelyn Brooks Higginbotham, *Righteous Discontent: The Women's Movement in the Black Baptist Church, 1880–1920* (Cambridge, Mass.: Harvard University Press, 1993); Darline Clark Hine, *Black Women in White: Racial Conflict and Cooperation in the Nursing Profession, 1890–1950* (Bloomington: Indiana University Press, 1989). See also Susan Smith, *Sick and Tired of Being Sick and Tired: Black Women's Health Activism in America, 1890–1950* (Philadelphia: University of Philadelphia Press, 1995); Kevin Gaines, *Uplifting the Race: Black Leadership, Politics, and Culture in the Twentieth Century* (Chapel Hill: University of North Carolina Press, 1996).

20. Steinberg, *Acts of God.*

21. Muhammad, *Condemnation of Blackness.*

22. Karen Sawislak, *Smoldering City: Chicagoans and the Great Fire, 1871–1874* (Chicago: University of Chicago Press, 1995).

23. Ibid., 1–3.

24. Charles Rosenberg, *The Care of Strangers: The Rise of America's Hospital System* (Baltimore: The Johns Hopkins University Press, 1995).

25. Sawislak, *Smoldering City,* 71, 72; Carl Smith, "Faith and Doubt: The Imaginative Dimensions of the Great Chicago Fire," in *American Disasters,* ed. Steven Biel (New York: New York University Press, 2001), 29–70.

26. Sawislak, *Smoldering City,* 77, 85–88.

27. Ibid., 88–93.

28. Erik Larson, *Isaac's Storm: A Man, a Time, and the Deadliest Hurricane in History* (New York: Vintage, 2000).

29. Elizabeth Hayes Turner, *Women, Culture, and Community: Religion and Reform in Galveston, 1880–1920* (New York: Oxford University Press, 1997), 34, 189.

30. Ibid., 194.

31. Ibid.

32. Turner, *Women, Culture, and Community.*

33. Ibid., 188, 190–91.

34. See Alan Dawley, *Struggles for Justice: Social Responsibility and the Liberal State* (Cambridge, Mass.: Belknap Press, 1993).

35. Foster Rhea Dulles, *The American Red Cross: A History* (New York: Harper, 1950), 1–3; John F. Hutchinson, *Champions of Charity: War and the Rise of the Red Cross* (Boulder, Colo.: Westview Press, 1996), 150–51.

36. Hutchinson, *Champions of Charity,* 150–51; Kristin Hoganson, *Fighting for American Manhood: How Gender Politics Provoked the Spanish-American and Philippine-American Wars* (New Haven: Yale University Press, 2000).

37. Hutchinson, *Champions of Charity,* 177–85; Carolina Moorehead, *Dunant's Dream: War, Switzerland, and the History of the Red Cross* (New York: Carroll and Graf, 1998).

38. Hoganson, *Fighting for American Manhood.*

39. Records of the American National Red Cross, RG 200, Box 36, File 494.2, National Archives and Records Administration; Hutchinson, *Champions of Charity,* 150.

40. Dulles, *American Red Cross,* 1.

41. Edmund Russell, *War and Nature: Fighting Humans and Insects with Chemicals from World War I to Silent Spring* (Cambridge: Cambridge University Press, 2001).

42. See Chad Louis Williams, *Torchbearers of Democracy: African American Soldiers in the World War I Era* (Chapel Hill: University of North Carolina Press, 2010).

43. Ibid.

44. Nancy Leys Stepan, *Eradication: Ridding the World of Diseases Forever* (Ithaca: Cornell University Press, 2011), 55–56.

45. Margaret Humphreys, *Yellow Fever and the South* (New Brunswick, N.J.: Rutgers University Press, 1992), 1–16.

46. Ibid.

47. Ibid., 1–16.

48. Stepan, *Eradication,* 55–56.

49. Ibid.

50. J. R. McNeill, *Mosquito Empires: Ecology and War in the Greater Caribbean, 1620–1914* (New York: Cambridge University Press, 2010), 2.

51. Russell, *War and Nature,* 2–3.

52. Ibid.

53. Ibid., 76.

54. Ibid., 77.

55. Muhammad, *Condemnation of Blackness;* John Haller, *Outcasts from Evolution: Scientific Attitudes of Racial Inferiority, 1859–1900* (Carbondale: Southern Illinois University Press, 1996).

56. Edmund Russell, "'Speaking of Annihilation': Mobilizing for War against Human and Insect Enemies, 1914–1945," *Journal of American History* 82, no. 4 (March 1996): 1505–29; Nayan Shah, *Contagious Divides: Epidemics and Race in San Francisco's Chinatown* (Berkeley: University of California Press, 2001).

57. See Rachel Carson, *Silent Spring* (Boston: Houghton Mifflin, 1962).

58. Barry, *Rising Tide.*

59. Joan Hoff Wilson, *Herbert Hoover: Forgotten Progressive* (New York: Waveland, 1992), 47–56; George H. Nash, *The Life of Herbert Hoover: The Humanitarian, 1914–1917* (New York: W. W. Norton, 1988); George H. Nash, *The Life of Herbert Hoover: Master of Emergencies, 1917–1918* (New York: W. W. Norton, 1996).

60. Ellis Hawley, *The Great War and the Search for a Modern Order: A History of the American People and Their Institutions, 1917–1933* (New York: St. Martin's Press, 1979), 20–35; Nash, *Life of Herbert Hoover,* 71, 45–74, 310–11, 477–78, 519; Nell Irvin Painter, *Standing at Armageddon: The United States, 1877–1919* (New York: W. W. Norton, 1987), 333; Wilson, *Herbert Hoover,* 7.

61. Hawley, *Great War,* 117–30; Dawley, *Struggles for Justice,* 318–19, 327–29, 331–33; Herbert Hoover, *American Individualism* (New York: Doubleday, 1922); William E. Leuchtenburg, *The Perils of Prosperity, 1914–1932* (Chicago: University of Chicago Press, 1958).

62. Wilson, *Herbert Hoover,* 68–69.

63. Hawley, *Great War,* 119.

64. "Our President Asks a Minimum Fund of $10,000,000 for Relief of the Flooded Southland," *Red Cross Courier,* May 16, 1927; Barry, *Rising Tide,* 188, 194–95.

65. Telegram from J. S. Conway, Acting Commissioner of Lighthouse, Commissioner of Lighthouses/Bureau of Lighthouses, Washington, D.C., May 5, 1927, Subject of Telegram: Mississippi River Flood Relief Work—Chronicling Report of Operations of Department of Commerce Floating Equipment and Personnel, National Archives and Records Administration, General Records of the Department of Commerce, Office of the Secretary, General Correspondence 83952–84076/1 Box no. 615.

66. Ibid., April 29, 1927.

67. Commission of Lighthouses, Department of Commerce, Memphis, Tennessee, April 27, 1927. Re: "Lighthouse Tender Wakerobin now departed south from Memphis on important mission demanded by present emergency. Likely period of use one month. Signed Spaulding in Charge of Transportation/Mississippi River Relief Committee"; Telegram Commission of Lighthouses, April 28, 1927. "Cap't Good in charge of fleet 3 river boats, one coal barge, left Memphis 10 a.m., should arrive in Vicksburg to (coal) 29th Natchez, as base, 30th, meeting there 6 Coast Guard Motor Boats assigned to fleet and 17 Coast Guard Survey Personnel with fleet"; Department of Commerce Steamboat Inspection Service, Washington, D.C., April 23, 1927, The Secretary of Commerce. Subject: In Relief Work in the Mississippi Flooded Area. National Archives and Records Administration, General Records of the Department of Commerce Office of the Secretary, General Correspondence 83952–84076/1 Box no. 615.

68. Hazel Braugh Red Cross Archive, Files on Flood Relief in the Mississippi Valley, Lorton, Va.; Red Cross Papers, National Archives and Records Administration, Record Group 200, Boxes 733–45; U.S. Army, Office of the Adjutant General, Record Group 94, Box 2417, National Archives and Records Administration.

69. "Red Cross Flood Relief Forces Holding Front Line," *Red Cross Courier,* June 1, 1927; U.S. Public Health Service, Record Group 90, Box 3 (NARA); U.S. Army Corps of Engineers, Record Group 77 (NARA); U.S. Army Office of the Adjutant General, Record Group 94, Box 2417 (NARA); Hazel Braugh Red Cross Archives, File on Mississippi Valley Flood Relief, Lorton, Va.; Red Cross Papers, National Archives and Records Administration, Record Group 200, Boxes 733–45.

70. "Holding Front Line," *Red Cross Courier*; U.S. Army, Office of the Adjutant General, Record Group 94, Box 2417 (NARA); U.S. Army Corps of Engineers, Record Group 77 (NARA).

71. "Holding Front Line," *Red Cross Courier*; Photographic archives on the 1927 Mississippi Flood at the National Archives and Records Administration in Bethesda, Md.. The Library of Congress in Washington, D.C.; New Orleans Public Library; Mississippi Department of Archives and History in Jackson, Miss.; and Louisiana State University Archives and Special Collections all maintain a strong contingent of photographs taken by the United States Coast Guard on levee breaches in the Mississippi Delta. See also images of the Mississippi River Commission: U.S. Army, Office of the Adjutant General, Record Group 94, Box 2417 (NARA); U.S. Army Corps of Engineers, Record Group 77 (NARA). On the historical interpretation of images, see John Tagg, ed., *The Burden of Representation: Essays on Photographies and Histories* (Amherst: University of Massachusetts Press, 1988); Shawn Michelle Smith, *Photography on the Color Line: W. E. B. Du Bois, Race, and Visual Culture* (Durham, N.C.: Duke University

Press, 2004); Reese Jenkins, *Images and Enterprise: Technology and the American Photographic Industry, 1839–1925* (Baltimore: The Johns Hopkins University Press, 1975); Paul Landau and Deborah Kaspin, eds., *Images and Empires: Visuality in Colonial and Postcolonial Africa* (Berkeley: University of California Press, 2002).

72. Patton, "High Water Blues."

73. "Our President Asks a Minimum Fund of $10,000,000 for Relief of the Flooded Southland," *Red Cross Courier*, May 16, 1927.

74. Ibid.

75. Ibid.

76. American Red Cross, *Mississippi Valley Flood Disaster of 1927* (Washington, D.C., 1928).

77. "Death and Famine," *Pittsburgh Courier*, May 7, 1927.

78. "Steps to Prevent Disease: Residents' Health Carefully Guarded," *St. Bernard Voice*, July 30, 1927.

79. "Flood Region Now Has New Menace: Lack of Sufficient Milk Has Caused Outbreak of Pellagra," *Louisiana Weekly*, August 6, 1927.

80. The long-term health effects of environmental disasters is an understudied subject of historical analysis. Studies focusing on environmental racism, toxic dumping, housing, and the long-term health complications such as cancer that have arisen among at-risk populations has been discussed in works such as Robert Bullard's *Dumping in Dixie: Race, Class, and Environmental Quality* (Boulder, Colo.: Westview Press, 1994); American Red Cross, *Mississippi Valley Flood Disaster*.

81. "Medical Profession in Volunteer Spirit Rises to Great Emergency" and "Nurses of Red Cross Service Again Respond Immediately to Call," *Red Cross Courier*, May 16, 1927; "Consolidating Health Gains by 30-Day Red Cross Follow-Up Program," *Red Cross Courier*, July 15, 1927.

82. "Medical Profession in Volunteer Spirit," *Red Cross Courier*; "Consolidating Health Gains," *Red Cross Courier*.

83. "Consolidating Health Gains," *Red Cross Courier*.

84. Edward Beardsley, *Health Care for Blacks and Mill Workers in the Twentieth-Century South* (Knoxville: University of Tennessee Press, 1990).

85. "Holding Front Line," *Red Cross Courier*.

86. Hawley, *Great War*, 144–46; Roland Marchand, *Advertising the American Dream: Making Way for Modernity, 1920–1940* (Berkeley: University of California Press, 1985); T. J. Jackson Lears, *Fables of Abundance: A Cultural History of Advertising in America* (New York: Basic Books, 1994).

87. "Radio Joins with Red Cross to Aid Mississippi Relief," *New York Times*, May 15, 1927.

88. Ibid.

89. Herbert Hoover, "An Appeal to the American People for Support: Mississippi Flood Sufferers," radio broadcast on the National Broadcasting Company Chain and Associated Stations from WMC, Memphis, Saturday Night, April 30, 1927, Herbert Hoover Presidential Library, West Branch, Iowa.

90. Film One: MP-72/296, "Mississippi River Flood of 1927"; Film Two: MP-74/393, "Untitled"; Film Three: MP-74/394, "The Mississippi Flood of 1927"; Film Four: MP-62/049, August 1928, "Master of Emergencies"; Newsreels of 1927 Mississippi River Flood and 1928 Campaign Film, Herbert Hoover Presidential Library, West Branch, Iowa. American painter John Steuart Curry's *Hoover and the Flood* in 1940 has been the subject of a brief historical analysis. Undertones of the painting reflect contemporary ideas of paternalism toward African Americans and Hoover as a saintly figure whose mere presence brings calmness and relief to all sufferers.

91. Proclamation of Calvin Coolidge, reprinted in the *Red Cross Courier,* May 16, 1927.

92. Newspapers researched include the *Chicago Defender, Pittsburgh Courier, Christian Science Monitor, Memphis Commercial-Appeal, New Orleans Daily Times, New Orleans Times-Picayune, New York Herald, New York Times, St. Louis Globe-Democrat, Louisiana Weekly, Jackson Clarion-Ledge,* and *Washington Afro-American.* Newspaper collections are located at the National Archives and Records Administration, Library of Congress, Mississippi Department of Archives and History (Jackson), Louisiana State University Rare Reading Room (Baton Rouge), Amistad Center at Tulane University (New Orleans), Old U.S. Mint Building (New Orleans), New Orleans Public Library, Louisiana State Archives (Baton Rouge), and Howard-Tilton Memorial Library (Tulane University–New Orleans).

93. "The Red Cross Appeal," *New York Times,* May 1, 1927.

94. Ibid.

95. "Boys and Girls Help 'Beat the Mississippi River': Denied Themselves to Give Comfort to Flood Sufferers," *Red Cross Courier,* July 1, 1927; "Flood Relief Fund Reaches $2,172,000," *New York Times,* April 27, 1927; "Aid in Flood Relief Asked by Cardinal," *New York Times,* July 11, 1927.

96. *Red Cross Courier,* undated article, Herbert Hoover Presidential Library, West Branch, Iowa; "Boys and Girls," *Red Cross Courier.*

97. Naomi Rogers, *Dirt and Disease: Polio before FDR* (New Brunswick, N.J.: Rutgers University Press, 1992), 170–88; David Oshinsky, *Polio: An American Story* (New York: Oxford University Press, 2005), 54–55; Jane Smith, *Patenting the Sun: Polio and the Salk Vaccine* (New York: W. Morrow, 1990).

4. Where Sixteen Railroads Meet the Sea

1. Gwendolyn Midlo Hall, *Africans in Colonial Louisiana: The Development of Afro-Creole Culture in the Eighteenth Century* (Baton Rouge: Louisiana State University, 1995); "Zydeco Preserves Creole Tradition," *Texas Catholic Herald*, May 1, 1981; Sybil Kein, *Creole: The History and Legacy of Louisiana's Free People of Color* (Baton Rouge: Louisiana State University Press, 2000).

2. "Our Mother of Mercy Catholic Church: Celebrating 75 Years of Evangelization and Education as a Beacon of Light in the Heart of the Fifth Ward," Internal Church History Publication.

3. Barry, *Rising Tide*; Spencer, "Contested Terrain."

4. Spencer, "Contested Terrain."

5. Joseph A. Pratt, "A Mixed Blessing: Energy, Economic Growth, and Houston's Environment," in *Energy Metropolis: An Environmental History of Houston and the Gulf Coast*, ed. Martin V. Melosi and Joseph A. Pratt (Pittsburgh: University of Pittsburgh Press, 2007), 23.

6. Ibid.

7. Ibid.

8. Ibid., 26–27.

9. Ibid.

10. Historian Bernadette Pruitt, in her forthcoming manuscript, provides much-needed historical attention to the migration of African Americans to Houston during the interwar years and the development of community institutions.

11. This term shows up in a series of articles by Bob Giles of the *Texas Catholic Herald* on the Frenchtown section of Houston. These articles were published between 1980 and 1983, describing the culture of Frenchtown.

12. Isabel Wilkerson, *The Warmth of Other Suns: The Epic Story of America's Great Migration* (New York: Random House, 2010).

13. Lewis, *In Their Own Interest*, 29–66, 167–99; Shirley Anne Wilson-Moore, *To Place Our Deeds: The African American Community in Richmond, California, 1910–1963* (Berkeley: University of California Press, 2000).

14. Allan Ballard, *One More Day's Journey: The Story of a Family and a People* (New York: McGraw-Hill, 1984).

15. Bernadette Pruitt, "For the Advancement of the Race: African American Migration and Community Building in Houston, 1914–1945" (PhD diss., University of Houston, 2001), 85. Creoles of color did not just move across the border to Texas but were part of a broader movement out west. Los Angeles, San Francisco, and Oakland received influxes of Louisiana Creoles of color after World War II.

16. Moore, *To Place Our Deeds;* Claytee D. White, "'Eight Dollars a Day and Working in the Shade': An Oral History of African American Migrant Women Working in the Las Vegas Gaming Industry," in *African American Women Confront the West, 1600–2000,* ed. Quintard Taylor and Shirley Moore (Norman: University of Oklahoma Press, 2008).

17. Denise Labrie is the daughter of Inez Prejean Calegon. Labrie recorded oral histories of her mother and aunt Mable Prejean Guillory describing the 1927 Mississippi River Flood. These oral histories are unpublished and in the personal possession of Denise Labrie. I am thankful to her for extending this oral history to me. See "Inez Prejean Calegon's Personal Account of What Happened to her Family the Morning of the Great Mississippi Flood of 1927," December 1999. Document is in the personal possession of the author.

18. Denise Labrie, Oral History of Inez Prejean. Denise Labrie also recorded the story of her aunt, Mable Prejean Guillory (Inez Prejean's sister). She named this oral history "The Louisiana to Houston Connection." This oral history was also graciously extended to me by Denise Labrie and recorded in December 1999.

19. Labrie, Oral History of Inez Prejean Calegon; Labrie, Oral History of Mabel Prejean Guillory. On the treatment of African American flood sufferers in Red Cross Relief camps, see Barry, *Rising Tide.* By mid-April the *Chicago Defender, Pittsburgh Courier,* and other black newspapers began printing stories on the violence and control that blacks experienced in the camps, particularly around Greenville, Mississippi.

20. Barry, *Rising Tide.*

21. Labrie, Oral History of Inez Prejean Calegon; Labrie, Oral History of Mabel Prejean Guillory.

22. Ibid.

23. Barry, *Rising Tide.*

24. Margaret Landry Attaway, Oral History Collection File on the 1927 Mississippi Flood, Louisiana State Archives and History, Baton Rouge.

25. Worster, *Dust Bowl.*

26. Attaway, Oral History Collection File.

27. Ibid.

28. Labrie, Oral History of Inez Prejean Calegon; Labrie, Oral History of Mable Prejean Guillory.

29. Grossman, *Land of Hope.*

30. "Oral History of Frenchtown, Houston, Texas: Conducted, Compiled and Transcribed by Knight and Associations, Inc. As Directed by Texas Department of Transportation, August, 2002." Publication is in the personal possession of the author.

I am indebted to Mr. Frank Broussard, president of the Frenchtown Community Association, for making this oral history collection available to me.

31. Grossman, *Land of Hope.*

32. Labrie, Oral History of Inez Prejean Calegon; Labrie, Oral History of Mable Prejean Guillory.

33. Ibid.

34. Ibid. In transcribed notes of the interview with Mable Prejean Guillory, Labrie vividly describes Mable Prejean Guillory crying emotionally in recalling the hurricane in Brazoria County and how the family had to start over yet again. This was a powerful part of the family's collective consciousness.

35. Labrie, Oral History of Inez Prejean Calegon; Labrie, Oral History of Mable Prejean Guillory; 1930 United States Federal Census, Houston, Harris County, Roll 2351, page: 62B, Enumeration District 142, Image 969.0, Clayton Genealogical Library, Houston, Tex.

36. "Frenchtown", *Houston Chronicler,* February 23, 1992, Houston Public Library, Vertical Files on Frenchtown.

37. Ibid.; 1930 United States Federal Census, Houston, Harris County, Roll 2351, page 63B, Enumeration District 142, Image 971.0, Clayton Genealogical Library, Houston.

38. United States Federal Census, Houston, Harris County, Roll 2351, page 63B, Enumeration District 142, Image 971.0, Clayton Genealogical Library, Houston.

39. "Frenchtown," *Houston Chronicler.*

40. Census records for 1930 were invaluable for teasing out job opportunities for residents of Frenchtown. One particular section of the census inquired about present employment, and the responses demonstrated the range of opportunities for migrants to Houston. Also, an unpublished oral history of the Frenchtown community provided valuable information on migration and labor, as well as social and cultural activities within the community. See "Oral Histories of Frenchtown, Houston, Texas."

41. Grossman, *Land of Hope.*

42. Ibid.

43. "Oral Histories of Frenchtown," 27, 38, 39, 45, 54–56, 63, 64, 71.

44. "Houston's Creole Quarter: Inside the Little-Known Community of Frenchtown, Traditions Still Live, but the Culture Is Slowly Dying," *Houston Post,* March 19, 1989, Archives of the Archdiocese of Galveston-Houston.

45. "Oral Histories of Frenchtown," 75–91.

46. Ibid. Interview in the home of Mr. John Gordon of Frenchtown conducted by the author on December 13, 2008. Ben Stuberville and his family show up in the 1930 U.S. Census. See 1930 United States Federal Census, Houston. Harris County, Roll

2345, page 87A, Enumeration District 50, Image 175.0, Clayton Genealogical Library, Houston.

47. Sybil Kein, *Creole: The History and Legacy of Louisiana's Free People of Color* (Baton Rouge: Louisiana State University Press, 2000).

48. Howard Beeth and Cary Wintz, eds., *Black Dixie: Afro-Texan History and Culture in Houston* (College Station: Texas A&M University Press, 1992), 88.

49. Ibid., 89.

50. See Irma Watkins Owens, *Blood Relations: Caribbean Immigrants and the Harlem Community, 1900–1930* (Bloomington: University of Indiana Press, 1996); Mary C. Waters, *Black Identities: West Indian Immigrant Dreams and American Realities* (Cambridge, Mass.: Harvard University Press, 1999).

51. Pruitt, "For the Advancement of the Race."

52. See Alan Kraut, *The Huddled Masses: The Immigrant in American Society, 1880–1921* (Arlington Heights, Ill.: Harlan Davidson, 1982).

53. "Oral Histories of Frenchtown," see interview of Mrs. Inez Calegon, Mrs. Mable Guillory, and Mr. Ulysses Laverque. Many children would later attend school at Our Mother of Mercy Catholic Church.

54. Cyprian Davis, "God of Our Weary Years: Black Catholics in American Catholic History," in *Taking Down Our Harps: Black Catholics in the United States*, ed. Diana Hayes and Cyprian Davis (Maryknoll, N.Y.: Orbis, 1998), 39.

55. Milton Sernett, *Bound for the Promised Land: African American Religion and the Great Migration* (Durham, N.C.: Duke University Press, 1997).

56. Ballard, *One More Day's Journey.*

57. Sernett, *Bound for the Promised Land.*

58. Denise Labrie, "Our Mother of Mercy: The Community of Frenchtown Builds a Church," published in *Zydeco Magazine*, date unknown; "Our Mother of Mercy Catholic Church," Internal Church History Publication.

59. "Our Mother of Mercy Catholic Church," Internal Church History Publication; "Our Mother of Mercy's 75th Year," *Josephite Harvest*, March 2005.

60. Ibid.

61. "Josephite Fathers," *Texas Catholic Herald*, April 3, 1981.

62. "Our Mother of Mercy Catholic Church," Internal Church History Publication.

63. Kimberley L. Phillips, *Alabama North: African-American Migrants, Community, and Working-Class Activism in Cleveland, 1915–45* (Urbana: University of Illinois Press, 1999); Peter Gottlieb, *Making Their Own Way: Southern Blacks' Migration to Pittsburgh, 1916–30* (Urbana: University of Illinois Press, 1997).

64. Wilkerson, *Warmth of Other Suns.*

65. Phillips, *Alabama North.*

66. "Frenchtown Is Dying... But Memories Linger On," *Texas Catholic Herald,* May 8, 1981, Archives of the Archdiocese of Galveston-Houston; "Frenchtown Is Dying... But Memories Linger On," *Houston Chronicle,* September 18, 2005.

67. "Oral Histories of Frenchtown," 19.

68. Roger Wood, *Texas Zydeco* (Austin: University of Texas Press, 2006), 96–97.

69. Michael Tisserand, *The Kingdom of Zydeco* (New York: Arcade Press, 1998); Barry Jean Ancelet, *Cajun and Creole Music Makers* (Jackson: University of Mississippi Press, 1999).

70. Wood, *Texas Zydeco,* 96–97.

71. Tisserand, *Kingdom of Zydeco.*

72. Much of the information I use about Creole identity in Texas, including Zydeco, comes from the oral history collection of Frenchtown residents conducted by Knight and Associates. See also "Zydeco Preserves Creole Tradition," *Texas Catholic Herald,* May 1, 1981.

73. Wood, *Texas Zydeco,* 116, 127–30.

5. Every Day Seems Like Murder Here

1. Patricia Sullivan, *Lift Every Voice: The NAACP and the Making of the Civil Rights Movement* (New York: New Press, 2009), 152.

2. Roy Wilkins, *Standing Fast: The Autobiography of Roy Wilkins* (New York: Penguin, 1982), 119–27; George S. Schuyler, *Black and Conservative: The Autobiography of George S. Schuyler* (New Rochelle, N.Y.: Arlington House, 1966), 198–204; Oscar R. Williams, *George S. Schuyler: Portrait of a Black Conservative* (Knoxville: University of Tennessee Press, 2007), 86–89; Sondra K. Wilson, ed., *In Search of Democracy: The NAACP Writings of James Weldon Johnson, Walter White, and Roy Wilkins (1920–1977)* (New York: Oxford University Press, 1999), 158; "NAACP Levee Camp Investigators Jailed and Threatened in Mississippi," January 13, 1933, NAACP Press Release, Mississippi Flood Control Subject File, 1930–1934, NAACP Papers, Library of Congress, Washington, D.C. (hereafter NAACP Flood Control File).

3. Wilkins, *Standing Fast,* 119–27.

4. Ibid.; Schuyler, *Black and Conservative,* 198–204; Williams, *George S. Schuyler,* 86–89.

5. Wilkins, *Standing Fast,* 121.

6. Ibid., 119–22

7. Ibid., 122.

8. Ibid., 119–27.

9. Ibid.; Schuyler, *Black and Conservative,* 198–204.

10. Roy Wilkins, "Mississippi Slavery in 1933," *Crisis,* April 1933.

11. Ibid.

12. Ibid.

13. Wilkins, *Standing Fast,* 123.

14. See Barry, *Rising Tide*; Steinberg, *Acts of God.*

15. Karen O'Neill, *Rivers by Design: State Power and the Origins of U.S. Flood Control* (Durham, N.C.: Duke University Press, 2006), 143–47.

16. Barry, *Rising Tide,* 423; O'Neill, *Rivers by Design,* 147.

17. O'Neill, *Rivers by Design.*

18. Farah Jasmine Griffin, *"Who Set You Flowin'?,"* 18–19; Leroi Jones, *Blues People: The Negro Experience in White America and the Music That Developed from It* (New York: William Morrow, 1963), 96; Charlie Patton, "Down the Dirt Road Blues," Yazoo L-1020.

19. See William Hemphill Family Papers, Special Collections, Duke University Library.

20. Edward Soja, *Postmodern Geographies: The Reassertion of Space in Critical Social Theory* (London: Verso, 1989), 1–18, 76–93; Michel Foucault, "Questions on Geography," in *Power Knowledge: Selected Interviews and Other Writings, 1972–1977,* ed. Colin Gordon (New York: Pantheon Books, 1980), 63–77.

21. Alex Lichtenstein, *Twice the Work of Free Labor: The Political Economy of Convict Labor in the New South* (New York: Verso, 1996), 2–3; Douglass Blackmon, *Slavery by Another Name: The Re-Enslavement of Black Americans from the Civil War to World War II* (New York: Random House, 2008).

22. Lichtenstein, *Twice the Work,* 2–7.

23. Harvard Sitkoff, *A New Deal for Blacks: The Emergency of Civil Rights as a National Issue: The Depression Decade* (New York: Oxford University Press, 1978), 35.

24. Alan Lomax, *The Land Where the Blues Began* (New York: Pantheon Books, 1993), 212–56; William Hemphill Family Papers, Special Collections, Duke University Library, Durham, N.C.; Barry, *Rising Tide,* 122–23.

25. See Jones, *Labor of Love,* 80–94.

26. Wilkins, *Standing Fast,* 123.

27. Ibid.

28. William Jones, *A Tribe of Black Ulysses: African American Lumber Workers in the Jim Crow South* (Urbana: University of Illinois Press, 2005), 2–3.

29. Ibid., 2–3.

30. Ibid., 3–4. Jones describes the influence and demands of black lumber workers in the early twentieth century on the political, social, and economic transformation of the southern region. Importantly, he also describes the conscious movement of local

farmers into the seasonal lumber industry work as a way of supplementing wages. The result meant more stability and economic mobility for families. He argues that when lumber industries throughout the South began pushing against seasonal employment and for more long-term investments by workers in the 1920s, black lumber workers responded by demanding policies that reinforced workplace ethics, family life, and leisure in these newly developed lumber communities.

31. Ibid.

32. American Federation of Labor Report on Levee Camps, December 5, 1931; Helen Boardman Report on Levee Camps, August 1932, NAACP Flood Control File.

33. Washboard Sam, "Levee Camp Moan." I obtained a recording of this song from the Hogan Blues Archive, Tulane University.

34. American Federation of Labor Report on Levee Camps, December 5, 1931; Helen Boardman Report on Levee Camps, August 1932, NAACP Flood Control File.

35. Figures taken from the Mississippi Valley Branch of the Associated General Contractors, quoted in the *Chicago Defender,* August 12, 1933.

36. "List of Contractors on Levee Work on Mississippi River and Tributaries," NAACP Flood Control File.

37. John Cowley, "Shack Bullies and Levee Contractors: Bluesmen as Ethnographers," *Journal of Folklore Research* 28 (1991), Special Double Issue, "Labor Song: A Reappraisal."

38. "List of Contractors," NAACP Flood Control File.

39. Lomax, *Land Where the Blues Began,* 235–50. Walter Brown was also interviewed by Lomax in the 1970s. Lomax's work is problematic and has been rightly criticized by numerous scholars, but it provides a useful window into limited aspects of levee camp life.

40. Barry, *Rising Tide,* 191.

41. Ibid., 190–92.

42. John Cowley, "Shack Bullies and Levee Contractors."

43. Barry, *Rising Tide.*

44. American Federation of Labor Levee Camp Investigation, December 5, 1931, NAACP Flood Control File.

45. David Rosner and Gerald Markowitz, *Deadly Dust: Silicosis and the Politics of Occupational Disease in Twentieth-Century America* (Princeton: Princeton University Press, 1991); Martin Cherniak, *The Hawk's Nest Incident: America's Worst Industrial Disaster* (New Haven: Yale University Press, 1986); Alan Kraut, *Silent Travelers: Germs, Genes, and the Immigrant Menace* (Baltimore: The Johns Hopkins University Press, 1995); Arthur F. McEvoy, "Working Environments: An Ecological Approach to Industrial Health and Safety," *Technology and Culture* 36 (April 1995): S153.

46. Gene Campbell, "Levee Camp Man Blues."

47. American Federation of Labor Levee Camp Investigation, December 5, 1931, NAACP Flood Control File. The AFL was the first to report on the conditions of levee camps in the Yazoo Delta. It is possible that Holt Ross and Thomas Carrol, the two men who conducted the report, may have drawn the wrath of William Green, president of the AFL. Ross later told the NAACP that he was fired as a labor organizer for the AFL because of the report. Ross also published an article on his findings in the AFL's *Federationist* called "Levees, Labor and Liberty," in March 1932.

48. American Federation of Labor Levee Camp Investigation, December 5, 1931, NAACP Flood Control File.

49. Helen Boardman Report on Levee Camps, August 1932, NAACP Flood Control File.

50. Barry, *Rising Tide.*

51. See Wilson, *Herbert Hoover.*

52. William Leuchtenburg, *Franklin D. Roosevelt and the New Deal, 1932–1940* (New York: Harper and Row 1963); Alan Brinkley, *Franklin Delano Roosevelt* (New York: Oxford University Press, 2009); Harvard Sitkoff, *A New Deal for Blacks* (New York: Oxford University Press, 1978).

53. David Levering Lewis, *W. E. B. Du Bois: The Fight for Equality and the American Century, 1919–1963* (New York: Henry Holt, 2000), 244.

54. Spencer, "Contested Terrain."

55. John Barry provides a terrific description of the reports in *Rising Tide,* 381–91.

56. Letter from Ella Hutson to Herbert Hoover, July 20, 1927, Herbert Hoover Presidential Library, West Branch, Iowa.

57. Ibid.

58. Editorial by W. E. B. Du Bois, *Crisis,* November 1927. Copy located at the Herbert Hoover Presidential Library, West Branch, Iowa.

59. "Investigation of Labor Camps Along the Mississippi Flood Control Project," September 30, 1932, NAACP Press Release; "Aroused Negro Public Opinion Forced Hoover Levee Probe, Says White," 1932, NAACP Press Release; Walter White to James A. Cobb, Municipal Court, Washington, D.C., November 16, 1932; Walter White to Rev. H. S. Bigelow, Odd Fellows Temple, Cincinnati, Ohio, December 2, 1932. All documents are located in the NAACP Flood Control File.

60. Barry, *Rising Tide.* This second Moton committee is largely absent in the literature on race and labor.

61. Leuchtenburg, *Franklin D. Roosevelt;* Sitkoff, *New Deal for Blacks.*

62. Cobb, *Most Southern Place on Earth,* 184–85; Sitkoff, *New Deal for Blacks,* 44, 49, 52–55; Stewart, *"What Nature Suffers to Groe"*; C. Vann Woodward, *The Strange*

Career of Jim Crow (New York: Oxford University Press, 1955); Pete Daniel, *The Shadow of Slavery: Peonage in the South* (Urbana: University of Illinois Press, 1972).

63. See Charles G. Holle, First Lieutenant, Corps of Engineers, Report of Investigation of Labor Conditions–Flood Control–Mississippi River, Submitted to The President of the Mississippi River Commission, January 30, 1933. National Archives, College Park, Md.; Record Group 77, E 109, Box 83, 2525–1110/1.

64. See John S. Haller, *Outcasts from Evolution: Scientific Attitudes of Racial Inferiority, 1825–1939* (Carbondale: Southern Illinois University Press, 1994); Matthew Frye Jacobson, *Whiteness of a Different Color: European Immigrants and the Alchemy of Race* (Cambridge, Mass.: Harvard University Press, 1998).

65. Holle, "Report of Investigation of Labor Conditions."

66. Ibid.

67. Wilkins, *Standing Fast,* 123.

68. "Investigation of Labor Camps Along the Mississippi Flood Control Project," September 30, 1932, NAACP Press Release; Helen Boardman Report on Levee Camps, August 1932, NAACP Flood Control File.

69. Helen Boardman's research experiences are part of the Mississippi Flood Control Subject File, 1930–1934, NAACP Papers, Library of Congress.

70. Lewis, *W. E. B. Du Bois,* 9.

71. Ibid., 8–9.

72. Ibid.

73. "Investigation of Labor Camps Along the Mississippi Flood Control Project," September 30, 1932, NAACP Press Release; Helen Boardman Report on Levee Camps, August 1932, NAACP Flood Control File.

74. Lytle Brown, Major General and Chief of Engineers to Walter White, Secretary for the NAACP, August 25, 1932, NAACP Flood Control File.

75. Walter White to Lytle Brown, August 29, 1932; Andrew Hurley, Secretary of War to Walter White, August 31, 1932, NAACP Flood Control File.

76. "Investigation of Labor Camps Along the Mississippi Flood Control Project," September 30, 1932, NAACP Press Release, NAACP Flood Control File.

77. Ibid.

78. Ibid.; "War Department Fails in Attempt to Hush up Testimony of Flood Control Slavery: General Pillsbury Excludes Press But Miss Boardman Hands Out NAACP Release," 1932, NAACP Press Release, NAACP Flood Control File.

79. "Investigation of Labor Camps Along the Mississippi Flood Control," September 30, 1932, NAACP Press Release, NAACP Flood Control File.

80. "Interrogation of Miss Helen Boardman by Brigadier General G. B. Pillsbury," September 22, 1932; "Investigation of Labor Camps Along the Mississippi Flood

Control Project," September 30, 1932, NAACP Press Release; Helen Boardman Report on Levee Camps, August 1932, NAACP Flood Control File.

81. Leuchtenburg, *Franklin D. Roosevelt.*

82. "No Funds for Hoover Committee Probe: NAACP Pushes Wager Resolution," 1932, NAACP Press Release, NAACP Flood Control File; "Nation-Wide Mass Meetings to Urge Senate Levee Probe," December 4, 1932, NAACP Press Release, NAACP Flood Control File.

83. Lewis, *W. E. B. Du Bois,* 251.

84. Ibid.

85. Kenneth Goings, *The NAACP Comes of Age* (Bloomington: Indiana University Press, 1990); Letter from Walter White to Dr. H. Claude Hudson, president of the Los Angeles branch of the NAACP, November 17, 1932, NAACP Flood Control File.

86. Alan Brinkley, *Franklin Delano Roosevelt* (New York: Oxford University Press, 2009).

87. Arthur M. Schlesinger Jr., *The Age of Roosevelt: The Coming of the New Deal* (Boston: Houghton Mifflin, 1958), 87–92.

88. F. H. Payne, Assistant Secretary of War to Walter White, October 10, 1932; Roy St. Lewis, Assistant Attorney General to Walter White, September 22, 1932, NAACP Flood Control File.

89. Leuchtenburg, *Franklin D. Roosevelt.*

90. Letter from Walter White to Roy Ellis, Committee on Labor, December 20, 1932, Report Attached to Letter; "3 Mississippi Flood Control Areas Lose $1,412,226 Yearly for Negroes," 1932, NAACP Press Release, NAACP Flood Control File.

91. "3 Mississippi Flood Control Areas Lose $1,412,226 Yearly for Negroes," 1932, NAACP Press Release, NAACP Flood Control File.

92. Letter from Walter White to Roy Ellis, Committee on Labor, December 20, 1932, Report Attached to Letter; "3 Mississippi Flood Control Areas Lose $1,412,226 Yearly for Negroes," 1932, NAACP Press Release, NAACP Flood Control File.

93. "Expect Levee Probe Committee to be Named in Last Congress Hours," March 3, 1933, NAACP Press Release, NAACP Flood Control File; "Open Levee Slave Probe: Wagner to Head Quiz in South," *Chicago Defender,* April 15, 1933; Wilkins, *Standing Fast,* 126.

94. Schlesinger, *Age of Roosevelt,* 87–92; Leuchtenburg, *Franklin D. Roosevelt,* 57–60.

95. "Levee Contractors Present Code Raising Pay of Labor," August 4, 1933, NAACP Press Release, NAACP Flood Control File; Sitkoff, *New Deal for Blacks,* 47–48, 52–55; Roy Wilkins, Assistant Secretary of the NAACP to Ludwell Denny, Associate Editor, Scripps Howard Newspapers, October 11, 1933, NAACP Flood Control File. Research by the Public Works Administration would be useful for the discussion

of levee camp workers after 1933. Unfortunately, the administrative file of the PWA was discarded and is unavailable.

96. Sitkoff, *New Deal for Blacks,* 53–55.

97. Ibid.

98. Wilkins, *Standing Fast,* 126.

99. "Levee Contractors Present Code Raising Pay of Labor," August 4, 1933, NAACP Press Release; Letter from Roy Wilkins to Robert R. Church of Memphis, October 4, 1933, NAACP Flood Control File.

100. Letter from Walter White to Rev. Mother M. Katharine, Sisters of the Blessed Sacrament, Cromwells Heights, Pa., July 10, 1934; Letter from Roy Wilkins to Major General Edward M. Markham, Chief of Engineers, War Department, October 3, 1934; Letter from W. L. Byrd, Vicksburg, Mississippi, to NAACP, November 3, 1933, NAACP Flood Control File.

101. Richard White, *The Organic Machine: The Remaking of the Columbia River* (New York: Hill and Wang, 1995), x.

Conclusion

1. Michele L. Landis, "Fate, Responsibility, and 'Natural' Disaster Relief: Narrating the American Welfare State," *Law and Society Review* 33, no. 2 (1999).

2. Ibid., 264–65.

3. Ibid., 265.

4. Ibid.

5. Steinberg, *Acts of God.*

6. Ibid., 175.

7. Steinberg, *Acts of God.*

8. Ibid.

9. Cobb, *Most Southern Place on Earth*; Leuchtenburg, *Franklin D. Roosevelt*; Alan Brinkley, *The End of Reform: New Deal Liberalism in Recession and War* (New York: Random House, 1995).

10. Lucille Bogan, "Red Cross Man," recorded in 1933, Banner.

11. Ibid.; Guido Van Rijn, *Roosevelt's Blues: African-American Gospel Songs on FDR* (Jackson: University of Mississippi Press, 1997), 43–66.

12. Walter Roland, "Red Cross Blues," recorded in 1933, Banner.

13. Cobb, *Most Southern Place on Earth,* 184, 193, 195–98.

14. Keith Wailoo, Karen O'Neill, Jeffrey Dowd, and Roland Anglin, eds., *Katrina's Imprint: Race and Vulnerability in America* (New Brunswick, N.J.: Rutgers University Press, 2010).

15. Paul Garon, *Woman with Guitar: Memphis Minnie's Blues* (New York: Da Capo, 1992), 45–56; Robert Santelli, *The Big Book of Blues* (New York: Penguin, 1993).

16. Garon, *Woman with Guitar,* 45–56; Kansas Joe and Memphis Minnie, "When the Levee Breaks," recorded in 1929, Columbia Records.

17. Clyde Woods, "Do You Know What It Means to Miss New Orleans? Katrina, Trap Economics, and the Rebirth of the Blues," *American Quarterly* 57 (December 2005): 1005.

18. Wailoo et al., *Katrina's Imprint.*

19. "Families on the Move Find a Friend in Texas," *Houston Chronicle,* September 18, 2005.

20. Frenchtown Historical Marker, taken by the author on August 1, 2009.

21. Thomas Sugrue, *The Origins of the Urban Crisis: Race and Inequality in Postwar Detroit* (Princeton: Princeton University Press, 1996).

SELECTED DISCOGRAPHY

Alexander, Texas. "Levee Camp Moan Blues." OK 8498.

Andrews, Mose. "Mississippi Storm." ARC (Unissued).

Anonymous. "The Red Cross Store." *Negro Songs of Protest.* Rounder 4013.

Bogan, Lucille. "The Levee Blues." PM 12459.

———. "Red Cross Man." Recorded July 17, 1933. Banner 33072.

Brown, Lee. "Mississippi Water Blues." DE 7744.

Campbell, Gene. "Levee Camp Man Blues." Recorded May 1930. BR 7154.

Carter, George. "Rising River Blues." Recorded February 1929. Yazoo 1012.

Crap Eye. "Levee Camp Holler." Recorded August 9, 1933. LC.

Crawford, James. "Flood and Thunder Blues." Recorded July 1928. GE 6536.

Crawford, Rosetta. "Down on the Levee Blues." Recorded October 5, 1923. OK 8096.

Davis, Walter. "Red Cross Blues." Recorded August 2, 1933. Bluebird B5143.

Delaney, Mattie. "Tallahatchie River Blues." Recorded February 1930. Vol. 1480.

Dorsey, Thomas (Georgia Tom). "Levee Bound Blues." *Complete Recorded Works,* vol. 2 (1930–34).

———. "Mississippi Bottom Blues." Yazoo L/041.

Easton, Amos. "Rising River Blues." DOCD 5267.

Gibson, Clifford. "Levee Camp Moan." Recorded December 1929. B1.

Harris, Pete. "The Red Cross Store." LC.

Hicks, Robert (Barbeque Bob). "Mississippi Heavy Water Blues." CO 14222.

———. "Mississippi Low Levee Blues." CO 14316.

Higgins, Billy. "The Levee Blues." Ajax 17125.

Hill, Bertha (Chippie). "Mississippi Waters Blues." OK (Unissued).

Hooker, John Lee. *John Lee Hooker: The Country Blues of John Lee Hooker,* 1959. Riverside Records.

Jefferson, Blind Lemon. "Rising High Water Blues." Recorded in 1927.

Johnson, Lonnie. "Backwater Blues." Recorded May 3, 1927. Okeh 8466.

———. "Broken Levee Blues." Recorded March 13, 1928. Okeh 8618.

———. "Flood Water Blues." Recorded November 1937. DE 7397.

———. "Southbound Backwater." Recorded April 25, 1927. Okeh 8466.

Kansas Joe and Memphis Minnie, "When the Levee Breaks." Recorded June 1929. Columbia 14439.

Leadbetter, Huddie. "Red Cross Store." Recorded February 13, 1935. LC (Unissued).

———. "Red Cross Store Blues." Recorded June 15, 1940. Bluebird B8709.

Martin, Carl. "High Water Flood Blues." CH 50074.

Martin, Sara. "Goin' Down to the Levee." Recorded July 12, 1923. Okeh 8304.

Moore, Prince (Kid). "Mississippi Water." DOC D5180CD.

Patton, Charley. "High Water Everywhere." Recorded in 1929.

Pearson, Alice. "Greenville Levee Blues." DOCD 5497.

Roland, Walter. "Red Cross Blues" (parts 1 and 2). Recorded July 17, 1933. Banner 32822 and 33121.

Scott, Sonny. "Red Cross Blues." Recorded July 18, 1933. VO 25012.

Smith, Bessie. "Backwater Blues." Recorded February 17, 1927. Columbia C24–47474.

———. "Homeless Blues." Recorded September 28, 1927. Columbia CG30818 1972.

Terry, Sonny. "The Red Cross." LC (Unissued).

Wallace, Sippie. "The Flood Blues." Recorded May 6, 1927. Okeh 8470.

Washboard Sam. "The Levee Blues." BB B6556.

———. "Levee Camp Moan." *Complete Recorded Works in Chronological Order,* vol. 6 (1941–42). DOCD 5176.

Washboard Trio, "Red Cross Blues." Recorded July 17, 1941. LC (Unissued).

Weldon, Will (Casey Bill). "Flood Water Blues." Recorded March 1936. VO 03220.

Yates, Blind Richard. "The Levee Blues." Recorded April 1927. PA 7521.

INDEX

Page numbers in italic refer to images.

RICHARD M. MIZELLE JR. is assistant professor of history at the University of Houston. He is the coeditor of *Resilience and Opportunity: Lessons from the U.S. Gulf Coast after Katrina and Rita.*